# DEMOCRACY IN LATIN AMERICA

# DEMOCRACY

## *in*

# LATIN AMERICA

## BETWEEN HOPE AND DESPAIR

## IGNACIO WALKER

### TRANSLATED BY

### KRYSTIN KRAUSE, HOLLY BIRD, AND SCOTT MAINWARING

*University of Notre Dame Press*
*Notre Dame, Indiana*

*Library of Congress Cataloging-in-Publication Data*

Walker, Ignacio.
    Democracy in Latin America : between hope and despair / Ignacio Walker ;
translated by Krystin Krause, Holly Bird, and Scott Mainwaring.
        pages cm
    Includes bibliographical references and index.
    ISBN-13: 978-0-268-01972-3 (pbk. : alk. paper)
    ISBN-10: 0-268-01972-X (pbk. : alk. paper)
    1. Democracy—Latin America. 2. Latin America—Politics and government.
I. Krause, Krystin, translator. II. Bird, Holly, translator. III. Mainwaring, Scott,
1954– translator. IV. Title.
    JL966.W35     2013
    321.8098—dc23
                                2013000479

FOR ALBERT HIRSCHMAN

# CONTENTS

# PROLOGUE

This book is a dialogue between academia and politics. My life has traveled paths between both. After a decade dedicated to law, first as a student and later as a human rights lawyer during the Pinochet dictatorship (1973–1990), my life turned to political science and active politics with a single fixation: the consolidation of democracy and respect for human rights in Chile and in Latin America.

I belong to a political generation marked by two vital dates: September 11, 1973, with the military coup that interrupted one of the oldest democracies in Latin America, and October 5, 1988, with the plebiscite that put an end to Pinochet's dictatorship and opened up the way to democracy. Both processes — the breakdown and the transition to democracy — instilled in many of us the need to think deeply about the past, present, and future of democracy in the region.

In the 1980s, I dedicated myself to a systematic reflection on the processes of the breakdown of democracy and the initial processes of transition to democracy. I did this first as a graduate student at Princeton University, where I received a Ph.D. in political science, and later as part of an outstanding team at the Center for Latin American Studies (CIEPLAN) in Santiago, Chile, under the leadership of Alejandro Foxley.

In the 1990s and in the first decade of the 2000s, we put into action all that we had learned, suffered, and above all, longed for and dreamed based on certain fundamental values and academic rigor. Given the past experience of great political failure, this time we felt we could not fail— for our own sake and for the tremendous expectations placed on the processes of democratization by the people of Latin America. Victims of so much deception and frustration throughout history, they maintained hope for a future of economic and social progress, where the dignity and rights of all people would be respected.

I was appointed director of political relations at the Secretariat General of the Presidency (1990–1994), under the leadership of Edgardo Boeninger, in the transitional government to democracy headed by Patricio Aylwin. It was like getting a second Ph.D., this time in political action, within a transition to democracy that I consider to have been successful. Subsequently, I was elected as member of the National Congress for two consecutive terms (1994–1998 and 1998–2002) coinciding with the government of President Eduardo Frei Ruiz-Tagle (1994–2000). From 2004 to 2006 I served as minister of foreign affairs under President Ricardo Lagos, and in 2009 I was elected senator for an eight-year term from 2010 to 2018. In 2010, I was also elected president of the Christian Democratic Party through 2012.

I emphasize my political trajectory because this book goes beyond the academic. Without forgoing the rigor and systematic analyses that stem from my academic formation, I wanted to leave space for experience itself, both personal and collective, in order to attain a fuller understanding of politics and democracy in Latin America.

The following reflections attempt to give an account of the abundant available literature about democracy in the region, especially in recent decades, organizing it in a systematic manner, but with the support of a political trajectory that follows other paths. I believe that this combination of academic perspective and real-world experience enhances the understanding of political and economic development in this part of the world.

My own life, both political and academic, and the lives of others of my generation bear witness to the dilemmas that we faced between the waves of democracy and authoritarianism in the past decades, both in Chile and throughout Latin America. It is no accident that most political leaders in Chile today are between the ages of fifty-three and fifty-seven:

at the time of the 1973 military coup we were between the ages of fifteen and nineteen. The political tragedy that we lived, from the breakdown of democracies in the late 1960s and early 1970s through the transitions to democracy that began in the late 1970s, inspired in us, more than in any other generation, a determined commitment to systematic reflection.

After I completed my law degree at the University of Chile in 1978, when Pinochet's dictatorship was in full swing, I had the chance to enter one of the best law firms in the country. I decided, given my beliefs and the political context in which we were living, that I could not follow the path of practicing freely as a lawyer while human rights were being violated in Chile. I became a lawyer for the Vicaría de la Solidaridad (the Vicariate of Solidarity) under the determined, clear-sighted, and prophetic leadership of Cardinal Raúl Silva Henríquez. It was the post–Vatican II Catholic Church, committed to the dignity and rights of the human person. I lost all my cases as a human rights lawyer (1979–1982), but I felt deeply fulfilled as a person. Above all, I came to understand that respect for human rights constitutes the moral foundation of democracy.

I left the vicariate not because of the bad results I obtained in the court cases, which reflected a judiciary complicit, either deliberately or through negligence, in the crimes of Pinochet's dictatorship. Rather, I left to pursue a new passion in life. I wanted to study the factors that had led to the democratic breakdowns in Chile and in Latin America. I wanted to understand. It seemed to me that none of this had occurred merely by chance or was simply a product of the greed and evil deeds of the United States and the militaries, which frequently took the blame for the processes of democratic breakdown and the coups d'état that were part of the authoritarian wave set off in Brazil in 1964.

After dedicating nearly a decade to law, I began doctoral work at Princeton University. I read a great deal and systematically studied political theory, comparative politics, and international relations. I never imagined that I would become a practitioner in these fields as a political advisor, congressman, senator, minister of foreign affairs, and party president. The synthesis between theory and practice has always been a source of peculiar fascination to me. Politics without ideas or, conversely, ideas not grounded in the broad scene of politics, are only half-fulfilled realities that fail to mutually enrich each other.

Upon my return to Chile, I had the privilege of joining a team of researchers from CIEPLAN, which throughout the years has been a center of learning for many of us in the fields of politics, economics, and public policy. Much could be said about the field and the contributions of think tanks in the recent history of the region. The systematic study of reality they pursue enriched our research and its contribution to the public sphere, both in Chile and in Latin America. When I left my research work to serve in the Concertación, a center-left coalition that governed between 1990 and 2010, I found that many of Chile's achievements during that time—which undoubtedly have their deficiencies, errors, and shortcomings as well—have roots in the academic and intellectual formation offered by institutions such as CIEPLAN. Our experience there left us little space for improvisation and a lot of space for the development of ideas, as well as professional and systematic work in the sphere of public policy.

The rest of the story I have already explained. Now, by rewriting this prologue and publishing this book in English with some minor changes (it was originally edited and published in Chile in 2009 by Uqbar Publications and CIEPLAN), I hope to contribute to the ever-present challenge of consolidating a stable and respectable democracy in Latin America.

After twenty years of Concertación leadership, the public willed that we hand over power to the opposition following the election of a right-wing government in January 2010. I did so, with the power invested in me as senator and as president of the Christian Democratic Party, with the same intention I have had all these years: to serve the nation in search of the common good by doing whatever can and should be done, whether in my own government or that of the opposition, in politics or in academia.

This book contains a sort of synthesis, in a systematic and detailed analysis, of my reflections during the decades I have spent as a politician and academic witnessing the ups and downs of democracy in Latin America.

The basic content of this book is inspired by the course that I gave as a visiting professor and Laporte Distinguished Fellow at the Princeton Institute for International and Regional Studies (PIIRS) and the Woodrow Wilson School of Public and International Affairs during the 2007–2008 academic year. After losing contact with political science for more than fifteen years, I had the opportunity to read a great deal of academic material in a short period of time, which helped me to systematize my reflections on the theme that I address in this book. I wish to express special thanks to Jeremy Adelman, Deborah Yashar, and Katherine Newman, who welcomed me and made possible my stay at Princeton for the academic year. Special thanks to my students in the aforementioned course, as well as in my freshman seminar, Chile: From Revolution to Reform and Beyond. I cannot express enough my endless gratitude—my own, and that of Cecilia and our children—to the very dear friends that we made at Princeton, such as Albert and Sarah Hirschman (may both rest in peace), Paul Sigmund, Arcadio Díaz-Quiñones, Alma Concepción, Nancy Bermeo, and Peter Johnson. As a student, professor, and visiting researcher, I always found at Princeton a stimulating environment in both the human and intellectual spheres. If there is something of which the United States can feel legitimately proud, it is its exceptional system of universities, which I was first able to access in the 1980s thanks to the Fulbright Commission and the Ford Foundation.

By the same token, I also wish to mention the great contributions to my life and my process of academic and intellectual formation made by the University of Notre Dame and the Kellogg Institute for International Studies, created by the visionary Father Theodore Hesburgh, C.S.C. From my first term as a visiting fellow in 1987, in the depths of the volatile transition to democracy in Latin America, until today, I have found the intellectual environment very stimulating. It has helped me to formulate, reformulate, and question many of the ideas addressed here. My special gratitude goes out to professors Timothy Scully, C.S.C., and Scott Mainwaring, two great friends. I have had the privilege, on various occasions, of serving on the advisory boards of the Kellogg Institute and the Program in Latin American Studies at Princeton (in the case of the latter, until the present day), benefiting from numerous conversations with a diverse group of academics from the United States and Latin America.

I wrote a first draft about some of the ideas contained in this book following an invitation by professors Mainwaring and Scully to deliver a speech at CIEPLAN in Santiago in a late 2005 seminar, Democratic

Governability in Latin America. At that time, I was serving as minister of foreign affairs. The presentation was later published in *Foreign Affairs en Español* under the title "Democracia en América Latina" (Walker 2006). Subsequently, Mainwaring and Scully edited the book *Democratic Governance in Latin America,* published in 2009 by Stanford University Press, containing a second paper that I wrote with Patricio Navia, entitled "Political Institutions, Populism, and Democracy in Latin America." During my stay at Princeton I published a third paper, "Democracy and Populism in Latin America," as a working paper for the Kellogg Institute for International Studies (Walker 2008). A version of this paper appeared in *Dissent* in autumn of 2008 as "The Three Lefts of Latin America." Finally, I published the paper "Democracia de Instituciones" in *A medio camino: Nuevos desafíos de la democracia y del desarrollo en América Latina* (CIEPLAN/Uqbar Editores, 2009), edited by Fernando H. Cardoso and Alejandro Foxley. This paper was also published in *Estudios Públicos* (Walker 2009) under the title "Por una democracia de instituciones para América Latina." With the exception of this last paper, which appears with a few minor changes as the final chapter of this book, these papers have served as groundwork for a work I have conceived not as a compilation of previously published papers, but rather as an entirely new product. The papers and the reflections contained in this book have had a place in A New Economic and Social Agenda for Latin America, a project led by CIEPLAN and the Fernando H. Cardoso Institute from 2006 to 2008, and financed by the Inter-American Development Bank (IDB), the Spanish Agency for International Cooperation and Development (AECI), and the United Nations Development Programme (UNDP). My special gratitude goes out to these five institutions.

Truth be told, my original idea was to write a textbook. This became a necessity when, as I was giving the Democracy in Latin America course at Princeton, I could not find a satisfactory book in English or Spanish. The number of books and papers published in English and Spanish about democracy in Latin America is endless. I could not, however, find a comprehensive text directed to both experts and the broader public. Ever since then, I had thought about writing a text like this one. This is the reason for the abundant references found throughout these pages, many of which I have provided as counterpoint to some of the principal academic contributions on the theme in question, which come from a wide variety of authors, primarily from the United States.

Along the way, what I had initially envisioned as a textbook began to form part of the central argument of this book, in the form of an essay. At a time when political science is transforming itself into a subset of mathematics and applied statistics, I felt it important to recover history, without which there is no true political science. Likewise, it is important to recover the genre of the essay, characteristic of Latin America, even within the context of a systematic approach with the academic rigor required by the subject I address here.

Central to my thinking while writing this book was an interesting talk by Professor Frances Hagopian at the twentieth anniversary celebration of the Kellogg Institute for International Studies, in which she warned about a double danger in the field of political science: of hyperspecialized focus (risk of narrowing), which involves a marked inability to speak beyond a narrow circle of experts, and of the exact opposite (the risk of generalizations), a focus which, generally, we Latin Americans have used and abused. The genre of the essay, so prevalent in Latin America, often falls prey to this second danger. Nevertheless, given the present trend toward hyperspecialization in political science based on models and statistics, it seems to me that a focus that breaks free of dependent and independent variables, correlations, and regressions, such as the one contained in this book, allows the work to be read outside of a small circle of experts.

In fact, this is an objective that I deliberately pursue. I have attempted to make complex subjects and the sophisticated theories that have arisen around them more familiar to a broader audience. As I indicated before, I have serious reservations about the current trends in political science, with their constant and almost obsessive attempts to measure everything. I am reminded of Machiavelli's classic statement, in the preface to book two of *The Discourses*, that "human affairs are ever in a state of flux." Thus, we must take into account the complexity and dynamism of historical processes. Political science without history is political science without content. As a former student of Sheldon Wolin, I turn often to classical authors such as Thucydides, Machiavelli, and Tocqueville, who helped me to understand the true nature of the political phenomenon.

I wrote the prologue to the Spanish version of this book while once again at CIEPLAN. As Alejandro Foxley said after the end of his term as minister of foreign affairs in Chile (2006–2009), returning to CIEPLAN is like "coming home." At CIEPLAN we began our reflection about Chile and Latin America, and there we shall continue with what we have labeled "the new stage": a stage focused more on Latin America than on Chile, focused on that desire shared over so many years to make political democracy, economic growth, and social equity compatible in the new age of globalization, with its shadows and its lights and, above all, its enormous possibilities.

Finally, I am grateful for the comments that several academic colleagues offered on the initial drafts of these chapters. Special thanks to Ivan Jaksic (chapter 1), Oscar Muñoz (chapters 2 and 4), Scott Mainwaring (chapter 3), and Patricio Meller (chapter 7) for their very helpful suggestions. The eighth and final chapter, the only one that was previously published, received the comments and contributions of Edgardo Boeninger (RIP), Maria Hermínia Tavares, Scott Mainwaring, Fernando Luiz Abrucio, Marcus André Melo, and Cristóbal Aninat. I am also grateful to political scientist Sergio Toro for his very pertinent comments and suggestions on the final draft of the book, and to Eugenio Tironi and Francisco Saffie for their comments on the prologue and introduction. None of them bear any responsibility for the content of this book.

# INTRODUCTION

It is a paradox of our region and time period that, while Latin America experiences the most widespread presence of democracy in its history, there remains a general perception that these democracies are fragile. There is talk of a democratic "deficit," or the problem of democratic governability in Latin America.

Between 2005 and 2010 there were eighteen presidential elections in the region[1]—that is, in every country in Latin America except Cuba, which remains the sole dictatorship in all the thirty-four countries of the Americas, understood as stretching from Canada in the north to Patagonia in the south. These elections are examples of electoral democracy, which entails the realization of free, transparent, and competitive elections. This sort of democracy, one aspect of the minimalist or procedural concept of democracy found in the tradition of Joseph Schumpeter (1942) and Robert Dahl (1971), is emerging most substantively

---

1. Bolivia (December 2005), Peru (April and June 2006), Mexico (July 2006), Nicaragua (November 2006), Venezuela (December 2006), Guatemala (September and November 2007), Argentina (October 2007), Paraguay (April 2008), El Salvador (March 2009), the Dominican Republic (May 2008), Ecuador (April 2009), Panama (May 2009), Uruguay (October 2009), Honduras (November 2009), Chile (December 2009 and January 2010), Costa Rica (February 2010), Colombia (May and June 2010), and Brazil (October 2010).

in the region. The following elements are part of a procedural definition of democracy in this tradition: the existence of open and competitive elections—without fraud, coercion, or proscriptions—that determine who establishes public policy and permits the possibility of alternation of power; universal suffrage for adults; and the guarantee of certain traditional civil rights, such as freedom of expression, the right to organize, and due process (Mainwaring and Shugart 1997b, 14). Others include as a defining feature of democracy the successful subordination of the military to the legitimately established authorities.

Although I am not entirely satisfied with this concept and will elaborate later on the type of democracy that is desirable, this "third wave" of democratization (Huntington 1991) is a significant advance from the earlier, authoritarian wave that began with the coups d'état in Brazil (1964), Peru (1968), Uruguay (1973), Chile (1973), and Argentina (1976). Huntington's famous book distinguishes between the long wave of democratization between 1828 and 1926, the short wave between 1943 and 1962, and the present (third) wave, beginning in 1974. Let us recall that at the end of the 1970s, only three countries in Latin America were holding free, transparent, and competitive elections: Colombia, Venezuela, and Costa Rica.

The eighteen presidential elections between 2005 and 2010 were accompanied by a great political and electoral mobilization, perhaps the first of its kind in the history of Latin America (Hagopian and Mainwaring 2005). There have also been qualitative advances in democratization. In South America, for the first time in history, a union leader (Luis Inácio Lula da Silva in Brazil), two women (Michelle Bachelet in Chile and Cristina Fernández in Argentina), and an indigenous leader (Evo Morales in Bolivia) have been elected president of their countries. Meanwhile, Haiti celebrated what might be the most democratic presidential and parliamentary elections in its history in 2006.

This progress, however, comes with a series of questions regarding the solidity of these processes in the context of the great heterogeneity of Latin America. The best evidence of the difficulties of consolidating a stable democracy (in clear contrast with the strength of electoral democracy) is that in the third wave of democratization, fifteen democratically elected presidents have not completed their constitutional terms.[2] To put it in journalistic terms, this paradox is well stated in the title of the article "América Latina: Democrática e ingobernable" in the Chilean magazine *Siete+7* (November 29, 2002). It alludes, on one hand, to the region's healthy record of electoral democracy and, on the other, to its serious deficiencies in terms of governability. That contrast surfaces throughout this book, which is an analysis of the achievements and shortcomings of democracy in Latin America. The following reflections attempt to contribute to the necessary, urgent, and permanent task of exploring both the possibilities and the difficulties of establishing a stable democracy in Latin America within the context of acceptable conditions for good governance. The thesis of this book is that, throughout the past century, Latin American history has been marked by the search for responses or alternatives to the crisis of oligarchic rule, with the notable difficulty of replacing the oligarchic order with a democratic one. The most common response in Latin America to the oligarchic crisis and the subsequent waves of democratization and authoritarianism has been populism. We are still in this process of "de-oligarchization," demonstrated by the rise of neopopulism in our very recent history. Liberalism has been marginal, more typical of the elites than of the popular masses and more akin to authoritarianism than to democracy. The latter has had its ups and downs, materializing in a confused and inconsistent manner, more an aspiration than a reality.

Indeed, both before and after the transition to independence, there existed an oligarchic order in the economic, social, and cultural spheres, taking on different political forms, in both colonial and postcolonial times. It was an order that was elitist, hierarchical, and, as it turned out,

---

2. Hernán Siles Zuazo (1985), Gonzalo Sánchez de Lozada (2003), and Carlos Mesa (2005) in Bolivia; Abdalá Bucaram (1997), Jamil Mahuad (2000), and Lucio Gutiérrez (2005) in Ecuador; Fernando Collor de Mello in Brazil (1992); Jorge Serrano Elías in Guatemala (1993); Carlos Andrés Pérez in Venezuela (1993); Joaquín Balaguer in the Dominican Republic (1994); Raúl Cubas Grau in Paraguay (1999); Alberto Fujimori in Peru (2000); Raúl Alfonsín (1989) and Fernando de la Rúa (2001) in Argentina (see Valenzuela [2004] and Latinobarómetro [2008]); and Manuel Zelaya in Honduras (2009).

exclusionary, but it was an order, after all. After its collapse at the beginning of the twentieth century, in what we have labeled the crisis of oligarchic rule, disorder rather than a new political order ensued—the latter understood as an alliance between the middle and the popular classes—with serious institutionalization problems. It sometimes resembled democracy, but often resembled authoritarianism, at times with republican and revolutionary features, depending on when and where it took place.

This oligarchic crisis happened irregularly over time. In some cases, it took place prematurely and radically, as it did in the Mexican Revolution in 1910. In other cases, it occurred rather late, as in Central America, Peru, and Bolivia in the 1950s and 1960s. In general, and especially in South America, the oligarchic crisis transpired during the 1920s and 1930s. In the search for replies or alternatives to this crisis, revolutionary traditions arose, such as those of Mexico in 1910, Bolivia in 1952, Cuba in 1959, and Nicaragua in 1979. Diverse forms of authoritarianism also appeared, including some traditional authoritarian regimes (Fulgencio Batista in Cuba, Anastasio Somoza in Nicaragua, Rafael Trujillo in the Dominican Republic, François Duvalier in Haiti, Alfredo Strössner in Paraguay, Marcos Pérez Jiménez in Venezuela, and Gustavo Rojas Pinilla in Colombia, not to mention the authoritarian regimes of the nineteenth century). The region also had some populist authoritarian presidents (Juan Domingo Perón in Argentina and Getúlio Vargas in Brazil, to mention two emblematic examples), and some took the form of "bureaucratic-authoritarian" regimes, such as the military regimes of the Southern Cone (Argentina, Brazil, Chile, and Uruguay) in the 1960s, 1970s, and 1980s. Democracy scarcely appeared. Chile, Uruguay, and Costa Rica have long democratic traditions, although Chile and Uruguay did fall into authoritarianism in the 1970s. Colombia and Venezuela also had democracies, though with many "buts" and reservations to be accounted for. Finally, the democracies inaugurated in the "pacts" in the late 1950s after the dictatorships of Rojas Pinilla in Colombia and Pérez Jiménez in Venezuela evolved into two-party, elitist, exclusionary democracies. The case of Colombia led Alexander Wilde (1982) to describe it in the title of his book as *Conversaciones de caballeros*. What is certain is that populism did exist in Latin America, or at least a certain "national and popular" model, as it has also been called. One of its principal characteristics has been and, as I shall argue, continues to be its marked ambiguity toward representative democracy and its institutions.

Different academic theories have attempted to explain both the possibilities and limitations of democracy in Latin America. Following a systematic review of some of the principal theories, based on an analysis of the interactions of political, economic, and social factors, I maintain that it is primarily the actors, institutions, and public policies that make the difference between progress and regression in Latin American democracy. I eschew all determinism, avoiding those theories that emphasize the conditions, requisites, prerequisites, or "structural" determinants— economic, social, political, or cultural—to explain political processes such as the waves of democracy and authoritarianism in the region. I do so without failing to recognize the importance of the structural factors that underlie political phenomena, but that hardly explain the changes and transformations of (and in) political regimes. I conclude that it is *"democracia de instituciones"* (democracy of institutions) that is better suited to securing stable democracy in Latin America, under acceptable conditions for governability.

I write this introduction and finish writing this book in the middle of the most acute economic crisis in the last seventy years, with all the doubts, questions, and uncertainties about the future that such a crisis causes. I do so with the firm purpose of affirming the value of democracy and a longing for no more authoritarian regressions, while maintaining the realism and the necessary degree of skepticism acknowledging that, in light of our own history, there are no irreversible paths towards democracy. This book does not ignore the difficulties of consolidating democracy in the region, but expresses a clear option in favor of it. Reflecting on the history of democracy in Latin America systematically and in a comparative perspective, I affirm that democracy is not reserved to countries of a certain level of development or of certain cultural characteristics. I argue that Latin America is not condemned to authoritarianism and underdevelopment.

I argue in chapter 1 that, although the attempts to establish a representative and constitutional government stem from the processes of independence themselves, various circumstances, ideologies, and institutional arrangements worked against the establishment of stable democracy in the region throughout the nineteenth and twentieth centuries. Actually existing liberalism, positivism, revolution, corporatism, patrimonialism, clientelism, socialism, and populism were some of the principal attempts to respond to the crisis of oligarchic rule, opening the way to a new social and political order. All of these attempts, in one way or another, revealed serious tensions and contradictions with democracy as a form of government. None of that, however, should obscure the attempts that, from early on, took place in the region after the establishment of constitutional democracy.

In chapter 2, I analyze the shift from the era of exports (1870–1920), based on outward-looking growth, to import substitution industrialization directed by the state as perhaps the most important aspect of the oligarchic crisis from the point of view of development strategies. In some ways, the process of industrialization was one aspect of the most widespread efforts for democratization in Latin America. It involved the incorporation of the newly emerging working and middle social classes and the absorption of labor, a product of the great migrations to the cities from the rural areas (urbanization). Nevertheless, it was not long before heavy criticism and self-criticism emerged around this new model of development through industrialization and inward growth. At the core of these critiques was the question of "export pessimism" and the protectionism and developmentalist nationalism characteristic of this model, which became its Achilles' heel. The poor results of industrialization, especially the widespread reality of poverty and inequality, produced many frustrations at the social level and spurred heated intellectual debate in a climate of widespread and acute ideologization, polarization, and conflict. For some scholars (O'Donnell 1979), the breakdown of democracy in the late 1960s and early 1970s was related to the characteristics of this development strategy based on a certain type of industrialization.

In chapter 3, I reflect on some of the principal characteristics of democratic breakdowns, transitions, and consolidation in Latin America. In an attempt to systematize the abundant literature available on this topic, I explain the processes of breakdown by way of internal more than external factors, and political factors more than economic ones, arguing that there was nothing inevitable about them. I explain the analytical differences between democratic transition and consolidation and maintain that the recent processes of democratization in Latin America and in the world as a whole appear to toss out the majority of theories in the field of social science regarding the difficulties of establishing and consolidating democracy. Of these theories, some placed excessive emphasis on the economic and/or social requisites or prerequisites for democracy, or on certain factors related to political culture, or on the presidential form of government. All of these arguments contributed to the impression that democracy was reserved for countries with a certain degree of economic development (high) and certain types of social structures (complex ones), cultural characteristics (Protestant, tolerant, pluralist), or forms of government (parliamentary). Despite all these limitations, democracy has been more robust than the literature predicted for a region like Latin America (underdeveloped, Catholic, and presidentialist). It is this case that I will analyze—without ignoring the serious weaknesses associated with new democracies, primarily in the sphere of governability—in chapter 5.

In chapter 4, I hold that we see a double transition in Latin America in the 1980s and 1990s, from authoritarianism to democracy, and from import substitution industrialization (based on protectionism and state-led growth) toward a new strategy based on external openness and trade liberalization in the new era of globalization. I analyze the characteristics of a very complex transition from one development strategy to another, whether under authoritarianism or democracy, with advances and setbacks and multiple contradictions. I argue that one cannot simply speak of a new "neoliberal era" or "neoliberal democracy," for the process underway in the region is much richer, much more complex, diverse, and interesting, than those expressions suggest. Most recently we have observed the transition from a phase of marked ideological content (neoliberal) shown in the Washington Consensus, to a much more pragmatic stage in the 2000s, the political economy of the possible.

In chapter 5, I argue that much remains to be done to establish stable democracy in the region. Even with great advances in electoral democracy, there remains a great deficit in the quality of institutions and democratic governability. Along with emphasizing certain dilemmas that have characterized Latin American politics in the last century—peoples or oligarchies, development or dependence, reform or revolution, democracy or dictatorship—I focus on the chiaroscuros of the present process of democratization. These include semidemocratic or hybrid situations, which account for the distance that continues to separate electoral democracy from an authentically representative democracy (a theme that I will systematically analyze in the final chapter). I examine the tensions between the neopopulism that has arisen since the mid-1990s and representative democracy and its institutions. In this analysis, I make especial note of Hugo Chávez; while he is the most strident and visible figure in the region, Chávez and his regime are the exception and not the general rule.

Chapter 6 is my contribution to the heated academic debate over presidentialism and parliamentarism. Beginning with Juan Linz's pioneering works on this subject, which became popular in the 1980s and gave rise to intense debate, I analyze the advantages and disadvantages of one form of government over another, only to conclude that there is nothing intrinsic to either presidentialism or parliamentarism that helps to explain political stability or instability in the region. In recent Latin American history a formula appears that tends to undo the apparent contradiction between presidentialism and multipartism, by way of what is known in the surrounding literature as "coalitional presidentialism." While I develop a critical vision of presidentialism, I call for an unbiased look at the subject. I suggest that, rather than holding to dogmatic conceptions, we need to think about an "options menu" of different institutional arrangements and combinations of diverse natures, with the objective of political stability and democratic governability. Although presidentialism—like the Andes Mountains—has a strong presence in the region, we cannot discount, a priori, innovation in institutional arrangements.

In chapter 7, I explore the profound economic, social, and cultural transformations of the last two decades, regarding the rise of what I call the new social question in Latin America. This concerns those countries in which underdevelopment was the reality until the 1960s and 1970s, but which now find themselves to be middle-income countries and economies halfway between underdevelopment and development. In this context, and from the perspective of the future, the present levels of tax burden and social spending are unsustainable. In the realm of social policies, we need to shift from a traditional, static focus, with a narrow emphasis on poverty and extreme poverty, to a new, dynamic focus including the universalization of benefits and/or social rights and accounting for the emerging middle classes in the process of development. Along with emphasizing the tremendous diversity of the region, which impedes generalizations and simplistic analyses, this chapter proposes that a focus on social cohesion is the most appropriate for facing the reality of poverty, inequality, crime, and corruption.

In the eighth and final chapter, I affirm that the democracy of institutions best responds to the new needs and challenges of economic, social, and political development in Latin America. The contrast between the eighteen democratic elections that took place between 2005 and 2010 and the fifteen governments that did not complete a constitutional term between 1985 and 2010 illustrates the chiaroscuros of political and institutional development in recent Latin American history. On one hand, electoral democracy is consolidated with free, competitive, and transparent elections and non-negligible levels of electoral participation. On the other hand, however, there is a strong democratic deficit, primarily between aspirations and reality. From the perspective of democratic governability, the great challenge for Latin America today and into the future is transitioning from electoral democracy to an authentically representative democracy, which I take as synonymous with democracy of institutions.

# CHAPTER 1

# THE SEARCH FOR ALTERNATIVES TO OLIGARCHIC RULE

At different times and in various forms, liberalism, positivism, revolution, corporatism, clientelism, patrimonialism, socialism, and populism have been some of the ideologies and institutional arrangements attempted in the search for a new social and political order to replace oligarchic rule. Among these, populism has been Latin America's most paradigmatic response to the oligarchic crisis and the emergence of the "social question" in the early twentieth century. All of these ideologies and institutional arrangements have included an understanding of democracy that is full of tensions and contradictions. Yet despite these tensions, seeds of democratic development existed in liberal and republican ideology of the nineteenth century (and even in positivist ideology, especially following its search for the idea of modernity).

## LIBERALISM

Beginning with the struggles for independence, ruling elites envisioned a representative and constitutional government. The political processes then taking place in Europe and the United States of America and the re-publicanism and constitutionalism already present in the Hispanic world strongly influenced this republican concept. Republicanism—and, by the same token, liberalism—was not simply imported from Europe. Al-though this is not the place to discuss the theoretical and historiographi-cal differences and disputes between republicanism and liberalism (see Aguilar and Rojas 2002), the latter was one of the most influential ide-ologies of the nineteenth century, especially among the ruling elites. The actually existing liberalism seen in Latin America in the second half of the nineteenth century and throughout the twentieth was more con-nected to economic freedom and authoritarianism than to political free-dom and democracy. As a political philosophy, liberalism did not take root in social and political processes beyond some vague references to the idea of freedom found in constitutional texts. Struggles for universal suffrage came belatedly and in a partial and contradictory manner (with few exceptions) following the search for an authentically democratic and representative government. In the history of liberalism in Latin America, democracy was the exception and not the general rule.

The republican and liberal ideas that the forgers of independence heard about and defended had their origins in the North American and French revolutions of 1776 and 1789, respectively. Their reception by the Latin American elites was often disconnected from the cultural, so-cial, and political reality of the region. By the end of the colonial era, the monarchies of Spain and Portugal exhibited a type of enlightened des-potism with the first liberalizing reforms in the economic sphere, break-ing with the rigid, monopolistic control of trade between the Iberian Peninsula and the overseas colonies. The other effect of the Bourbon re-forms in Spain and the Pombaline reforms in Portugal, with their ratio-nalist, reformist, modernizing and liberalizing components, was a strong administrative recentralization, which conservative forces in the newly formed American republics reinforced time and again during the nine-teenth century. The Latin American reception of Spain's Cádiz Consti-tution of 1812 varied, while at the same time the restoration of Ferdi-nand VII to the throne in 1814 reinforced efforts to secure the precarious constitutional democracy forged since 1810. The outcome of the wars for independence was not necessarily the ideology of freedom and democracy (despite the various essays that displayed such sentiment), but rather anarchy, *caudillismo*, militarism and civil wars, accompanied more often by conservative and authoritarian solutions than by liberal and democratic ones.

The forerunners of Latin American independence (such as Francisco de Miranda and Simón Bolívar in Venezuela; Antonio Nariño in Colombia; Manuel Belgrano and José de San Martín in Argentina; and Bernardo O'Higgins in Chile) worked diligently for independence and separation from Spain, but were less concerned with freedom and democracy. Most of these men defended republican notions, understood as a form of government contrary to monarchy and based on a representative, elective, and constitutional system of government (Aguilar and Rojas 2002, 82). Some, however, ended up advocating the monarchic cause, while others openly opted for dictatorial rule. After Napoleonic forces invaded the Iberian Peninsula, the monarchy was literally transferred to Brazil. It wasn't until 1889 that Brazil established a republic. All of this occurred in clear contrast to the case of the United States, which embraced liberty and the republican cause without ambiguities (notwithstanding its own internal contradictions), with democratic elements that deepened and developed throughout the nineteenth century. From the beginning, the Declaration of Independence advanced the principle of equality, and the Founding Fathers passionately debated the Constitution and institutions in order to make them more consistent with the common ideology of liberty and the republic.

In Latin America, the nineteenth century was marked by constant struggles between liberals and conservatives. While liberals opened the way for federalism, with the United States exerting some influence, conservatives defended centralism. Liberals pushed to limit or even eliminated ecclesiastical privileges and advocated the separation of church and state. In contrast, conservatives allied themselves with the Catholic Church and its prerogatives. And while liberals introduced the idea of individual rights based around a vague idea of economic progress and free trade, conservatives defended many of the institutions of the old regime, especially within the social order.

Liberal ideas emerged during the struggles for independence and in the years immediately following, influenced by writer José María Luis Mora in Mexico; President Bernardino Rivadavia (1826–1827) in Argentina (principally in the province of Buenos Aires in connection with the Constitution of 1826); in Honduras with the Constitution of 1824 and the newly formed (and ultimately unsuccessful) United Provinces of Central America; and by the irruption of the *pipiolos*, or liberals, in the constitutional experiments of the 1820s in Chile. The liberal impulse was driven forward under the Colombian president Francisco de Paula Santander (1832–1836), a pragmatic liberal who promoted political, constitutional, and religious reforms associated within a model of constitutional government and rule of law. Experiments linked to liberal ideology were few and far between, ending in failure and the reinstatement of conservatism.

After a series of constitutional experiments in the 1810s and 1820s, political stability became a necessity to fend off disorder and anarchy. This stability was most often achieved under authoritarian rule. Among these authoritarian leaders were Juan Manuel de Rosas, who commanded Argentina from 1829 to 1852 and in 1835 demanded unlimited power to exercise dictatorial control over the provinces; Dr. José Gaspar Rodríguez de Francia (1812–1840) in Paraguay; José Antonio Páez, who governed until the 1840s in Venezuela, more a military caudillo than a dictator in the style of Rosas; General Antonio López de Santa Anna in Mexico, who suspended the Federalist Constitution in 1824 to open the way for his authoritarian exercise of power; José Rafael Carrera, who defeated the liberalizing attempts of Francisco Morazán between 1823 and 1837 in Central America, instituted a conservative order, restored ecclesiastical privileges and jurisdictions, and dominated the political scene in his authoritarian manner until his death in 1865; and finally, the presidential authoritarianism created by Diego Portales in Chile, even under a political format of impersonal authority and the legal and orderly transfer of power.

In the 1850s, a new political generation emerged to counter the conservative and authoritarian onslaught, with the objective of promoting liberal reforms in the region. Historians call the period between 1850 and 1880 the peak of liberal reforms in Latin America (Bushnell and

Macaulay 1988).[1] This new political generation, the first to authentically represent liberal ideals, sought profound political and constitutional reforms and laid the foundation for a liberal order. Such was the case of Benito Juárez (president of Mexico from 1858 to 1872), a Zapotec Indian who barely spoke Spanish until age twelve and who carried out what historians call "the Reform" (1855–1861) in Mexico, primarily based on the Constitution of 1857. The Law of Juárez (1855) put an end to ecclesiastical and military privileges and jurisdictions, generating heated disputes with the conservative sectors that resulted in political and social upheaval (Halperin 1993). Contrary to the corporate system and conservative centralism that commanded the country until the 1850s, the Constitution of 1857 set up a regime based on individual liberties and a federal system. It introduced universal suffrage (despite various limitations) for the first time. Meanwhile, the Catholic Church excommunicated any person who swore to respect and defend the Constitution. General Porfirio Díaz (president of Mexico from 1876 to 1911) headed the regime that served as a model for further Latin American political development, based on a combination of political authoritarianism and economic liberalism. Ironically, the very motto that Porfirio Díaz had used against the attempted reelection of Lerdo y Tejada in 1876 ("No reelection, effective suffrage") was used again a quarter century later to remove Díaz from power, culminating in the Revolution of 1910. The short-lived attempts of Francisco Madero's government to take up the liberal ideology of José María Luis Mora and Benito Juárez (lasting fifteen months between 1911 and1913) confirmed the ongoing difficulties of consolidating the ideals of constitutional government and a democratic and liberal order in Latin America.

Following in the footsteps of Francisco de Paula Santander (president of Gran Colombia from 1819 to 1826; president of the Republic of New Granada from 1832 to 1837), General José Hilario López's liberal Reform (1849–1853) was another attempt to install a liberal order in Latin America. Implemented after the election that ended the conservative rule of General Tomás Cipriano de Mosquera (1849), it initiated

---

1. In the following lines, I pay special attention to the work of Bushnell and Macaulay (1988) and Halperin (1993).

a period of great upheaval and violent confrontation between liberals and conservatives. The liberal Constitution of 1853 established the right to vote, (nominal) federalism, the abolition of slavery, and the separation of church and state (with a strong anticlerical sentiment that included the expulsion of the Jesuits from Colombia). After the conservative reaction against these reforms and the civil war of 1858 to 1861, the liberal triumph of 1863 led to a new constitution, which lasted for twenty-two years. Its regulations included the confiscation of church properties, the confirmation of federalism, and the guarantee of individual rights and universal suffrage. In 1870, a system of free and universal primary education was established. Nevertheless, the tone was set for constant confrontations between liberals and conservatives in the form of the civil wars and violence that have been characteristic of Colombia even until our era. Finally, after the civil war of 1876, a crisis of exports and foreign trade marked the end of the "liberal era" in Colombia and led to the dictatorship of Rafael Núñez (1880–1888). Written during this centralist and conservative administration, the Constitution of 1886 made the achievements and reforms of the liberal era disappear. Almost half a century of conservatism (including the Thousand Days' War from 1899 to 1903) followed after Núñez decreed a process of conservative "Regeneration" in the 1880s, continuing until a liberal, Enrique Olaya Herrera, was finally elected in 1930. Social structures, however, remained virtually untouched, driving a strong radicalization of one faction of Colombian liberalism. The assassination of one representative of this radicalization, Jorge Eliécer Gaitán, on April 9, 1948, triggered a new period of violence, culminating in the dictatorship of Gustavo Rojas Pinilla (1953–1957).

Something similar to Juárez's liberal regime (although in a more moderate form) occurred in Argentina after the end of the Rosas dictatorship in 1852. A new political era and generation came into being, adopting a liberal, progressive, and federalist nature. It was formed in the context of the struggles between Buenos Aires and the rest of the provinces, and one of its most evident and lasting achievements was the Constitution of 1853. These liberal reforms included the establishment of a federal system, the guarantee of individual rights, the separation of powers, religious freedom, and the abolition of slavery and of military and ecclesiastical privileges, among others. Not included, however, was the true extension of the right to vote—which was already implied in the law of universal suffrage of 1821—an issue that would not be resolved until 1912 under President Roque Sáenz Peña (1910–1914). Among the precursors of liberal reform in Argentina, Domingo Faustino Sarmiento, president of the republic from 1868 to 1874, and intellectual leaders such as Juan Bautista Alberdi and Bartolomé Mitre stand out. Still, the liberal reforms carried out in Argentina, especially those between 1850 and 1870, ended like so many other attempts to bring about similar reforms in Latin America, with the emergence of a dictatorship—in this case the dictatorship of General Julio Roca in the early 1880s. The presidencies of Roca (1880–1886 and 1898–1904) concluded the turbulent process of forming a national state, including the "federalization" of Buenos Aires. Roca's command, first as a military man and later as a politician, spanned almost two decades of Argentine politics, from the late nineteenth century to the early twentieth century. Indeed, Natalio Botana has pondered labeling this period a "hidden *porfiriato*" (2005, 34).

A similar political generation appeared in Chile in the 1850s and, under the influence of Francisco Bilbao, adopted the radical Society of Equality, a combination of political liberalism and utopian socialism. The emergence of liberal ideology took on different forms from the 1850s to the 1880s—some doctrinaire, some more pragmatic. These forms included a tendency toward religious tolerance (clerical-anticlerical struggles marked the period and gave rise to the party system in the 1850s) and the necessity of limiting the enormous political power of the executive branch established by the Constitution of 1833 and the presidential authoritarianism of the ten-year periods of José Joaquín Prieto, Manuel Bulnes, and Manuel Montt (1830–1860). This last aspect led to the formation of the curious Liberal-Conservative Fusion, destined to strengthen the power of parliament and the parties, and a regime of freedoms backed by both liberals and conservatives. It culminated in the political reforms of 1874, including the establishment of universal suffrage. Liberal president José Manuel Balmaceda (1889–1891) attempted to undo these reforms, strengthening the power of the executive branch. This, among other factors, led to civil war in 1891 which, unlike in the rest of Latin America, did not result in a dictatorship but rather in a distorted presidentialism—the badly labeled "parliamentary regime" (1891–1920)—in the midst of a comprehensive regime of public liberties.

The end of the nineteenth century saw a renewed push for the liberal ideology in Central America. Such was the case of the presidency of José Santos Zelaya in Nicaragua, beginning in 1893. Once again, however, the liberalizing reforms in Central America were most often accompanied by authoritarian politics. One such case is Justo Rufino Barrios, who, following Guatemala's Liberal Revolution of 1871, later became president of the republic (1873–1885). The "republican dictatorships" (Skidmore and Smith 2005) of Central America confirmed the widespread presence of economic liberalism and political authoritarianism in the region, bolstered by the alliance of the oligarchs and the military. External control increasingly accompanied this internal control, chiefly on the part of the United States, which in turn was becoming a world superpower (especially after World War I). Strategic and economic ideas surrounding manifest destiny (introduced under the Monroe Doctrine in 1823) were transforming the Central American republics into veritable protectorates of the United States under the premise of "civilizing" the newly formed (and chaotic) Latin American republics. Gunboat diplomacy and "big-stick ideology," utilized since the presidency of Theodore Roosevelt (1901–1909), transformed Central America and the Caribbean into a sphere of influence for the United States by way of interventions and constant occupations. In the economic realm, the famed United Fruit Company came to refer to the "banana republics" in the region. Meanwhile, the Batistas (Cuba), Somozas (Nicaragua), and Trujillos (Dominican Republic) gained power, along with all those promoters of republics that boldly proclaimed economic freedom alongside authoritarian politics.

In the nineteenth century, as we will see in following chapters, the story of Latin America was that of "slow adaptation to the global economy" (Skidmore and Smith 2005, 38). Along the way, the doctrine of liberalism came to mean economic freedom more than political freedom. The peak of liberal ideology between 1850 and 1880 corresponds to what one historian has called the construction of a "neocolonial" economic order, marked by trade, economic freedom, exportation of raw materials, and the triumph of economic liberalism (Halperin 1993, 128). During this slow and irregular incorporation into the global economy, rather than sustaining a liberal and democratic political regime, liberalism fed progress, free trade, and exporting efforts within a social order that maintained basic continuity in the years before and after independence. From the *Científicos* under Porfirio Díaz in Mexico to the Chicago Boys under Pinochet in Chile (1973–1990), liberal authoritarianism, rather than liberal democracy, has been the trend in the region. Even if liberalism was the "dominant ideology" (Bushnell and Macaulay 1988, 12 and 287) throughout the nineteenth century (even more so than in the twentieth), and even if this developing and doctrinaire liberalism later gave rise to processes of democratization, these trials were marked by unresolved tensions and contradictions that often resulted in authoritarian politics. The more recent experience of bureaucratic-authoritarian regimes in the Southern Cone is really just a more refined (and relentless) present-day version of liberalism that protects economic freedom at the expense of political freedom. Indeed, the constitutions dictated by the Batista, Somoza, and Trujillo families were among the most liberal of their time periods, but nonetheless preserved social structures and oligarchic order by way of authoritarian politics.

None of this should lead us to believe that liberalism in Latin America has been simply a façade or a thinly veiled form of authoritarianism. The ideology of liberalism and the attempts to establish a representative and constitutional government within a republic have had to coexist with the need for a new political order—a veritable "state in form," as Alberto Edwards (1959) has labeled the case of Chile—in the wake of collapsed monarchies. As Daniel Negretto wrote, "There were not many viable options for a political order in the Hobbesian world that the republican project faced in Latin America in the nineteenth century" (in Aguilar and Rojas 2002, 34). The various attempts and struggles to establish a liberal ideology and a representative democracy occurred within this context of tensions and contradictions that were never resolved. Yet, in spite of its limitations, liberalism prevailed as the dominant ideology of the nineteenth century.

## POSITIVISM

Positivism was one of the first systematic attempts to address the question of modernity in the region, as opposed to the premodern ways of the old oligarchic regime. Positivism was championed in various Latin American countries from the 1880s until the 1920s, but its greatest influence was in Mexico and Brazil. It was not, however, a result of liberalism—rather, it critiqued liberalism. Neither did it stem from political democracy, as it promoted an elitist and hierarchical view, making use of authoritarian structures and concepts more than democratic ones.

In the second half of the nineteenth century, there were various attempts to modernize the economic, social, and political structures. Along with this modernization came efforts to achieve a greater level of order and political stability in a century marked by civil war, *caudillismo*, and all sorts of dictatorships, as well as the interminable disputes between liberals and conservatives, federalists and centralists, clericalists and anticlericalists. Immigration from Europe, the presence of foreign capital (mainly British), the first signs of a new economic infrastructure, the creation of a bureaucracy that would be consistent with "legal-rational" authority (to use Max Weber's terminology), and the creation of armed forces capable of guarding the new borders formed by the failure of Bolivar's great dream of a Gran Colombia—all these were expressions of the search for rationalization and, above all, for a new philosophy that could support the desire for progress and structural modernization (Wiarda 2001, 146).

Positivism, even more than liberalism, proved to be one of the potential responses to these problems, especially among the elites. From the first signs of economic progress in the 1850s and onward, political stability became imperative. It overcame the reactionary position of the church, the military, and the oligarchy, which were perceived as the last bastions of the old regime. All of this came together in the idea of "order and progress," the expression of positivist philosophy in Latin America.

Here we turn to Auguste Comte (1798–1857), one of the fathers of sociology, who proposes the thesis of an organic order of the universe in an attempt to decipher the scientific laws that govern the universe and society. Positivism is the final of three stages—theological, metaphysical, and scientific—characterized by a rationalist and modern vision of social phenomenon. With its critique of individualism and the liberalism of John Locke, this organic vision of society resonated with the Latin American elites who strove for order and progress, articulated concretely in the drive for education, infrastructure, a modern bureaucracy, and professional armed forces. All of this was expressed through a certain social engineering, done from above, capable of shaping society and its structures, opening the way for modernity and progress, and replacing the traditional scholasticism with a new, positivist political philosophy.

This positivist vision manifested during the dictatorship of Porfirio Díaz in Mexico (1876–1910). Enacted by the *Científicos*, a sort of technocracy of the period, it led to a period of authoritarian political stability and unprecedented economic progress. Political authoritarianism and economic liberalism were the formula of the Porfiriato, characterized by the emergence of a new middle class rife with contradictions that would build up until the outbreak of revolution in 1910.

In the case of Brazil, the technocratic elites and military academies introduced positivism with the intention of structural modernization, resulting in the motto ("Order and Progress") seen on the Brazilian flag following the belated establishment of the republic (1889). Although linked to the emergence of the republic, the military and technocrats gave this positivist push an elitist and authoritarian character, similar to the case of Mexico. This made the military an active presence in Brazilian politics throughout the twentieth century. The alliance of technocrats and the military, of ideas of economic liberalism in the direction of progress and modernization and authoritarian political structures, would become paradigmatic of Latin American political and economic development in the twentieth century. Neither liberalism (incipient, partial, and contradictory), nor republicanism (an ideal more than a political reality), nor positivism (elitist, hierarchical, and vertical) were suitable to replace the old oligarchic order with a new, democratic one. Nevertheless, seeds of democratic development could be found in these three concepts throughout the nineteenth century.

## REVOLUTION

In the frustrating transition from the old oligarchic regime to the new so-cial and political order, many of the contradictions brewing in the eco-nomic, social, and political structures resulted in revolutionary actions that developed through the twentieth century. It is notable (especially because the Bolshevik Revolution would follow only seven years later) that Mexico was the first to appear on the scene, its revolution breaking out in 1910. Revolutionary ideology captured the imagination of elites throughout the twentieth century. These revolutions, however, went hand in hand not with democracy, but rather with authoritarianism.

Gary Wynia (1984) proposes that revolutions, understood as the violent transformation of economic, social, and political structures and the replacement of an old regime by a new social order, have been rather scarce in modern Latin American history. If this is the case, it is also true that revolution has formed a legitimate part of the region's search for re-sponses to the crisis of oligarchic rule. Wynia himself asserts that Mexico's violent revolution in 1910 led to the replacement of an oligarchy (the Por-firiato and the oligarchic regime that remained despite the modernizing reforms of Porfirio Díaz) by a new oligarchy, the Institutional Revolution-ary Party (PRI). Meant to be a compromise among differing revolutionary factions, the PRI was established by Plutarco Elías Calles (1924–1928) and was later reinforced by Lázaro Cárdenas in the 1930s.

Thus, there was a definite substitution of one dictatorship for an-other (the "perfect dictatorship," as Mario Vargas Llosa would call it), giving way to the hegemonic PRI that could establish a new political order—no small feat, given Latin America's instability and political dis-order—but not democracy. Neither the blood shed by Francisco Madero, Emiliano Zapata, Pancho Villa, Venustiano Carranza, and Álvaro Obre-gón, all killed in the years that followed the revolution, nor the new cor-porate structures put in place by the PRI were able to transform the old oligarchic order into a new democratic one. The new oligarchy governed in an orderly and legal fashion, providing the country with political sta-bility and a certain degree of economic progress, but not with democracy. The transition to democracy did not take place in Mexico until the year 2000, with the transfer of power from Ernesto Zedillo (1994–2000) to

Vicente Fox (2000–2006) after a complex process of reforms, advances, and setbacks that began in the late 1960s.

The PRI and the *priísta* state were characterized by a corporate, inclusive, and clientelistic structure that functioned from above to control and co-opt not just different revolutionary factions and leaders, but also the social sectors they supported: workers, peasants, the armed forces, and the "popular sector," an ambiguous label that included intellectuals and other sections of society. If the new regime was indeed extraordinarily efficient and capable of securing the legal and orderly transfer of power (done regularly every six-year period), it was only possible thanks to the undisputed and quasi-monopolistic rule of the PRI and its effective control over society. According to Wynia, the PRI was not only able to replace one oligarchy with another, but also ended up imposing the same technocratic logic that was in place under the *Científicos* (although in a more complex and sophisticated form) during the presidencies of José López Portillo (1976–1982), Miguel de la Madrid (1982–1988), Carlos Salinas de Gotarí (1988–1994), and Ernesto Zedillo. This last administration facilitated the transition to democracy, handing over power to Vicente Fox in 2000.

Why, Huntington (1968) asks, can the Mexican Revolution be considered successful while the Bolivian Revolution is considered unsuccessful? Huntington is not interested in the form of government (dictatorship or democracy), but rather in the degree of government and the ability to construct a political order. The Mexican Revolution and its subsequent institutionalization were extremely effective and successful at replacing a certain highly personalized political order, the Porfiriato, with a new, highly institutionalized order, the PRI.

Huntington believes the difference between Mexico and Bolivia lies in the high levels of institutionalization in the PRI compared with the low level of institutionalization in the Bolivian Revolution, unstable both in its beginnings and its development. The Mexican Revolution of 1910 was preceded by a dictatorship, but also by a period of great economic dynamism accompanied by great social contradictions and a high personalization of power. The Mexican Revolution was successful not only because of its great display of violence (a million casualties), which is inherent to any genuinely revolutionary process, but also because of its subsequent successful institutionalization which, together with the myth of the revolution itself (a myth that unified Mexican society), permitted the transition from the old regime to the new one.

According to Huntington's analysis, none of this was present in the unsuccessful Bolivian Revolution of 1952. Against the backdrop of the infamous and bloody Chaco War, a coup d'état by midranking officials and young leaders of the Revolutionary Nationalist Movement (MNR) in 1943 was a precursor to revolution. The objective of the 1952 revolution was not just to claim the electoral triumph won by Víctor Paz Estenssoro in 1951—the MNR leader went into exile when his legitimate victory went unrecognized—but rather to substitute an oligarchic political order with a revolutionary one, all the while dealing with the eternal disputes over power between Paz Estenssoro and Hernán Siles Zuazo (Paz Estenssoro's vice-president and twice president in his own right) that continued until the 1990s.

What went wrong with the 1952 revolution? In the first place, Huntington argues, the seizure of power by the young officials and MNR leaders involved little violence (three thousand casualties in comparison with the one million dead in the Mexican Revolution). Secondly, the different leaders of the revolution remained on the scene while Paz Estenssoro tried to remain in power. In the Mexican Revolution, in contrast, almost all the leaders were physically and violently eliminated, ending all attempts to stay in power and necessitating a formula of institutionalizing (and thus resolving peacefully) the succession of power. Third, there was no attempt in the Bolivian Revolution to centralize institutions capable of subordinating all groups to one political authority. Instead, a co-government evolved between the MNR and the Central Obrera Boliviana (COB) that was very distinct from the PRI's corporate arrangement of integration and subordination of emerging social forces. Finally, Huntington concludes, there was a strange absence of antiforeigner sentiment in the Bolivian Revolution, as the chief owners of the mines were Bolivians (Simón Patiño and Carlos Aramayo, among others). Meanwhile, there was a certain degree of sympathy from abroad, even from the United States. There may have existed, then, an anti-oligarchic component, but not the anti-imperialist sentiment that is trademark of almost every revolution, at least in Latin America. Postrevolutionary Bolivia witnessed just about everything except the consolidation of a democratic government. Only since the mid-1980s has Bolivia begun to have a degree of democratic political stability, at least compared to its own history.

If the ideologies of liberalism, positivism, and revolution have taken a more authoritarian than democratic route in the endless search for alternatives to oligarchic rule, corporatism (as well as its close relatives, clientelism and patrimonialism) has also not lived up to the expectations and demands of a democratic regime.

## CORPORATISM

Just as positivism had an important presence in Latin America between the 1870s and 1920s, corporatism was likewise influential in the 1930s and 1940s, the period between wars. Dating back to medieval times, shaped by Thomist thought and strongly rooted in Catholicism and Hispanism, corporatism reflects an organic concept of society that is as distant from liberalism as it is from Marxism. For this reason, perhaps, it took root in Latin America. The crash of 1929 and the subsequent crisis of liberal capitalism and the communist threat following the Bolshevik Revolution of 1917 created the conditions for the emergence of corporatism in both southern Europe (Italy, Spain, and Portugal) and Latin America—both regions strongly influenced by Catholicism.

Corporatism corresponds to a way of articulating the relationship between society and the state through a system of representation, or mediation, of interests. Sometimes, especially in the Catholic tradition, it has been identified with the concept of "intermediate bodies" with "hierarchically ordered categories of differing functions" (Philippe Schmitter, quoted in Cohen and Pavoncello 1987, 117). It is historically linked (especially in the Middle Ages) to the privileges of the church, nobility, and the military. Since the 1930s in Latin America, corporatism corresponded to a way of articulating the interests of workers, businesses, and the state, searching for harmony among the social classes as an alternative to class warfare and individualistic liberalism. Corporatism assumes some form of control by the state from above and a degree of privilege—while not monopolistic—for the particular interests represented in society. It thus differs from a horizontal, pluralistic notion that includes nonhierarchical representation from a variety of interests and based on competition and willful intent.

The culminating moment of corporatism in Latin America came during the interwar period. Differing from one place to another, corporatism had various influences, including the fascism of Benito Mussolini, who, in the 1930s, attempted to coordinate the interests of work and capital through action by the state, and Pope Pius XI's 1931 social encyclical *Quadragesimo Anno*. Often understood as a sort of third way between liberal capitalism and Marxism, corporatism established itself in various Latin American countries. It appeared under the PRI regime in Mexico and likewise under Getúlio Vargas's formula of Estado Novo in Brazil in the 1930s. Similarly, the MNR in Bolivia, the American Popular Revolutionary Alliance (APRA) in Peru, and the actions of young Catholic politicians known as National Falange in Chile were strongly shaped by corporatist ideology. If corporatism did not prosper, it was because of the defeat of fascism in Italy. Furthermore, the discredit of authoritarian and corporatist methods in Franco's Spain and in Oliveira Salazar's regime in Portugal, among others, undermined the important influence that corporatism had gained in the 1930s. The resurgence of liberal capitalism in the West and communism in the USSR after World War II likewise undermined the corporatist model.

Central to corporatism was the attempt to overcome not just the crisis of liberal capitalism, but also oligarchic predominance, finding new ways to mediate the relationship between the state and society. In Latin America, corporatism took both conservative and progressive forms. We may look, for example, to the original experience of the Revolutionary Government of the Armed Forces in Peru under Juan Velasco Alvarado (1968–1975), an experiment that took its shape from the third way between capitalism and communism, based on organic and corporatist thought (Lowenthal 1975). Though based on the same doctrine of national security as the bureaucratic-authoritarian regimes of the Southern Cone, it differed from them by emphasizing the challenges of development more than anticommunist logic. The Revolutionary Government of the Armed Forces stressed inclusion rather than exclusion of various social sectors. Ultimately, according to Julio Cotler (in Lowenthal 1975,

62), despite its almost complete failure, one of the few achievements of the 1968 revolution was that "the military government ended the oligarchic phase in Peru's history."

In fact, it was the Peruvian experience from 1968 to 1975 that inspired Alfred Stepan's (1978) theory about the relation between society and the state in Latin America, based on an organic and corporatist understanding of the state. Stepan claims that neither liberal (or liberal-pluralist) theories nor Marxist theories could adequately convey the true nature of the relationship between the state and society, as both theories share a negative view of the state. Rather, with its Catholic and Hispanic influences and its background in Aristotle, Roman law, and natural law, Latin America evinced a positive view of the state as an agent of the common good. This theory, known as organic statism, has at its core the idea of the state's autonomy, a clear contrast to liberalism and Marxism, where the state is seen as a reflection or epiphenomenon of social and economic structures. In the language of the social sciences, the organic-state concept considers the state an independent variable rather than a dependent variable. This elitist and hierarchical theory expressed the reality of Peru's revolutionary military government, as well as the region as a whole—a region in which elites shape society from above through the action of the state. Corporatism is a particular arrangement grounded in this more abstract form of the organic-statist model.

Despite the fact that corporatism was attempted in various Latin American countries and in various forms as an alternative to oligarchic predominance, it did not lead to democracy. Patrimonialism and clientelism, which evolved from corporatism, have likewise failed to contribute to a democratic form of government.

## PATRIMONIALISM

Patrimonialism is a traditional authority, as established in Max Weber's classic typology. It refers to government (or, more broadly, to the state and the political community itself) as the private dominion of the ruler, as if it were an extension of his or her home or domain (patrimony). It reflects the necessity of adapting to political communities larger than the small sphere of the home. Patrimonial authority governs its subjects as if they were personal dependents. Under this traditional form of domination, "the ruler treats his political administration as a personal matter, and in the same way, he exploits political power as an aspect of his private property" (Bendix 1977, 334 and 345).

Weber distinguishes between the different types of legitimization of domination, addressing the question of why humans obey other humans. Types of domination include the traditional form, which is the authority of the "eternal yesterday," the customs of the patriarch or prince of the old days; charismatic domination, relating to special gifts of individual leadership and the devotion and trust inspired in others by the plebiscite leader, demagogue, or party leader; and finally, legal-rational domination, in which authority is based on legal statutes and competence within rationally created laws (Gerth and Mills 1946). Patrimonialism is thus a personalized and traditional exercise of power, relationship, and exchange, differing from the modern, bureaucratic, legal form of authority (which is necessarily impersonal).

Patrimonialism is characterized by "bureaucracy permeated by personal relationships of clientelistic nature" (Roth and Heeger, quoted in Theobald 1982, 550). It is a common phenomenon in the developing world, arising as a traditional form of domination capable of coexisting with modern structures, despite the obvious tensions between them. In the case of Latin America, much attention has been given to patrimonialism in Brazil. With Brazil in mind, Riordan Roett (in Theobald 1982, 551) defines patrimonialism as a highly flexible and paternalistic public order based on the exchange of favors (especially in the form of public employment), in which the ruler uses resources as a form of co-optation and control.

According to Brazilian political scientist Bolívar Lamonuier, patrimonialism not only explains many of the events in Brazil's democratic period from 1946 to 1964, but also persists today, especially in the relationship between politics and the business world. "Brazil has a patrimonialistic structure, in that the state holds the wealth. Its power is overbearing. . . . To be a great Brazilian businessperson, one needs a symbiotic relationship with the government, because the government has a hand in everything" (Interview in *O Estado de Sao Paulo*, July 13 2008). This helps to explain why corruption is a persistent problem within power structures in Brazil and throughout Latin America. The relationship between the state and the private sector (and interest groups in general) corresponds to the relationship between the boss and the client. Inherent to patrimonialism, it is also seen in the related phenomenon of clientelism.

Whether authoritarian or democratic, patrimonialism has been a permanent characteristic of Latin American politics. The power of the state, levels of discretion by authorities, the absence of the rule of law and institutions that safeguard transparency, and the lack of accountability make widespread corruption a concern in Latin American political systems. We will return to this theme later. Meanwhile, I wish to point to patrimonialism and clientelism as the foundation of this reality and the difficulty of consolidating a modern and genuine representative democracy. The personalization of power that is characteristic of patrimonialism, clientelism, and populism (as well as *caciquismo* and *caudillismo*) presents a serious challenge to establishing modern and stable democracy in the region.

From a republican perspective, blurring the line between the public and private threatens the basic principle of the republican vision — the clear, unequivocal distinction between the public and private spheres. Autonomy and dignity in the public sphere in terms of the private interests represented in society are characteristic of the republican vision. In Latin America, the reality of widespread patrimonialism and clientelism poses a threat to this republican principle.

## CLIENTELISM

Patrimonialism and clientelism are virtually inseparable, conceptually speaking, and are usually found under a personal and premodern articulation of the relationship between the state and society. Like patrimonialism, clientelism can coexist with modern structures. By definition, clientelism refers to the exchange of favors and loyalties within a traditional boss-client relationship.

When we speak of patronage, political machines, and clientelism in Latin America, we refer to the personalized relationship between those who govern and those who are governed, based on reciprocity between an inferior and a superior and the unequal appropriation and use of resources (Lemarchand and Legg 1972, 151). This contrasts with the Weberian ideal of bureaucratic relations, based on rationality, anonymity, impersonality, and universalism. These qualities are absent in clientelism, which is based on emotional, personalized, particularized, reciprocal relations between social and political actors. A network of reciprocity is created around this exchange of favors and personal loyalties. Counterintuitively, clientelism can actually be an agent of modernization, taking advantage of the strongly centralized state structures in Latin America, which lend themselves to a relationship between the state (the boss) and interest groups (the clients). It's no surprise, then, that patrimonialism and clientelism play a part in the search for a response to the oligarchic crisis.

By their own logic, however, patrimonialism and clientelism present obstacles to structural modernization and democratization. Networks of reciprocity and personal loyalties help to explain the region's struggles with development strategies. As we will see in the next chapter, this characteristic became more accentuated under the paradigm for development dominant from the 1940s to the 1970s and focused on strengthening the power of the state without also adequately strengthening the power of the rule of law. Although they pushed for various market reforms, the development strategies that emerged under the recent bureaucratic-authoritarian regimes were not successful in this regard. In fact, they represented the most brutal form of concentration of state and political power since the struggles for independence.

Contrary to what one might conclude from our reflection so far, I will later argue that these characteristics of Latin American political culture and structures and the various attempts to initiate a new democratic order have not been an insurmountable obstacle to establishing democracy. In fact, I will question the deterministic theories that have been so in vogue in the social sciences and that explain if not the impossibility, then the difficulty of establishing and consolidating democracy in the region. Latin America's cultural, economic, social, and political characteristics and structures do not condemn the region to authoritarianism. For now, it will suffice to point out that the historical experience of "real liberalism," positivism, revolution, corporatism, patrimonialism, and clientelism has been in constant tension with constitutional democracy in the efforts to replace an oligarchic order with a new one.

## SOCIALISM

Before moving on to a more detailed analysis of the relationship between populism and democracy, I want to mention the rise and development of socialism as one of the many alternatives in the search for answers to the oligarchic crisis. Socialism, as developed in Latin America, certainly does not escape the tensions and contradictions with democracy outlined above. Neither nineteenth-century liberalism nor twentieth-century Marxism truly achieved popular support (Wiarda 2001) in the context of colonial and postcolonial structures and political culture that have demonstrated serious resistance to liberal individualism and Marxist collectivism. Although the struggles of the Latin American left were in a sense linked to the struggle for structural democratization, they remained in constant tension with democratic institutions, labeled "formal" or "bourgeois" democracy. Only in recent history has democratic socialism emerged in an important sector of the Latin American left, at the center of which is an appreciation of democracy as inherently good.

The first signs of socialism in Latin America arose in the early twentieth century, linked to the struggles of the working classes, the so-called social question, and the new phenomenon of industrialization, urbanization, and migration from the rural sectors to the city that characterized the region at the time. As in Europe, the initial forms of social organization occurred primarily in mutual benefit societies, unions, and strikes, while a tense relationship existed in the political sphere between Marxists and anarchists. Unlike in Europe, however, the subsequent development of Latin American socialism was a mixture of nationalism and populism with an indigenous influence more significant than Marxist or anarchist. The conflict in 1917 Russia was between the Bolsheviks and Mensheviks, while in the rest of Europe the conflict existed between the communist left of Lenin and Antonio Gramsci and the social democratic left of Eduard Bernstein and Jean Jaurès, among others. Socialism and the Latin American left, in contrast, evolved from a combination of populism, nationalism, and indigenous movements and revolutionary Marxist socialism. The latter was expressed differently throughout the twentieth century but was consolidated (especially after the Cuban Revolution in 1959) into waves of convergence and opposition between the region's socialist and communist parties.

Political democracy was never valued intrinsically in any of these phases, whether under the influence of Marxism or anarchism, populist or Marxist socialism, the communist or socialist left. Rather, the position of the left, defined in terms of class struggle and revolution, systematically and consistently denounced democratic political institutions as a means of capitalist domination and a cosmetic form of democracy. It also severely criticized the European left and social democracy, which placed so much emphasis on reformism and trying to construct a capitalist system "with a human face." This critique became particularly sharp after the triumph of the Cuban Revolution, which radicalized the Latin American left and created tension between orthodoxy (communism) and heterodoxy (socialism). The latter's thesis of leapfrogging—which questioned the idea of moving from capitalism to socialism and from socialism to communism in a long process in which the internal contradictions of each mode of protection matured—put the orthodox communists on the defensive. It created the impression of (and apparently the right conditions for) advancing socialism without intermediate stages such as democratic-bourgeois capitalism.

The first to raise the leapfrogging thesis was the Peruvian intellectual José Carlos Mariátegui, who also denounced the "reformist populism" of Víctor Raúl Haya de la Torre, the force behind Peruvian Aprismo. Although their perspectives differed, both proposed leftist alternatives by way of the indigenous question, emphasizing a strong Latin Americanist and anti-imperialist theme. Mariátegui's ideas, published in *Amauta* magazine (which was widely read among Latin American leftist intellectuals) and in his *Siete Ensayos de Interpretación de la Realidad Peruana* (*Seven Interpretive Essays on the Peruvian Reality*), addressed how to transition from feudalism, large estates, servitude, and imperialism to socialism. The transition would be neither liberal nor bourgeois and would have an indigenous perspective as its starting point—indigenous not just in the ethnic sense, but in the broader sense of social classes in their political, economic, and social dimensions. (Here, the Peruvian intellectual turned to the theoretical tools of Marxism and applied them to the Latin American reality.) Mariátegui developed the association between *indigenismo* and revolutionary nationalism, which he summarized in his concept of "Indo-American socialism" (Rojas Mix 1991, 296). It focused on revolution by the indigenous, proletarians, and peasants against capitalism and the feudal regime, skipping over the intermediate stages predicted by classical Marxism, including the bourgeois-democratic revolution. Mariátegui's thought, along with Mao's, was adopted in its most extreme form in the 1970s and 1980s by the Shining Path. In a less extreme form, and with a greater indigenous component, it has inspired Evo Morales's recent "democratic and cultural revolution" in Bolivia.

But it was Haya de la Torre's Aprismo rather than Mariátegui's project that reached the grassroots sectors in Peru, creating tension with Mariátegui's thought and the Marxist left. While Mariátegui's exile in Europe under Augusto Leguía (1919–1930) led him to study the theoretical contribution of Marxism to the Russian experience, Haya de la Torre's exile in Mexico kept his focus on Latin America, concentrating on the region's indigenous roots. Haya de la Torre gravitated to reformism rather than revolution and class compromise under the direction of the middle class rather than class struggle led by the proletariat and peasants. For Haya de la Torre, the problem of Indo-America came out of the question of indigenous identity transformed into political action in a societal project that went "from an internationalism of an oppressed race to a nationalism of a class pact," or "continental nationalism," as Luis Alberto Sánchez labeled it (Rojas Mix 1991, 285). Sharing Mariátegui's concern for the indigenous question in a pro–Latin American and anti-imperialist sense, Haya de la Torre committed himself to a socialism that focused on nationalism, populism, and reform more than Marxism and revolution.

The philosophy of Haya de Torre and APRA thus materialized in Latin America. Aprismo had various counterparts within the heterogeneous Latin American left, such as Víctor Paz Estenssoro's MNR in Bolivia, the PRI (especially under Lázaro Cárdenas, 1934–1940) in Mexico, the Chilean Socialist Party, and with less ideological intensity, *Varguismo* in Brazil and *Peronismo* in Argentina (Waiss 1954). The "populist pact" was the trend among the Latin American left, which hindered the rise of a Marxist left that supported class warfare and revolution.

The Cuban Revolution revived the Marxist left, along with the idea of leapfrogging stages, creating tension with the orthodox vision of the Communist Party, which understood history as gradual and occurring in stages. The rigors of the Cold War drove the 26th of July Movement of 1953 from a more nationalist than revolutionary focus to a Marxist and Leninist focus, to the point that Marxism and Leninism became the guiding force of a communist regime that allied itself with the USSR and expressed unyielding critiques of representative democracy and its institutions. As we know, the Cuban Revolution provoked a strong radicalization among the Latin American left during the Cold War, resulting in the rise of the Revolutionary Armed Forces of Colombia (FARC), the Sandinista National Liberation Front (FSLN) in Nicaragua, the Farabundo Martí National Liberation Front (FMLN) in El Salvador, different versions of *Guevarismo*, the Revolutionary Left Movement (MIR) in Chile, and other forms of Latin American ultraleftism, including the Montoneros and Tupamaros in Argentina and Uruguay, respectively. The tradition of a socialist and Marxist left that supported class warfare and revolution revived, only to distance itself from any appreciation of political or representative democracy. If populist socialism was marked by ambiguity and a merely instrumental appreciation for political democracy, the Marxist socialism that spread after the Cuban Revolution was marked by relentless opposition to bourgeois democracy and its institutions. Even the original experience of the Allendista Way to Socialism, via "democracy, pluralism, and freedom," did not escape the tensions within the Latin American left, until it culminated in the failure of the experiment of Salvador Allende and the Popular Unity coalition in Chile (Walker 1990).

Only under the third wave of democracy has an authentic democratic socialism emerged for the first time in Latin America, based on the affirmation of the intrinsic (not merely instrumental) value of democracy as the venue for political action. I shall examine that process in chapter 5.

## POPULISM

Populism emerged in the middle of an authoritarian wave in Latin America that fell between a long wave of democratization (1828–1926) and a short one (1943–1962). The rise of populism in the 1930s and 1940s occurred during a time of negative attitudes toward liberalism, liberal capitalism, and liberal democracy. This period between wars witnessed the rise of Nazism, fascism, and Stalinism in Europe, and corporatism and populism in Latin America. At the core of this process was the discrediting of liberal or representative democratic institutions, in sharp contrast with the neopopulism of our recent history, which emerges in a context of unprecedented prestige for the ideology and institutions of representative democracy.

The crisis of oligarchic rule stood at the center of the rise of Latin American populism. The working and middle classes had begun to demand their rights in terms of greater social and political inclusion. The following paragraphs are an account of some of the principal characteristics of populism in the region as it developed in the 1930s.

The first characteristic of Latin American populism has to do with its national and popular element. It was "popular" in its anti-oligarchic definition, and it was "national" in its anti-imperialist stance. It was also popular in terms of its resistance to the old oligarchic regime and especially to the hegemony of the old landowning aristocracy. It was anti-imperialist in its rejection of foreign control of natural and basic resources and the national economy, a sentiment expressed in the intense nationalism developed during the interwar period in both Latin America and the rest of the world.

The real dilemma to be resolved was between the oligarchy and the people, understood as a moral category more than a sociological one. The popular masses and urban workers, such as the *descamisados* (shirtless ones) and the *cabecitas negras* (little black heads) in Argentina under Perón, became the substance of the populist movement, which was indeed a movement more than a partisan organization in itself. Whatever was good for the people was good for the country as a whole.

From the very beginning, there was unresolved tension between populism and Marxism. The principal tension was not the capitalist conflict between the proletariat and the bourgeoisie, as laid out in the Marxist analysis of class struggle and revolution, but rather the conflict between the people and the oligarchy. Thus, from the very start, tension existed between the populist movement and the Marxist parties on the left. The populist leaders of the era (such as Perón in Argentina and Vargas in Brazil) always sought to avoid intensifying class struggle and actively critiqued Marxism and revolution. In fact, the fear of the expansion of Marxism and communism following the Bolshevik Revolution led many Latin American populist leaders to enforce the anti-oligarchic and anti-imperialist reforms so typical of their movement. This mentality became ingrained in the young military minds of the time, from whose ranks many populist and militantly anticommunist leaders emerged (including Perón himself.)

Secondly, Latin American populism took the form of a social and political alliance, especially among the popular and middle classes. This is perhaps one of the most interesting characteristics of Latin American populism. When we refer to the populist movement of the 1940s and 1950s, we mean the "populist coalition," a multiclass alliance between the lower and middle classes, or rather among capital, labor, and the state (as was the case of Vargas from 1951 to 1954 and Juscelino Kubitschek from 1956 to 1961 in Brazil).

This multiclass coalition was another point of tension between populism and Marxism, revolving around the old debate over the existence or inexistence (and characteristics) of a proper middle class, or a "national bourgeoisie" whose interests did not necessarily coincide with those of the old oligarchy and landowning aristocracy. Innumerable debates and tensions arose among leaders and intellectuals, populists and Marxists, including debates within the Communist International (Comintern) during its various stages of development. The moment of greatest convergence between the two perspectives occurred in 1935, during Comintern's Seventh Congress, which endorsed Georgi Dimitrov's Popular Front against fascism, thereby prioritizing the antifascist struggle over the anticapitalist one. The result was a broad alliance among the lower and middle classes, struggling against fascism and for structural modernization and democratic deepening. This populist coalition held great potential for democratization and modernization. This potential, however, was incomplete and ambiguous in its expression and was in constant conflict with the institutions of representative democracy, especially in their liberal sense.

A third characteristic of populism was the crucial role of the state, which was thought of in almost mythical terms as the vehicle of salvation for the dispossessed. Just as we can speak of a "populist coalition," we can also speak of a "populist state." Indeed, populism is almost by definition oriented toward state action. It accounts for an important state component. It is still debatable whether the state played an important role in Latin American development since the 1930s due to the lack of a private sector (or national bourgeoisie) that could take charge of development, or whether such a private sector did not exist because the state was overly active in economic development. The state certainly played a strong role in the economy, as seen in the emergence and later evolution of a "developmentalist" or entrepreneurial state and state-directed import substitution (ISI), especially since the 1940s.

As the region developed, the state became the salvation of the working masses, the people (*pueblo, povo*), and urban workers in their struggle against oligarchic rule, the landowning aristocracy, and the old regime. The state became the main instrument of progress and well-being—or, at least, this was the perception among the popular and middle classes and their representatives in the populist coalition.

The role of the state also brings to mind the fourth characteristic of populism, the attempt to modernize social and political structures through industrialization as a development strategy. This aspect was absent from the initial phase of populism in Latin America, which based itself more in intuition than in theory. Since the late 1940s, however, the theories of Raúl Prebisch and the UN Economic Commission for Latin America (ECLA) provided a theoretical framework for the development strategies of the populist coalition, focusing on the modernization of economic and social structures. Industrialization came to be seen as the means by which urban workers and the surplus labor resulting from urbanization and the massive migrations from the countryside could be absorbed. It would provide the working masses with new opportunities for well-being and progress. We will examine the advantages and disadvantages of this model in the next chapter.

The fifth characteristic of populism is the relationship between a charismatic leader and the working masses, a feature that is common to both the old and new populism. Almost by definition, populism refers to a charismatic leader's direct appeal to the people in the context of weak institutions, whether that leader is civil or military, authoritarian or democratic. The personalization of power is one of the most distinct and consistent traits of Latin American populism, from the 1930s until today. Populism assumes a low level of institutionalization. In fact, at the center of the tension between populism and democracy there seems to be a trade-off between populism and institutions, especially when we understand democracy as a "system of institutions" (Przeworski 1991). The tensions between populism and democracy are closely related to the conflict between personalization and the institutionalization of power.

The sixth characteristic is the intrinsic ambiguity between populism and the institutions of representative democracy. In populist logic, it is the incorporation of the masses, usually by means of some form of social or political alliance, that matters most. It can be said, then, that there is an element of democratization in both old- and new-style populism, but democratization understood in social rather than political terms. Populism encourages the incorporation of the masses, but not necessarily through institutions of representative democracy, which populists view with suspicion. As Enzo Faletto (1985, 70) writes, "Populism emerged as a response to the crisis of oligarchic rule, but, at the same time, it broke from the liberal idea of democracy."

Politically, populism generally took on an authoritarian form rather than a democratic one. This was the case, for instance, of Juan Domingo Perón in Argentina (1946–1955; 1973–1974) and Getúlio Vargas in Brazil (1930–1945; 1951–1954), the two most emblematic examples of old-style Latin American populism. This is not to say that there was no democratic or electoral component of these populist experiences. Perón himself came to power by free, transparent, and competitive elections in 1946 (although that was not the story in the 1951 elections, which are generally considered a case of electoral fraud). Perón emerged as a leader by virtue of his role as a colonel in the 1943 military coup, making fascism an important influence in his formative years. In the case of Brazil, one must distinguish between the stage of Estado Novo in the 1930s, with its fascist, corporatist, and authoritarian influences, and the Vargas who was democratically elected in 1950. Nonetheless, Vargas always favored a strong government more than a constitutional government and was "happier governing as an authoritarian leader than as a liberal democrat" (Wynia 1984, 141). Like Perón, Vargas dominated the Brazilian political scene in a decidedly personal manner.

Although this authoritarian tendency was largely characteristic of Latin American populism, the populist phenomenon remains complex and ambiguous, with plenty of cases leaning more towards democracy than authoritarianism. Such was the case of APRA in Peru and the Democratic Action (AD) in Venezuela, in spite of the latter's important link to the leaders of the 1945 military coup (the October Revolution).

The fact remains that the majority of populist experiences in the 1940s and 1950s were closer to authoritarianism than democracy. The incorporation of the working masses into the social process certainly contained an element of democratization, but in no sense did any of these populist experiences adhere to the institutions of representative democracy. In fact, both the old and new brands of Latin American populism have striven to construct a type of democracy distinct from the representative variety.

Up until now, I have tried to avoid applying one definition to populism, for I have always believed that trying to define populism only strips it of the ambiguities that are inherent to the concept itself. For that reason, I have focused on characteristics rather than definitions. Perhaps the most eloquent way of describing populism without defining it is by referring to a letter that Perón wrote in 1953 to his friend Carlos Ibáñez del Campo, who had been elected the president of Chile in 1952. In the letter, Perón (in Hirschman 1979, 65) gives his friend advice garnered from his own experiences on the art of governing.

> My dear friend: Give the people, especially the workers, everything you can. When it seems you are giving them too much, give them even more. You will see results. Everyone will try to scare you with the threat of economic collapse, but this is all a lie. There is nothing more elastic than the economy, which everyone fears so much because they do not understand it.

This excerpt helps us to understand the legacy of populism in Argentina and in Latin America and its unique concept of the "elasticity" of the economy, which gave rise to inflation and hyperinflation, as well as chronic macroeconomic instability. This, in turn, helps us to understand the difficulties of consolidating stable democracy in the region.

Looking beyond the emblematic case of Peronism in Argentina, the rise of the worker movements since the early twentieth century ultimately led to a reconfiguration of the Latin American political scene. The social and political alliances of the newly emerging sectors, based on the new relationship between the state and labor organizations, were at the center of this process. Perhaps its most lasting effect has been the progressive weakening of oligarchic rule (especially in South America), giving rise to new political and social alignments.

Collier and Collier (2002), state that the new relationship between the state and labor organizations that came out of different patterns of incorporation into the labor movement reconfigured the political arena. These patterns of incorporation include "radical populism" (the case of Mexico and Venezuela), "labor populism" (in Argentina and Peru), various forms of "electoral mobilization" of the new labor organizations (in Uruguay and Colombia), and finally, "depoliticization and control" (in Chile and Brazil). Beginning with diverse forms of repression and control, states and political actors used various political and social alliances to incorporate themselves into labor organizations. This transition to modern social structures was linked to the rise of a new politics of the masses. In some cases, there arose alliances of "adjustment" with the dominant classes, while in other cases populist alliances sprang up between the lower and middle classes. Generally, the state played the role of mediator in class conflicts and arbiter between the employers and workers within corporate arrangements that institutionalized the labor movement and its organizations. As Guillermo O'Donnell (1979, xi) writes in the prologue of his book, the core goal of this process was "ending oligarchic domination and predominantly agrarian societies in these countries," especially in South America.

What ultimately became of populism in Latin America? Three phenomena stunted its further development, at least in the form it took from the 1930s to the 1950s: First, the second (and short) wave of worldwide democratization that followed World War II. Second, the problems with the state-directed import substitution industrialization that was central to the populist coalition. Third, the tremendous impact of the Cuban Revolution and the dilemma of "reform or revolution" that was characteristic of the region in the 1960s and early 1970s, replacing that of "oligarchies or people."

This is not to say that populism has completely disappeared from the region. Several leaders adhered to relatively populist economic policies in times of extreme polarization in Latin America, including João Goulart in Brazil in the early 1960s, Juan Velasco Alvarado in the late 1960s in Peru, and Salvador Allende in the early 1970s in Chile. Finally, the new bureaucratic-authoritarian regimes that arose beginning in the mid-1960s and the market reforms they established played a large part in defeating the old form of populism, the developmentalist state, the populist coalition, and the policies associated with ISI and the "national and popular" model. Only in the late 1990s would populism be reborn in a new form, keeping some elements of old populism and changing others. We will examine the phenomenon of neopopulism and its relation to democracy in chapter 5.

## THE DELAYED, SLUGGISH, AND UNFINISHED CONSTRUCTION OF DEMOCRACY IN LATIN AMERICA

As Valenzuela and Posada-Carbó (2008) state, "How to organize a legitimate representative government was the central theme in the political process driving independence." Two hundred years after the invasion of the Iberian Peninsula by Napoleon's troops in 1808, one could say that we are still attempting to consolidate an authentic representative government. Analyzing the situation from a comparative perspective, Valenzuela and Posada-Carbó maintain that there were attempts in Latin America to establish a form of "democratic constitutionalism" based on universal suffrage and inspired by the Cádiz Constitution of 1812. In fact, in some cases, these attempts went further than attempts made in the United

States. For example, the abolition of slavery in the newly formed republics created favorable conditions for "universal" suffrage for males (in spite of all its limitations), especially when compared to the United States' record of exclusion of Native and African Americans from voting. In this sense, the new Latin American democracies were not necessarily an anomaly, at least when compared to other political systems, including Europe. Furthermore, democracy in the nineteenth-century United States did not escape the pathologies of fraud, voter intimidation, and violence. The incipient electoral processes in Latin America, based on the gradual extension of suffrage and electoral institutions, were one aspect of "democracy before democracy" (Valenzuela, in Posada-Carbó 1996). Even if this process was not linear—and there were several limitations and regressions in the extension of suffrage in the following years—there was at least a serious attempt to establish some type of constitutional and representative democracy in the region.

There was initial skepticism among the leaders of the emancipatory movement regarding the possibility of establishing a democratic regime, taking into account the factors of the political culture, institutions, and structures in Latin America in light of the colonial legacy. One of the most eloquent testimonies in this regard was that of Simón Bolívar, which conveys the decided skepticism about the newborn republics' ability to govern themselves. In his famous Jamaica Letter of 1815, Bolívar (in Pierson 1950) exposes his doubts about the possibility of forming a representative and constitutional democracy in Latin America:

> This is why it is so difficult for us to achieve freedom. As far as public affairs are concerned, we were left in a stage of perpetual infancy. . . . The facts have shown us that completely representative institutions are inadequate considering our character, our habits, and our level of education. . . . As long as our fellow citizens do not acquire talents and virtues like those of our brothers to the north, a government of the people, far from being a good thing, will bring us ruin.

Additionally, the militarization of Latin America associated with the independence movements became one of the main barriers to establishing representative democracy in the newly formed republics (Halperin 1993, 76 and following). A career in the military became one of the fastest ways to achieve ascending social mobility. But other processes, Halperin believes, did facilitate democratization: the abolition of slavery (which came earlier in some countries than in others); the replacement of the colonial-era caste system and greater possibilities for social mobility for mulattos and mestizos (even though the social order itself remained largely intact); the rise of the new urban elite, whose interests did not necessarily coincide with the traditional elites; and the fact that the Catholic Church was losing prestige and power (though not its base of popular support).

We might add that the alliance between the oligarchy and the military, especially in Central America, became one of the primary obstacles to the establishment of representative democracy. The historical reality of *caciquismo* and *caudillismo* (which gained strength after independence and during the nineteenth century) posed another difficulty in securing constitutional democracy in the region.

Still, all of this should not lead us to underestimate the various efforts in the direction of constitutional democracy since the dawn of the new republics, especially in regard to the extension of suffrage. In fact, recent historical revisionism has helped us to see that liberal and republican ideology—and, potentially, democratic ideology—was more present in the region's political development than is commonly thought. The efforts to extend suffrage gained strength after the imprisonment of Ferdinand VII (held captive by Napoleon from 1808 to 1813), which inspired the idea that sovereignty was returning to the people. The election of representatives to appear before the Central Junta of Seville after the Napoleonic invasion, as well as the liberal, democratic model of the Cádiz Constitution, created a sort of electoral fever in the region amid the struggles for independence. Even if the authoritarian wave of the 1830s and future events often interrupted and reversed these processes, when we compare Latin America to Europe and the United States at the time, we see abundant legislation and repeated attempts to open the way for representative democracy and its institutions. Despite the restrictions on suffrage and the multiple cases of government intervention and electoral fraud, the political history of nineteenth-century Latin America also includes "elections prior to democracy" (Posada-Carbó 1996).[2]

In a book that is perhaps the most systematic study to date of the history of democracy in Latin America, Paul Drake (2009) affirms that, although the region has shifted between "tyranny and anarchy" from the 1800s to 2006 (to use Bolívar's own expression), this has not prevented a long history of struggles to establish democracy that are rooted in the very processes of independence. Despite having a bad reputation for despotism, Latin America can boast of having one of the world's longest and richest histories of experimenting with democracy. The principal dilemma, as Drake describes it, has been "how to reconcile political systems that advocate equality in theory with societies that are divided by extreme forms of socioeconomic inequality" (2). Along with the dilemma between tyranny and anarchy, the democratic experiments have fluctuated between "protected" (i.e., elitist) democracy and "popular" democracy, with a tendency toward the latter. Neither of these two types, however, embraced the classical concept of liberal democracy like the form seen in the United States and the writings of Thomas Jefferson. Rather, both types have taken on paternalistic or outright authoritarian forms while leaning either left or right, depending on the circumstances and the time period.

Although a sizeable portion of the nineteenth century was marked by political violence, foreign and civil wars, attempted military coups, and anarchy, the period between 1880 and 1930 shows significant economic prosperity. The economy thrived on the drive to export, benefiting from the favorable conditions for foreign trade and the international economy. Despite the attempts to consolidate what various authors call an "oligarchic republic" (Hartlyn and Valenzuela 1994; Smith 2005; Drake 2009), the rare cases of political stability were usually found in authoritarian forms, from Porfirio Díaz in the north to Julio Roca in the south.

2. I have benefited greatly from the discussions, papers, and abundance of work presented at the seminar The Origins of Democracy in Latin America, 1770s–1870s, held at the Kellogg Institute for International Studies at the University of Notre Dame in September 2008.

Hartlyn and Valenzuela argue that Latin American democracy (especially in terms of the development of parties and party systems) has been present mainly in eight countries since the 1930s, with a longer tradition of elections and alternation in Chile, Uruguay, Costa Rica, Venezuela, and Colombia, and in a weaker form in Argentina, Brazil, and Peru. It is notable that, with the exception of Costa Rica, all are South American countries. The authors argue that the struggle to consolidate authentically representative regimes in the region has been "continuous and irregular," relating the democratic experiments of the early twentieth century to cases of "oligarchic democracies"—in other words, "regimes in which presidents and national assemblies arose through open competition, even if not totally clean, with the support of a limited electorate, and in agreement with the constitutional rules that mandated the law and which can be compared to the limited representative systems of Europe at the same time period" (1994, 12). Universal suffrage, established in Argentina in 1912 and Uruguay in 1918, helped to accelerate democratization. (Chile had established the first law of universal suffrage in 1874, although it took a long time to actually fulfill it.) Despite these advances, the profound disorder provoked by the economic crisis of 1929 hindered further democratic development—made evident by the fact that six of the eight countries mentioned above suffered military coups during the difficult years of the depression. The end of World War II spurred a new democratic "moment" to the extent that, in 1946, those eight countries simultaneously witnessed political democracy (at the time, there were eleven constitutional governments total in Latin America). This short wave of democracy, which faced interruptions starting in the late 1940s, was followed by a brutal and widespread authoritarian wave. By the end of the 1970s, only Costa Rica, Venezuela, and Colombia enjoyed free and democratic elections. Only since the 1980s can we speak of widespread democratization in Latin America, including Central America and Mexico. We will address this topic in chapter 3.

Democracy, understood as political democracy in its triple dimension of competition, constitutionalism, and inclusiveness or participation, has faced serious problems of consolidation throughout this process. In spite of these political and ideological difficulties, Hartlyn and Valenzuela assert that "the legitimacy of democracy as the best institutional system to govern a country and peacefully resolve conflicts is a fundamental part of the heritage of Latin American political culture since independence" (63).

A 2005 study by Peter Smith examined nineteen Latin American countries throughout the twentieth century, analyzing the quality of democracy in terms of cycles of political change and incidence and durability of electoral democracy (free and transparent elections). The study shows that 47 percent of the cases studied correspond to authoritarian regimes rather than democracies, 26 percent to democratic regimes themselves (electorally speaking), 18 percent to oligarchic regimes (especially in the first few decades of the 1900s), and 10 percent to so-called semidemocracies. There were 155 total changes of political regime throughout the twentieth century, demonstrating the characteristic political instability of the region. The period of "oligarchic competition" between 1900 and 1939 was followed by waves of democratization and authoritarianism. Meanwhile, electoral democracy did not become a widespread reality in the region until the 1980s, under the third wave of democratization. According to Smith, only Argentina, Chile, Colombia, and Uruguay were part of the first wave of democratization. Costa Rica, Venezuela, Bolivia, Brazil, Peru, and Ecuador joined in the second wave, which would include ten countries, bringing the total to nineteen. With the exception of Costa Rica and Mexico, Central America established electoral democracies under the recent third wave (Smith 2005, 32). Even so, there was a vast difference between electoral democracy and liberal democracy itself, where the latter is understood as guaranteeing civil liberties. We will address this theme further in chapter 5.

Until the 1920s (a little earlier in Mexico, a bit later in the rest of the region, and much later in Central America), political development in Latin America was based on an oligarchic regime and consequently experienced difficulties in consolidating an authentically representative and democratic government that could replace the old oligarchic order. The waves of democratization and authoritarianism during the arduous search for alternatives to oligarchic rule are the clearest expression of the difficulties involved in establishing a new political order in the region. As we will see later, when we examine the recent wave of democratization, there is no structural obstacle that prevents the establishment of democracy in the region. When all is said and done, democracy refers not only to the establishment of institutions, but also to the existence of a political process—a process of learning, of trial and error, of advances and setbacks. Indeed, as Smith (2005, 38) shows, the processes of redemocratization have been more effective in consolidating democracy, thanks to previously accumulated experiences of attempts, failures, regressions, and renewed attempts. This reality of redemocratization lends a certain advantage to South America over Central America. Nonetheless, there is no predetermined rule that would prevent Central America or countries recently witnessing their first wave of democratization, such as Mexico (save the brief democratic experiment of Francisco Madero), from establishing a stable democracy. The political instability endemic to Latin America explains many things, but it neither condemns nor predisposes the region to authoritarianism. Taken in the context of the profound changes in developmental paradigms in Latin America, the waves of democracy and authoritarianism have constituted a learning process—a painful one, to be sure, especially in light of the recent bureaucratic-authoritarian regimes—but a process by which the inherent value of political democracy is being rediscovered.

# CHAPTER 2

# TOWARD A NEW MODEL
# OF DEVELOPMENT

Economics is not my specialty. Nonetheless, it is impossible to understand political development and democracy in Latin America without also examining economic development. In fact, some of the most important theories about democratic breakdown, including those of Guillermo O'Donnell, point to the close relationship between political and economic factors.

Both this chapter, which deals with the new development model in Latin America in the 1930s and 1940s, and chapter 5, which deals with the development strategy carried out in the 1980s and 1990s, draw heavily upon the training I received at CIEPLAN. During the first phase of that institution's work (1976–1990; I joined in 1985), researchers undertook a systematic critique of the dogmatic neoliberal model introduced during the Pinochet dictatorship (1973–1990) by the Chicago Boys under the form of authoritarian capitalism. This model was executed in an almost pure, textbook form during that period. The critiques leveled against the dictatorship by democratic forces went hand in hand with critiques of this economic model.

It can be difficult to explain to the outside world the extreme dogmatism that unfolded under authoritarian capitalism, especially in Chile during the era of the Chicago Boys. I will never forget one particular example. Towards the end of Pinochet's dictatorship, CIEPLAN began a series of dialogues intended to bring together various leaders of social groups, unions, and businesses. One of the senior business leaders present described Chile as he saw it: "For me, the Chile before 1973 was a dictatorship. Chile after 1973, however, has given us unlimited freedom."

The Chicago Boys experiment emerged in the context of the crisis of the development model implemented in Latin America from the 1930s and 1940s. Foreshadowing the neoliberalism proclaimed by the Washington Consensus in the 1990s, the experiment was carried out in various countries, especially in the Southern Cone. It is impossible to understand the economic changes that took place during the transition and consolidation of democracy (see chapters 4 and 5) without an adequate understanding of the crisis of state-led import substitution industrialization (ISI) applied from the 1940s to the 1960s. I will dedicate the following lines to examining that process.

Chapters 2 and 4 draw heavily on the thought of Albert Hirschman, to whom I have dedicated this book. He has been a tremendous influence on us at CIEPLAN, as well as on many intellectuals and leaders, such as Fernando Henrique Cardoso and José Serra in Brazil, and others elsewhere in Latin America.

One of the central aspects of Latin America's oligarchic crisis was the questioning of the export-led growth model that formed the basis of the old oligarchic order. The search for alternatives to an outward-looking growth model based heavily on exports and free trade drove South America to a new model of inward-looking growth based on state-directed ISI. This shift in paradigm was triggered by the economic crisis of 1929. It took on a more defined form in the late 1940s with the theories of Raúl Prebisch and the ECLA and remained in place until the 1970s.

Latin America changed irrevocably during the transition from the old oligarchic order to a new order dominated by the middle class, with the participation of the emerging popular classes, and with a strong state presence. The search for a "second independence" of an economic nature—one that would bring greater autonomy by developing domestic markets and making the region less vulnerable to foreign economic shocks—inspired doubts, questions, and debates. If replacing the oligarchic order with a democratic one was difficult, replacing one development model with another was even more so. While there were advances in some areas, a final evaluation has yet to be made and many questions remain. In an attempt to decipher some of these complexities, I will look to history, among other things, to inform our search for a political and economic development model for Latin America that also achieves political stability, economic growth, and social equity.

Four models of economic development have been attempted in Latin America: mercantilist capitalism during the colonial era; liberal capitalism beginning in the late 1700s and taking on a more definite form in the mid-1800s (outward-oriented growth); the developmentalist model formed around ISI; and the new, outward-oriented growth model attempted since the 1990s in a context very different from the previous one. Some have labeled this latest model "neoliberal" (Ffrench-Davis 2005; Ocampo 2007; and Sunkel 2007). Nonetheless, this recent development strategy is more complex, more interesting, and more diverse than this label suggests. In this chapter, I will focus mainly on the third model of development, which coincides with the political and economic course of Latin America from the 1940s to the 1970s. Without denying the model's important achievements, I will provide some critical analysis. The democratic breakdowns in the late 1960s and early 1970s, as well as the bureaucratic-authoritarian regimes that arose, especially in the Southern Cone, had something to do with the problems and complexities of this development model, which marked a large portion of the twentieth century.

The development of mercantilist capitalism in Latin America show cased a type of economic development accomplished through the extraction of precious metals (mainly gold and silver, which were the main source of wealth in the Latin American colonies), a strong protectionism linked to colonial administrative structures, and the trade monopoly held by Spain and Portugal. From the beginning, economic development in Latin America came about through its insertion into a global economy that was turning away from mercantile capitalism and towards liberal capitalism (especially by the early nineteenth century) while the oligarchic social structure remained virtually unaltered.

Along with the extraction and exportation of gold and silver, agriculture played an important role in the first phase of development. Agriculture in the temperate zones differed from agriculture in the tropical areas, which was marked by the use of plantations and slave labor in the production of crops such as tobacco and sugar. The social structure shaped itself around the encomienda (an administrative grant given to colonists by the crown) and the hacienda (large-scale production units). Encomiendas began to disappear from Mexico, Peru, and other countries in the sixteenth and seventeenth centuries and were replaced by land "distributions" and various types of labor regimes. Meanwhile, the hacienda system underwent various transformations that consolidated export efforts first around the plantation economy and later around mining. Nonetheless, many elements of these systems, particularly the social structure, remained largely unchanged after independence and through the majority of the nineteenth century. In the fiscal realm, certain taxes financed the administrative structures of the colonies, and Spain and Portugal exercised a trade monopoly challenged only by contraband trade with England, Spain, Holland, and other nations.

The Bourbon Reforms in Spanish America and the Pombaline Reforms carried out by Brazil in the late eighteenth century helped to liberalize trade to and from Europe, planting the seed of intraregional trade. These reforms also reflected a modernizing aspect of the enlightened despotism of the time, which conflicted with centralizing tendencies in the administrative field—the other effect of these modernizing reforms. By the end of the eighteenth century, the Spanish American economy had achieved a considerable degree of growth. In 1800, its income per capita in U.S. dollars was around $245, compared to $239 in North America (Bulmer-Thomas 2003, 27). What caused Latin America to fall behind North America over time, so that in 2007, according to the April 2008 IMF *World Economic Outlook*, the average income per capita (all figures purchasing power parity) in Latin America was $8,257, compared to $45,845 in the United States and $38,435 in Canada? The answer lies beyond the scope of this book, but it has something to do with the insufficiencies of the ISI model as it was conceived and implemented from the 1940s onwards.

If the tumult of wars and processes of independence damaged the relative dynamism of the Spanish American colonies, the reforms mentioned above sowed seeds of greater economic liberalization that took root in the shift from mercantilist capitalism to liberal capitalism in the nineteenth century. This model of development was based on insertion into the global economy by means of international division of labor and specialization, as well as the exportation of raw materials to and the importation of manufactured goods from Europe. (The United States would replace Europe as a trade partner in the early twentieth century, particularly after World War I.) The second half of the nineteenth century and on, especially between 1870 and the end of World War I, marked a boom of free trade and export growth. Celso Furtado (1976, 51) states that "Latin America became an important contributor to world trade and a key source of raw materials for the industrialized countries." He further reports that the chief exports included agricultural produce from the temperate zones (Argentina and Uruguay), produce from the tropical zones (Brazil, Colombia, Ecuador, Central America, and the Caribbean, plus some regions of Venezuela and Mexico), and mining-related products (Mexico, Chile, Peru, and Bolivia).

According to Ocampo (2007), this "export era" (1870–1920), which had its roots in the early (and profound) Latin American insertion into the "era of mercantile capitalism," showed a marked improvement in terms of the exchange of commodities, to the point that "every country benefited from the greater integration into the global economy." However, this era was not accompanied by the development of liberal political institutions, as we saw in the previous chapter, and left the agrarian structure inherited from the previous era virtually untouched. It also displayed an inability to absorb the workforce generated around agriculture and the growing urbanization that accompanied industrialization and which was already taking place under export efforts. This model of outward-oriented growth created dependency on foreign markets. Given the cycles of financial boom and recession on the foreign market, this dependency became an Achilles' heel of that particular model of development. The absence of a national base and domestic markets that could provide a certain economic autonomy, in addition to the weakness of the newly formed states and institutions, posed further disadvantages.

These structural weaknesses—premodern, precapitalist, or semi-feudal structures, as well as excessive dependence on the foreign market, the lack of a national base, and vulnerability to foreign economic shocks, among others—were completely exposed in the 1929 economic crash, which reached "catastrophic proportions" in the region (Furtado 1976, 54). Economies that had come to depend primarily on foreign trade felt the repercussions very strongly. The international crisis of liberal capitalism had lasting effects on the Latin American economy, as shown by the slow but persistent transformation from a primary export economy to one based on ISI and inward-oriented growth. The only element of continuity was the agrarian system that remained practically unchanged across the region (with the exception of Mexico) for several decades at least.

This new model of development, with all its economic, social, and political implications, was not born in a classroom, nor did it spring from a theoretical model (which would not be clearly stated until the late 1940s). Rather, it arose from certain circumstances—primarily external—that produced a radical shift in the strategies for economic development in the region. In Chile, for example, ISI emerged as a result of the devastating 1939 earthquake and the need for a public agency (the Corporación de Fomento de la Producción de Chile: CORFO, or the Development Agency) that could contribute to the creation of an industrial infrastructure. As Joseph Love (1996, 209) writes, "Industrialization in Latin America was a fact before it was a policy, and a policy before it was a theory." The instability of the interwar period, especially the crisis and depression triggered in 1929, led to a revision of liberal theories based on export efforts, free trade, and specialization by way of international division of labor.

In the late 1700s, at the end of the mercantilist capitalist era, and again in the late 1800s and early 1900s (which marked the export era), the region's economies experienced significant economic dynamism. An extremely weak social and political base accompanied this dynamism, as evidenced by the emergence of the social question associated with the crisis of oligarchic rule and the primary export-led model that had formed the base of the old regime. The shocks of the period between wars and a variety of other external factors uncovered internal shortcomings that would be addressed by a new "national and popular" developmentalist model, which called for a second, economic independence.

Industrialization, nationalism, and the active intervention of the state formed the basis of the developmentalist model. This was more true in South America and Mexico than in Central America, which remained strongly tied to the primary export model (with the exception of a few cases, like Costa Rica, that are representative of a new economy and a new agro-export business class). If ISI was indeed born from the 1929 economic crisis and the instability of the interwar period, then the process of industrialization (indissolubly linked to a more active state) suffered a strong idealization over time that distorted the original sense of advancing toward greater economic autonomy in the region.

The origins of industrialization in Latin America are tied not only to these external variables, but also to the gradual expansion of the economy in the period of outward-oriented growth, which led to the creation of a domestic market around the production of consumer goods (Hirschman 1968). ISI emerged in the first decades of the twentieth century as industrial sectors pressured the state to involve itself more actively in that process. It was the industrial business leaders themselves who pushed for import substitution, which became a vital necessity after the decline of importation and foreign trade after the 1929 crisis. Similarly, the growth of intraregional trade created a broad domestic market that gradually expanded from the production of consumer goods (in the "easy" phase of industrialization and import substitution) to the production of intermediate and capital goods (in the "advanced" era of import substitution), especially in Brazil, Mexico, and Argentina.

According to Joseph Love (1996), Raúl Prebisch, who became the main theorist behind ISI in the late 1940s, was strongly influenced by the ideas of an Argentine industrialist, Alejandro Bunge, for whom he worked in his early years as an economist. Bunge was an important promoter of industrialization in Argentina, which until the 1930s had prospered by the theory of competitive advantage in its division of labor and specialization in meat and grain exports (with a strong dependence on English capital). By 1934, Prebisch had written about the "deterioration of the terms of trade," a concept that became the backbone of ISI by affirming that the prices of agricultural products fell more than the prices of industrial products, thus putting orthodox neoclassical economics into question. In 1937, Prebisch formulated his theory of unequal exchange, claiming that the possibility of growth based on export efforts was no longer viable in terms of economic development (Love 1996, 222). As Argentina's manufacturing production began to grow more significantly, this theory called for an industrial sector that would pressure the state to take a more active role in the economy and the production process. In 1944, Prebisch wrote about the "center" and the "periphery," referring to the developed and underdeveloped worlds, respectively. He proposed the need for the inward-oriented growth that formed the core of ISI, designed to break the dependence of the periphery (exporters of raw materials) on the center (exporters of manufactured goods). In the late 1940s, the ECLA established theories based on these two fundamental concepts—the deterioration of terms of trade and inward-oriented growth—thereby confirming the first signs of industrialization in the region.

The coups d'état conducted by Juan Domingo Perón and the Argentine military in 1943, and Perón's government itself (1946–1955), consolidated the basic ideas of strong nationalism, industrialization as a way to economic autonomy, active intervention by the state, and a critical attitude toward foreign capital (such as English and, later, U.S. capital). Import substitution, which had already begun in the export era and had gained strength in the first decades of the twentieth century, became the new strategy for development in Argentina, and, increasingly, in the rest of South America and Mexico. Such was also the case in Brazil under Getúlio Vargas's Estado Novo (1937–1945), and under his later administration of 1951 to 1954, as well as that of Juscelino Kubitschek (1956–1961). These regimes laid the basis for Brazilian industrial development.

Between 1948 and 1949, the ECLA adopted, formulated, and disseminated the ideas of Raúl Prebisch, among others (Werner Sombart, Mihail Manoilescu, Aníbal Pinto, and Charles Kindleberger, to mention just a few). Its theories were based on the premise that, by making the economy less vulnerable to external shocks and by seeking development through more autonomous terms, industrialization would solve the region's problems. A certain export pessimism marked this model, stemming from the ideas of the ECLA intellectuals (who dominated the Latin American intellectual scene). They theorized that export efforts and outward-oriented growth only succeeded in turning Latin America into the periphery, dependent on foreign markets, and led to the persistent deterioration of terms of trade that benefited the manufacturers and the developed countries (the center). These new theories became an economic doctrine—a veritable "manifesto," as Albert Hirschman called it—that remained practically unchallenged until the late 1950s and 1960s.

The rise of the so-called structuralist school, which questioned orthodox neoclassical economics based on the supposed Keynesian balance of the economy, advocated greater intervention by the state in the economic process. It called attention to the structural factors that hindered development in Latin America: premodern, agrarian structures based on the hacienda and the latifundio (large, commercial estate). Behind all these structuralist and developmentalist theories stood the old debate over development strategies in late industrializers such as Russia, Germany, and Italy. Alexander Gershenkron, whose ideas were of particular importance to the discussion, defended the need for an active role of the state in late-industrialization countries. According to Hirschman (1968, 70), borrowing from Gershenkron, Latin America constituted a case of "late, late industrialization," which was also the case in countries such as Japan and South Korea. The structuralist school and the theoretical framework behind this development model seemed to match the Keynesian thought of the time as well as Gershenkron's theories, all of which agreed on the necessity of more active intervention by the state.

Economic development in Latin America was quite diverse and heterogeneous, especially after the 1930s. According to Bulmer-Thomas (2003), ISI took root primarily in Mexico, Brazil, Argentina, Chile, Uruguay, and Colombia. Meanwhile, countries including Bolivia, Paraguay, and Peru, and those in Central America opted to maintain certain characteristics of the classical primary-export model while keeping the industrial sector weak. Indeed, the author asserts that attempts by such countries to enact industrialization turned out to be quite disastrous. Some of these countries tried "intensifying" export efforts around single-export economies (Venezuela with petroleum, Bolivia with tin, Cuba with sugar). Other countries diversified their exports (Peru, Ecuador, Paraguay, Central America), efforts that yielded different types of results. Despite their modifications, their systems remained more traditional than the ISI system adopted by the southern countries.

One certainly cannot say that industrialization was a unique model, or that it was adopted universally throughout the region despite certain common features. "The post war decades saw extremely disparate country experiences and practices, within a common framework of received wisdom on development strategies, internal demographic pressures, and external possibilities and threats" (Thorp 1998, 178). The region saw a range of fairly unequal trajectories that corresponded to the heterogeneity of Latin America, though the predominant model (especially in South America) was import substitution industrialization directed by the state.

The results varied from one country to another. The system was most successful in Brazil and Mexico, less so in Argentina, and yielded uncertain results in Chile and Uruguay, whose size (among other factors) caused many to question whether an inward-oriented growth strategy could be applied in smaller countries. Furthermore, countries such as Colombia, Mexico, Venezuela, and the majority of the Central American countries grew rapidly in the second half of the 1960s and the early 1970s. Broadly speaking, this new model of development gave rise to economic progress such that the average annual rate of growth of the gross domestic product was 5.5 percent in the region as a whole from 1950 to 1980 (with the greatest level of growth at 7.2 percent from 1968 to 1974). During the same period, the rate of per capita growth reached 2.7 percent (Ocampo 2007; Cardoso and Fishlow 1992), a considerable figure when viewed comparatively. There were undoubtedly advances in terms of the creation of infrastructure and an industrial base, especially in Brazil and Mexico. There were also improvements in terms of literacy, primary education, infant mortality rates, life expectancies, and the quality of life for salaried workers in the industrial and urban sector, who were able to incorporate themselves into the industrial development process. As they began to organize, these groups gained a voice in the political system and began to pressure the state to meet their demands. Often, as was the case in Brazil, Mexico, Argentina, Chile, and Uruguay, these groups formed the various political and social alliances inherent to the "populist coalition" that governed between the 1940s and 1970s. Although these alliances functioned under the radar of economic and social development, they allowed marginalized sectors that lacked organization and representation to obtain their share of substantial economic development.

Despite its advances, this new model of development began to show serious deficiencies and contradictions. At the same time, a heated political and academic debate about the advantages and disadvantages of this model began, starting in the late 1950s and running through the 1960s. Some of the intellectuals and advocates of the model, including the ECLA, raised doubts and questions about ISI. In addition to the structuralist school that had been dominant in the 1940s and 1950s, a new "monetary" school emerged, aimed at explaining the increasingly worrisome phenomenon of inflation. It placed the blame on fiscal and monetary irresponsibility rather than structural causes, pointing to excessive public spending and monetary emission as evidence. On the opposite end of the spectrum, dependency theory gained popularity among the Latin American left, with its focus on the international insertion of the Latin American economy, but in a different mode than previous theories. Meanwhile, certain theories arose to strike a balance between monetary and dependency theories. They appeared within the ECLA itself, as well as from intellectuals such as Albert Hirschman, who adopted a more eclectic position.

Let us briefly review the situation as it appeared in the late 1950s and the responses to it, not only theoretical and doctrinaire, but now also strongly ideological, according to the atmosphere of the region during the 1960s.

Disillusionment with the undesired effects of industrialization had been growing since the 1940s, and it was reflected in the thought and public expressions of some of its main supporters. Raúl Prebisch, for example, had pushed for industrialization in the region under the theory of deterioration of terms of trade and asymmetry between the center and the periphery. Nonetheless, after 1962, when he became the secretary general of the United Nations Conference on Trade and Development (UNCTAD), which strove to examine the new international economic order, Prebisch claimed that an industrial structure had emerged in the past fifteen years that was isolated from the outside world. High tariffs and strong protectionism increased to the point that "the proliferation of industries of every kind in a closed market has deprived the Latin American countries of the advantages of specialization and economies of scale, and owing to the protection afforded by excessive tariff duties and restrictions, a healthy form of internal competition has failed to develop, to the detriment of efficient production" (quoted in Hirschman

1968, 2). Speaking of Brazil's experience, Hirschman (3) quotes Celso Furtado, another great supporter of ISI, writing in 1966 that "In Latin America . . . there is a general consciousness of living through a period of decline. . . . The phase of 'easy' development, through increasing exports of primary products *or through import substitution* has everywhere been exhausted."

Were Prebisch in Argentina and Furtado in Brazil transformed into proto-neoliberals in the 1960s? Not at all. This was only one particularly eloquent manifestation of the problems faced by this new model of development in the 1950s and 1960s: "The initial and exclusive trust of Latin America in ISI as a way to industrialization was wearing out by the end of the 1950s. . . . By the beginning of the 1970s, this model had ceased to function, as the growing internal-external imbalance in the Latin American economy made clear" (Ffrench-Davis, Muñoz, and Palma 1997, 100). Hirschman disagrees that there was an "exhaustion" of industrialization, but many of the main supporters of ISI (including Prebisch and Furtado) nonetheless shared a critical diagnosis of the very model that they themselves had pushed (though with some characteristics and suppositions different than those present at the beginning). Both economists offer great criticism (or, rather, self-criticism) of the model, mainly in terms of its excessive protectionism, which had deprived the region of the great dynamism of the international economy in the 1950s and 1960s. These critiques are eloquently synthesized by Bulmer-Thomas (2003, 262), who asserts that, while the international economy was experiencing a phase of great expansion, Latin America had opted for a "self-imposed exile." In fact, Love reminds us that Prebisch's mentor Alejandro Bunge had always thought of industrialization as "a complement to export driven growth more than a substitute for it" (1996, 232).

That "self-imposed exile" was exactly the opposite of what had been attempted in Asia (initially in Japan and South Korea, then in Taiwan, Singapore, and Hong Kong, and later in China and India). They had based their development strategy on high levels of protectionism and a significant role of the state in the economy, but simultaneously on a strong push for foreign exports and macroeconomic stability. Over time, the experiences of the Asian countries became a fundamental example of the new (and fourth) model of development in Latin America, which I will analyze in chapter 4.

Just like so many similar processes in the economic, political, and social spheres, the development model of industrialization ended up being not just a theory, doctrine, or manifesto, but also part of the phenomenon of "ideological inflation" (Hirschman, quoted in Collier 1979) that characterized Latin America in the 1960s and early 1970s. From this context emerged the debate among structuralists, monetarists, and proponents of dependency theory, as well as what we might call a more eclectic position. The strongly polarized climate contributed in turn to the processes of democratic breakdown in the 1960s and 1970s. Could it be mere coincidence that the authoritarian regimes in Brazil, Chile, Uruguay, and Argentina emerged in the four most emblematic cases of state-directed ISI? Guillermo O'Donnell claims that this was not an accident and that between ISI (especially in the transition from producing consumer goods to producing intermediate and capital goods) and the advent of these authoritarian regimes there existed a Weberian "elective affinity." Others, such as Juan Linz, questioned O'Donnell's theories and emphasized the political and institutional factors that explained the processes of democratic breakdown. (I will discuss this debate in the next chapter.) Toward the end of the 1960s, there remained few supporters of the style of industrialization attempted under this new model of development, at least in the form in which it had been applied since the 1940s.

Before reviewing the heated intellectual debate in the 1960s, we might summarize the main shortcomings of this style of industrialization and its principal critiques as the following. First, the reality of export pessimism that accompanied this type of inward-oriented industrialization, grounded in strong nationalism, deprived the region's economies of a more active insertion into the global economy through export efforts, especially at a time of great dynamism in the international economy. In the period between 1950 and 1973, production in developed market economies grew at an annual rate of 5 percent (3.8 percent per capita). GDP tripled, while per capita income multiplied by a factor of 2.4 and exports grew at 9 percent annually. The period between 1960 and 1973 was the most dynamic phase for developed market economies as well as for less-developed countries (Ffrench-Davis, Muñoz, and Palma 1997, 84 and 99). We might add that between 1948 and 1973, international trade grew by an annual rate of 9.7 percent, while Latin America's participation in global exports fell from 13.5 percent in 1946 to 7 percent in 1960 (Bulmer-Thomas 2003, 264).

Second, there was an abandonment of agricultural development, with the exception of certain warnings against and attempts to correct the structural deficiencies of the hacienda and latifundio. While the process of industrialization put a strong emphasis on the production of manufactured goods, it failed to take advantage of the region's enormous agricultural potential.

Third, the critical question of macroeconomic instability manifested in the acute reality of inflation and hyperinflation, fiscal crises, and recurring problems with the balance of payments. These became one of the gravest consequences of constant pressures on the state, along with public policies that did nothing more than exacerbate the chronic macroeconomic instability.

Fourth, we must mention the tremendous inefficiencies and distortions that resulted not only from high tariffs and protectionism, but also from the use and abuse of various controls associated with this strategy of development—import quotas, manipulation of the exchange rates, and extensive subsidies, among others—which Ffrench-Davis, Muñoz, and Palma call "coarse, confusing, and inefficient" (92).

Finally, there was the reality of widespread poverty and inequality, the hidden face of a model that did not satisfy the enormous expectations held by the majority of the population. Despite some advances, quite a few problems remained unresolved, such as the significant social costs of poverty and inequality. According to Cardoso and Fishlow (1992), this was perhaps the most serious limitation of the development process during the postwar period in Latin America, to the extent that, by 1970, 40 percent of the population lived below the poverty line. Economic growth and industrialization coexisted with massive poverty, social tensions, regional imbalances, widespread political instability, and acute social injustice. "The stark poverty and the income distribution problem of Latin America measure the failure of the post-war development process" (Cardoso and Fishlow 1992, 217). While this may appear to be a harsh and even exaggerated critique of a nuanced process, it expresses the tremendous frustration that existed in significant social sectors in the region, including intellectuals and ruling elites.

As anticipated, the developmentalist strategy focused on the active role of the state as a promoter of industrialization. This was precisely the starting point for an intense intellectual debate that took place in the 1960s. For the structuralists, the state was the solution, while for the monetarists the state was part of the problem (Bulmer-Thomas 2003). Both theories addressed diverse themes, the most important of which was the causes of inflation, a widespread phenomenon in the region and a big headache for various governments. While the structuralists alluded to certain structural factors as a hindrance to development (such as the existence of the hacienda and the latifundio, which formed a real bottleneck in terms of agricultural modernization and development), the monetarists explained inflation as the result of excessive public spending and inorganic emissions, culminating in widespread macroeconomic instability.

The monetarist school reached its apex in the 1970s with the work of Milton Friedman and Friedrich Hayek—awarded the Nobel Prize in Economics in 1976 and 1974, respectively—and the governments of Margaret Thatcher in Great Britain (1979–1990) and Ronald Reagan in the United States (1981–1989), all of which targeted fiscal and monetary irresponsibility and the excessive economic action by the state. This line of thought prevailed in Latin America in the 1960s and 1970s. The new authoritarian regimes brought about sweeping reforms of the market, privatization and deregulation, greater control of fiscal spending, and different degrees of external openness and free trade, stronger in some cases (such as in Chile), and with less intensity and more protectionism and action by the state in other cases (such as in Brazil and Argentina). Indeed, the Brazilian military regime, like the Juan Carlos Onganía government in Argentina (1966–1970) and in contrast to Chile, Uruguay, and Argentina post-1976, was not precisely neoliberal in the economic sense. For instance, Ernesto Geisel's government (1974–1979) in Brazil was decidedly statist.

To summarize, the intense intellectual debate in the 1960s took place, on one hand, between structuralists and monetarists, referring principally to the causes of inflation, and on the other hand, between the theories of modernization and dependency, regarding the possibilities of and obstacles to modernization and development in Latin America.

Dependency theory emerged from the ideas of Latin American intellectuals who had been strongly influenced by the Cuban Revolution, Marxism, and theories about imperialism. They observed that, far from achieving greater economic autonomy in the region, import substitution industrialization had increased the dependence of the periphery countries on the center countries. This tendency, which originated in the era of colonialism and mercantilist capitalism, had deepened during the transition from the easy phase of industrialization to the advanced phase (mainly in countries such as Brazil, Mexico, and Argentina). The growing dependence, in terms of the need for new capital, new technology, and adequate external financiers, expressed itself in the growing levels of foreign investment and the multinational businesses that appeared like tentacles of imperialism in the underdeveloped and dependent countries during the era of advanced capitalism (later known as global capitalism).

According to Samuel and Arturo Valenzuela (1978), dependency theory can only be understood with reference to the theories of modernization that appeared in the social sciences during the 1950s. These were related, in turn, to the hegemony of the United States in the postwar period. In accordance with theories of modernization, underdevelopment came out of "traditional" values, institutions, and patterns inherited from colonial times, which represented the principal obstacles on the road to modernity and development. Modernization consisted of the removal of those traditional values, institutions, and patterns from both the economic and social spheres, and the diffusion of the values, institutions, and patterns of the developed countries to the underdeveloped countries. Thus, tradition and modernity were part of a continuum that ought to be viewed as a linear and evolutionary progression from tradition (backwardness) to modernity (development). Furthermore, the diffusion of capital and technology from the developed countries to the underdeveloped countries attempted to put an end to the dual character of Latin American societies, to the extent that a feudal-style society coexisted with a capitalist one.

In contrast to theories of modernization, dependency theories sustained that dependency was an exogenous factor imposed by the center onto periphery countries. "We are underdeveloped because we are dependent" was the fundamental assertion of early dependency theories. In that sense, dependency and underdevelopment were two sides of the same coin. The unit of analysis was not a "national" society, as in the modernization perspective, or cultural and institutional factors, but rather the historic insertion of Latin America in an international economy that, since colonial times, has been defined by the subordinate relationship between the periphery and the center. This was the reality of Latin America during the periods of mercantilism (1500–1750) and outward-oriented growth dependent on raw-material exports (1750–1914), the crisis of the "liberal model" (1914–1950), and the period of transnational capitalism in the 1960s, which brought with it new forms of dependence and subordination through the presence of transnational businesses (Valenzuela and Valenzuela 1978, 546). Each of the aforementioned periods had as a common denominator a type of international insertion based on dependent capitalism.

The early dependency theories (such as those of Theotonio dos Santos, Andre Gunder Frank, Ruy Mauro Marini, James Petras, and others) held to the central thesis that "rather than becoming a force for development, foreign penetration has created underdevelopment" (Chilcote and Edelstein 1974, 26). These theorists maintain that underdevelopment is not the original state of things, but rather one created by the growth of capitalism since the era of colonial expansion. Dependency is defined as "a situation in which the economy of certain countries is conditioned by the development and expansion of another economy to which the former is subjected" (26). This school of thought accuses theories of modernization of being ahistorical, asserting that development and underdevelopment are aspects in a single historical process based in the expansion of capitalism and dependency.

In opposition to the simplistic nature of the early dependency theories, Fernando H. Cardoso and Enzo Faletto (1979) wrote their classic book, *Dependency and Development in Latin America*. As its provocative title indicates, relationships of dependence do not condemn Latin American countries (and the Third World in general) to underdevelopment.

There was space for development, despite the structural limitations, as evidenced by the case of dependent development in Brazil. A trade-off between dependency and development did not necessarily exist. Rather than a general theory of dependency (in fact, the authors deny that such a thing exists), there are "situations" of dependence, which should be analyzed historically from case to case, since they vary between time periods and places. When considered historically, these situations of dependency correspond to a complex web of internal and external variables, showing that dependency must not be viewed simplistically as solely due to external factors. With a dialectical, historical, and structural focus, the authors avoid simplistic determinism by affirming that there is space for development, that alternatives exist, and that Latin America is not doomed to be underdeveloped. Along with the historical events that had led to Latin America's dependence, a new type of dependence based on the internationalization of markets emerged in the 1960s and 1970s, demonstrating the structural limitations of the previous experiences with the developmentalist state and the populist coalition. There were, then, certain limits to the possibility of national and autonomous development, to the extent that it required financial capital and new technologies and markets. In this new age of internationalization of markets and capitalism, the bureaucratic-authoritarian regimes in Latin America (as O'Donnell has labeled them) emerged out of a new alliance between the armed forces and technocrats (principally economists).

Finally, in addition to the opposing poles of the monetarists and structuralists and the theories of modernization and dependency, the debates of the 1960s represented more moderate positions, such as those linked to the structuralist school itself, ECLA, and the ideas of Albert Hirschman. ECLA and certain prominent intellectuals, such as Osvaldo Sunkel, attempted to call attention to the main problems with ISI that they had warned about previously, favoring a process of regional integration that could create a broader market for intraregional trade that complemented industrialization efforts with export efforts. Sunkel (1967), for example, openly declares "export or die" as the principal dilemma to be resolved. Speaking from a perspective clearly linked to the structuralist school, ECLA, and dependency theory, Sunkel asserts that the transition from the production of consumer goods to the production of intermediate and capital goods, as well as the need for foreign financiers, only worsened the region's dependency, vulnerability, and instability. Furthermore, ISI had begun to weaken and even stagnate as it failed to produce the expected benefits, especially the reduction of dependency on foreign markets. Along with accentuating the great vulnerability of the balance of payments, state-directed ISI had led to a relatively stagnant foreign sector (Sunkel 1967, 53). Besides advocating Latin American integration, Sunkel concludes that, in the face of the extremes of radical socialist revolution and the "country-subsidiary" (*país sucursal*) model, it was necessary to move toward a true model of national development that replaced dependence with interdependence and promoted the intensification and diversification of exports over a mono-export economy.

In agreement with those who emphasized the limitations of narrow national markets and the need to strive for regional integration, the creation of UNCTAD in the 1960s brought with it the idea of giving birth to a new international economic order that would create favorable conditions for the production and export of manufactured goods from the developing world. Attempts to broaden the horizon of domestic markets (albeit tinged with the constant export pessimism that privileged internal markets) included the creation of the Latin American Free Trade Association in 1960, the Central American Common Market in 1960, and the Andean Pact in 1969. There were very timid advances that varied widely over time and endured many advances and setbacks, resulting in outcomes very different than those seen in Asia. Eastern and southeastern Asian countries approached their own industrialization process with protectionist policies and significant intervention by the state, but always with involvement in the global economy, export efforts, constant searches for greater levels of competitiveness, and macroeconomic stability.

Along with denying the supposed "exhaustion" or "failure" of ISI and clarifying some of its historical and theoretical aspects, Hirschman (1968) asserts that there was not necessarily a trade-off between industrialization and export efforts, as some had thought in the 1940s and 1950s. He admits that there are problems with industrialization as it has been carried out in Latin America and that there exists a certain frustration or disenchantment in the region, especially in Brazil, which succumbed to a coup d'état in 1964 despite the many great expectations for success. At the center of these problems stood public policies implemented in support of industrialization, policies that overestimated the economy's tolerance of a variety of situations, including a sort of congenital incapacity of ISI to approach the challenge of export efforts. The main errors of these policies included the existence of protectionist-style import tariffs accompanied by zero tariffs for certain imported goods and a unilateral emphasis on import substitutions without combining industrialization with rigorous export efforts. "Industrialization of the nineteenth century latecomers was in fact frequently accompanied by both tariff protection and a vigorous export drive" (Hirschman 1968, 25). In the 1950s and 1960s, the subsidiaries of the multinational businesses present in Latin America had received instructions not to compete with the outside and to focus instead on domestic markets protected by high tariffs. What is certain is that, in accordance with Hirschman's analysis, there was a certain amount of maneuvering based on appropriate public policies and institutions that could (and knew how to) establish a system of incentives, and aimed at making industrialization compatible with export efforts. In the absence of these policies and institutions, a climate of disenchantment and frustration developed. Hirschman continues, "Industrialization was expected to change the social order and all it did was to supply manufactures! Hence one is only too ready to read evidence of total failure into any trouble it encounters" (32).

All of this occurred at very high cost and with serious inefficiencies and distortions of the public policies that were implemented, as well as a biased perspective in favor of import substitution and inward-oriented growth as the sole objective. It is easy to understand that, in the face of the external shocks of the interwar period, policies emerged that were destined to hasten the installation of import substitution already begun during the previous export phase. What is harder to understand is that these policies continued, despite their distortions, until the 1960s, when the global economy showed great dynamism and tremendous possibilities for developing nations. This is even harder to comprehend and justify when one considers the experience accumulated during three centuries of export efforts, whether under mercantilist capitalism or liberal capitalism, which had become part of the region's DNA.

I have addressed monetarist and structuralist theories on modernization and dependence, as well as some more moderate positions, because
they demonstrate not just the intellectual effervescence of the era, but also
the strong polarization of Latin American political ideologies, especially
after the Cuban Revolution (which would turn out to be as schismatic to
the region as the economic crisis of the late 1920s). The years 1929 and
1959 left their mark on the process of political and economic development in Latin America as true changes of paradigm, especially among the
elites. These changes resulted in frustration and disenchantment due not
only to the poor results of ISI, but also to a process that ended up suppressing the few (and weak) democratic experiences that occurred under
the second wave of democratization begun in the 1940s. The new authoritarian regimes that arose in the Southern Cone in the late 1960s and early
1970s began a fourth process of development, which started with neoliberal market reforms and continued after the auspicious processes of
democratization in the 1980s and 1990s.

# CHAPTER 3

# DEMOCRATIC BREAKDOWN, TRANSITION, AND CONSOLIDATION

My experience of democratic breakdown in Latin America has nothing to do with theory. I was seventeen years old and a senior in high school when a military coup overthrew the government of President Salvador Allende in Chile on September 11, 1973.

I studied at Saint George's College in Santiago, which was affiliated with the Congregation of Holy Cross (which is, in turn, associated with the University of Notre Dame). The military expelled the priests from the school and even deported some, accusing them of being Marxists. Since my beliefs were similar to the priests', and since I was not at all a Marxist (in fact, I was opposed to the Popular Unity government), I realized early on what was happening.

I took my exams with soldiers present in the classroom, in an atmosphere of vigilance and intimidation. Along with my classmates, I had to salute the flag every day following the coup, and we graduated in the presence of a commander of Group 10 of the Chilean Air Force, who had been appointed rector (president) of the school by the military junta through a special decree. Saint George's was a private Catholic school, which was seen as a threat to national security. Every morning from September to December 1973, personnel from a nearby military school arrived on buses, charged with looking after us (and national security).

I always recommend to my friends from other countries the movie *Machuca*, directed by Andrés Wood, who was a young student at the college at the time and who has captured through film the absurdity and the tragedy of the period.

What occurred in Latin America, and especially in South America ever since the coup d'état in Brazil in 1964, was a tragedy rather than nonsense or a simple misunderstanding.

I will never forget that fateful date, September 11, 1973.

In this chapter, I attempt to decipher some of the causes and characteristics of the waves of authoritarianism and democracy that we have witnessed in recent decades in Latin America. Over the years, I have learned and benefited from the interesting literature put out on this subject in the field of social sciences. In that light, this chapter differs from the others in that I attempt to review this literature, even at the risk of providing a slightly more detailed analysis of the subject matter.

As I have mentioned before, waves of democracy and authoritarianism have been a trend in Latin American political development during the last century, within the context of chronic political and economic instability. In this chapter I concentrate on the processes of democratic breakdown, transition, and consolidation in the region in order to decipher some of their characteristics and causes in light of the vast literature on the subject. Given this abundance of literature—especially in the field of comparative politics—and the usual lack of knowledge about it, I will focus on systematizing some of the principal theories for the benefit of a wider audience that goes beyond academia.

How can we explain the processes that drove democratic breakdown in the 1960s and 1970s in Latin America? How much of a connection is there between the model of economic development used from the 1940s to the 1970s and these processes of breakdown? Should we look mainly at the socioeconomic variables, the political-institutional ones, or a combination of both? How can we explain the processes of democratic transition and consolidation? What are some of their principal characteristics, and what relationship exists between them? What contributions can the literature make in understanding democratic breakdown, transition, and consolidation? These are some of the questions I will address in this chapter.

I maintain that the current wave of democratization in Latin America questions the majority of the theories developed in the social sciences, at least since the 1950s, in relation to the possibilities and difficulties of establishing and consolidating democracy in the region. The third wave of democratization has surprised us all, not just in Latin America, but throughout the world. For a while it appeared that democracy was reserved for countries that had certain economic, social, or cultural characteristics. The recent process of democratization, however, shows a persistence that never ceases to surprise us, especially given the widespread reality of poverty, inequality, corruption, and crime. If the greatest challenge (and the main problem) of political development in Latin America in the last century has been the attempt to replace the old, oligarchic order with a new, democratic one, then we are closer than ever to reaching that goal. Nonetheless, the auspicious processes of democratization begun in Latin America since the late 1970s have encountered numerous obstacles and setbacks, especially from the perspective of democratic governability (which I will address in more depth in chapter 5).

## DEMOCRATIC BREAKDOWN

It is well known that the second wave of democratization in Latin America—a "short wave," in Huntington's (1991) words—that began after World War II came to a tragic end with the new authoritarian regimes that emerged in the 1960s and 1970s, especially in South America. The initial optimism after the defeat of Nazism and fascism in Europe and the rise of new democracies in Latin America (in Costa Rica, Venezuela, Bolivia, Brazil, Peru, and Ecuador) in addition to the already present democracies (Argentina, Chile, Colombia, and Uruguay), created the impression that it was possible to establish stable democracy in the region. The "communist threat" was seen mainly as an external reality, a perception that would change radically in 1959 after the Cuban Revolution. In the postwar period, it was believed that the threat of subversion and disruption of representative democracy and its institutions was approachable from the logic of containment. This mindset served as the basis of the United States' foreign policy during the Cold War, which was a key influence on the region and contributed to the process of intense polarization. Perhaps with the exception of Chile and Uruguay, at least until 1973, the democratizing impulse after World War II was followed by new waves of authoritarianism and democracy, reaching a peak in the late 1960s and early 1970s.

The 1950s dictatorships of Rojas Pinilla and Pérez Jiménez in Colombia and Venezuela, respectively, were the first examples of the new authoritarian wave in South America. In both countries, the processes of transition to democracy had begun in the late 1950s through the pacts written by the ruling elites, creating the impression of a new democratizing wave in the region. Over time, however, it was evident that the democratizing processes initiated after the fall of both dictatorships gave rise to an elitist, oligarchic, duopolistic, exclusionary form of democracy, exacerbating tensions within the countries. The true signpost of exclusion in Latin America was the new authoritarian regimes that emerged in the 1960s and 1970s, especially in the Southern Cone.

Before I review the possible causes of democratic breakdown, going back to the climate of optimism surrounding the second wave of democratization, let me point out that the development of the social sciences (especially in the United States) contributed significantly to the optimism of the postwar period. Some of the major schools and theories in the social sciences, especially during the 1950s, proposed that economic development would lead to both political stability and democracy. Such was the "optimist equation" expressed in Seymour Martin Lipset's (1960) classic book, *Political Man*. By the mid-1960s and early 1970s, however, these theories were subject to radical questioning, first in light of the facts themselves, and later in intense intellectual and academic debate.

On one hand, Samuel Huntington argued that, far from leading to political stability, modernization has destabilizing effects. He writes, "It is not the absence of modernity, but rather the efforts to achieve it, that produce political disorder," adding that "modernity breeds stability, but modernization breeds instability" (1968, 41 and 43). Huntington asserts that in Latin America's case, this instability is reflected in the successful coups d'état that occurred in seventeen of the twenty countries in the region. Some years later, reflecting on the new authoritarian regimes that had appeared in Latin America, Guillermo O'Donnell (1979)—one of Latin

America's most outstanding political scientists, who died in 2011—concluded that a certain type of modernization, in the phase of "high industrialization," likely led to authoritarianism more than to democracy. At the center of these debates was the old discussion, dating back to Aristotle, about the relationship between socioeconomic structures and political-institutional variables. Let us briefly examine this debate.

In his 1968 book, *Political Order in Changing Societies*, Huntington proposes that the high levels of social mobilization and the expansion of political participation associated with modernization, especially when they occurred under low levels of political institutionalization, led to a decline in political order during the postwar period, undermining the authority, effectiveness, and legitimacy of the government. Thus, the destabilization of the political order can be explained by the existence of a gap between economic development, social mobilization, and political participation on one hand and political institutions on the other. Huntington argues that it is political institutions that make the difference between political development and underdevelopment. Modernity, which is brought about when political participation combines with adequate institutions, is synonymous with stability, while modernization is synonymous with instability. The relationship between the levels of political participation and institutionalization determines the existence of political stability or instability. When institutions cannot fulfill their proper role, social processes surpass them (leading, in its extreme form, to what Huntington named "mass praetorianism"). In some cases, this can lead to military intervention or even revolution, both understood as agents of modernization. The position of the United States' foreign policy during the postwar period was somewhat naïve in believing that economic development itself would lead to political stability. These were different goals, independent of one another. A linear causal relationship did not exist between then.

Huntington's contribution was extremely valuable in the field of comparative politics. Today the importance of institutions seems obvious to us, especially since the emergence of the neo-institutionalist school in the 1990s (Hall and Taylor 1996), a perspective now predominant in the fields of political science and economics. We must give Huntington credit, however, for systematically developing this theory in the face of the complex processes of modernization and the social and political change instigated in the twentieth century, especially in the postwar period.

One might critique Huntington's theory for his bias in favor of political order, or political stability, to the point that social change is seen (at least implicitly) almost as an anomaly or pathology. Furthermore, both these theories and a significant portion of political science developed in the United States in the 1950s and 1960s were functional to U.S. foreign policy, which supported the new authoritarian regimes in Latin America in the 1960s and 1970s. In the eyes of the U.S. administrations—and in Huntington's—these regimes capably produced a certain political order, which was valuable especially when confronting the communist threat during the Cold War. In Huntington's case, we must take into account that he focuses more on the degree of government than the form of government or the political regime itself (democracy or dictatorship) and looks mainly to the levels of political institutionalization in relation to processes of economic development, social mobilization, and political participation. This political order could appear under a democratic or authoritarian government, as long as there was an adequate level of political institutionalization. For example, besides being nondemocratic regimes, the PRI in Mexico and the USSR were successful cases of political institutionalization.

While Huntington argued that modernization was destabilizing in itself, O'Donnell argues, in *Modernization and Bureaucratic-Authoritarian Regimes: Studies in South American Politics* (published in Spanish in 1971 and in English in 1979), that a certain type of modernization during the phase of high industrialization likely led to bureaucratic-authoritarian regimes more than democratic ones. This authoritarianism was repressive and exclusionary in terms of the social sectors that had previously been activated under the national and popular model. The transition from the easy phase of industrialization (based on the production of consumer goods) to advanced industrialization (based on the production of intermediate goods and capital goods, within the context of dependent development in Latin America) led the military, business, and technocratic elites to repress those social sectors that had previously been activated under the populist coalition and to replace them with a new governing coalition. O'Donnell replaces the traditional (static) approach, such as

Lipset's "optimist equation" (the idea that economic and social development would most likely lead to democracy) with an alternative (dynamic) focus, maintaining that high levels of modernization would most likely promote bureaucratic-authoritarian regimes, given the concrete reality of the South American countries in the 1960s and 1970s.

This type of authoritarian regime was different from the traditional authoritarian regimes (which constituted the majority of historical authoritarian regimes in Latin America) and the populist authoritarian regimes such as those of Juan Domingo Perón and Getúlio Vargas in Argentina and Brazil, and of General Juan Velasco Alvarado in Peru following the 1968 military coup. Both types of authoritarian regime emerged in the context of low levels of modernization and social differentiation. The new bureaucratic-authoritarian regimes, in contrast, were based on high levels of modernization and social differentiation. The military assumed power, providing the new regimes with a high capacity for organization. These regimes were grounded in a doctrine of national security (which included a particular vision for economic and social development) and formed a new type of alliance between the military, the new technocratic sectors, which had displaced the popular sectors previously activated under the populist coalition, and the business sectors, which felt that their interests had been threatened. Together, these three sectors formed a "coup coalition" that furthered the process of capitalist (dependent) modernization.

The exclusionary character of this new type of authoritarian regime contrasts with the inclusive nature of the populist coalition that had emerged in the 1940s. Latin America had progressed (or regressed) from an inclusive, popular, national, and developmentalist alliance that based itself on a state-driven ISI model, to a military-based, authoritarian, bureaucratic, and exclusionary alliance aimed at furthering capitalist modernization. The deepening of the modernization process in countries like Brazil and Argentina (following the 1964 and 1966 coups, and before the end of the basic phase of industrialization) was linked to the new model of capitalist accumulation. The need for foreign capital, the subsequent presence of multinational businesses, and the new technologies associated with this process necessitated a new, authoritarian political order that could carry out the tasks of capitalist development. The need to repress and exclude the popular sectors grew in response to the property-owning class's perception that the previous demands of the popular sectors were excessive. The goal of such exclusion was to stabilize the economy against chronic macroeconomic instability based on inflation, fiscal deficit, and the recurring crisis of the balance of payments linked to the ISI model carried out in the previous decades.

In effect, then, the double process of high modernization and mass praetorianism was at the center of democratic breakdown and the advent of a new type of authoritarianism in South America. Contrary to what Lipset's optimist equation had suggested, "high modernization in contemporary South America [is] not associated with political democracy" (O'Donnell 1979, iii), but rather with this new type of bureaucratic-authoritarian regime. Social and economic development in South America's case had not led to the "democracy and/or political stability" (204) that the social sciences had predicted in terms of development and modernization. Rather, there was an "elective affinity" or a "strong tendency" (198) to associate the economic and social structures belonging to high modernization and industrialization with the new bureaucratic-authoritarian political structures.

The polemic surrounding O'Donnell's provocative study lasted at least a decade. At the center of the debate over O'Donnell's thesis was the causal relationship that the Argentine political scientist established between the degree of development, industrialization, and modernization achieved by some South American countries (principally Brazil and Argentina) and the resulting bureaucratic-authoritarian regimes, denoting a markedly deterministic focus. On one hand, the coups in Chile and Uruguay in 1973 appeared to contradict O'Donnell's theory, in that both countries appeared to be cases of "intermediate development" (more than high modernization or industrialization), making them supposedly more disposed to democracy. Despite the difference in levels of development, both countries ended up like Brazil and Argentina, with bureaucratic-authoritarian regimes that were decidedly exclusionary. Nevertheless, the biggest critique of O'Donnell's work was that his critics saw in it an excessively economic and determinist focus in his explanation of the rise of these new authoritarian regimes, based on certain structural characteristics in the economic and social development of Latin America.

Some critics argued that "bureaucratic-authoritarianism could not be explained simply as a consequence of the interplay of economic forces" (Collier 1979, 8). For example, Fernando H. Cardoso, one of the principal intellectuals behind dependency theory, maintained that the relationship between states (capitalist and dependent) and political regimes (understood as formal rules that connected political institutions with the political links between citizens and elected officials) was necessarily complex. The very same forms of states (capitalist and dependent) could coexist with a variety of political regimes (authoritarian, fascist, corporatist, and even democratic), showing that the bureaucratic-authoritarian form referred more to the characteristics of the political regime than to the state itself.

Perhaps the most cutting critique came from Albert Hirschman (in Collier 1979), who argues in "Against Economic Determinants" that the social sciences should avoid putting excessive emphasis on economic variables to explain political phenomena. Hirschman questions the existence of certain "intrinsic" demands in the economy whose structural characteristics helped to explain the rise of the new type of authoritarian regimes. He critiques O'Donnell's focus on certain intrinsic demands in the process of "deepening" of capitalist accumulation and the need to transition from an easy phase to an advanced phase of industrialization. Hirschman reminds us that there were alternatives—which did not necessarily lead to authoritarian regimes—to the supposed exhaustion of the easy phase of industrialization (which he also questions). He points out the need for more orthodox methods of managing the economy, putting greater emphasis on export effort and the necessity of creating new markets and pro-market policies, in contrast to the supposed elasticity of the economy commonly associated with the easy phase of industrialization, which had clearly been abused. With his critique of both the structuralist school, which had been predominant in Latin America, and the fundamentalist solutions of the new authoritarian regimes, Hirschman claims, "the search for one specific structural, economic difficulty underlying the rise of authoritarianism in Latin America seems to me unpromising" (81). It was necessary to search not for explanations linked to the structural economic transformations carried out in Latin America, but for phenomena like "ideological escalation" (and the responsibility of the intellectuals and ruling elites) that had led to failed experiments in the region. Faced with possible accusations of holding an eclectic position, Hirschman immediately responded, "I would rather be eclectic than reductionist" (Hirschman 1979, 98).

O'Donnell's indisputable theoretical contributions, the intense debate that his work spurred over modernization and authoritarianism, and the heavy critiques he received gave rise to a vast range of literature that explained the emergence of the new authoritarian regimes by means of political factors. Perhaps the most emblematic of this literature were the works of Juan Linz, who wrote about the processes of democratic breakdown in Latin America (Linz and Stepan 1978). Linz reflects on the how and why of democratic breakdown in the region. Discarding some of the structural, economic explanations, he opts for a "descriptive and probabilistic" focus (not a deterministic one, which results from a structuralist focus), emphasizing political variables and the role of history. The widespread reality of political violence, the existence of anti-systemic parties, disloyal opposition, the resulting power vacuum, and the role of political actors in general—all political variables—were more helpful in explaining the processes of breakdown than structural or economic variables. This implies that there was nothing inevitable about these processes, and that during crisis situations, political actors and processes can lead to a rebalancing of the political process, avoiding democratic breakdown.

Using Max Weber's analysis of the elements of legitimacy and effectiveness of political systems as his foundation, Linz assigns crucial importance to party systems. He argues that the crisis of democracies (according to Giovanni Sartori and his classification of party systems as "moderate" or "polarized") is related to multiparty systems that are extreme, polarized, and centrifugal, given the presence of parties that are more ideological than pragmatic. Within this context, the lack of efficiency (a political regime's ability to find solutions to basic problems) and effectiveness (its ability to implement these solutions) tends to undermine the basic agreements that, in turn, affect a system's legitimacy in terms of the beliefs shared by a substantial number of citizens and their adherence and loyalty to the rules of the game. In this manner, unresolved structural problems can affect the efficiency and, in the long term, the legitimacy of the system. Rarely, however, do they constitute an immediate cause of democratic breakdown. Rather, the causes of democratic breakdown are to be found in these shortcomings at the level of political intermediation, especially in the role of the ruling elites and party systems. Similarly, internal factors rather than external factors generally explain processes of democratic breakdown. The form of government (presidentialism versus parliamentarism) is also a political variable to be considered (a debate that I will address in chapter 6).

Like Linz, I believe that the processes of democratic breakdown can be explained by internal and political factors rather than external and economic (or structural) ones. In the United States especially, there is a certain inability to identify the domestic causes of Latin American political processes, including those connected to democratic breakdown. It is commonly believed that everything that happens in the world—especially south of the Rio Grande—is directly orchestrated by the north. I remember clearly when I arrived in the United States to pursue my postgraduate studies in political science in the early 1980s, during Ronald Reagan's first term, and amidst the heated debate between O'Donnell, Linz, and others, a significant number of U.S. leaders held the simplistic view that Nixon and the CIA had destroyed Chilean democracy and overthrown President Allende. Something similar could be said about the remaining processes of democratic breakdown in Latin America, which were decisively linked to the United States' foreign policy. Any other explanation was considered improbable, self-interested, or even suspicious, surely a product of the internal reactionary forces in the countries "down there." After living, studying, and teaching for several years in the United States, I discovered that the opposite was equally true; that is, that from the viewpoint of those of us who were immersed in the internal political processes of any country in the region, there existed—and still exists—a marked difficulty in understanding the external influences that affect internal events. Thus, the need arises for a more balanced position that can adequately account for the combined influence of internal and external factors.

I believe that internal factors are principally responsible for democratic breakdown in Latin America—in a similar way, in his outstanding and fascinating autobiography, *The Accidental President of Brazil*

(2006, 81), former President Fernando Henrique Cardoso very clearly states that "The coup had been entirely Brazilian—that is, it took place without direct US support." External factors should at most be considered "intervening variables"—no trivial matter—that deepened the internal crises or precipitated matters in a certain direction, without constituting a direct or immediate cause of democratic breakdown. Therefore, it seems obvious that the United States watched with relief and often gave its direct or indirect support to the military coups in Brazil (1964), Chile and Uruguay (1973), and Argentina (1976). It would take entire chapters to analyze U.S. foreign policy during the Cold War, with reference to the doctrine of national security and counterinsurgency techniques, the formation of elite military officials in the School of the Americas in Panama, and the economic interests of U.S. investors and multinational companies. All of this merits a detailed, case-by-case analysis with a solid empirical base, avoiding ideological prejudices and caricatures. It is a very different matter, however, to deduce a causal and direct relationship between these external factors and processes of democratic breakdown. We shall see that, in terms of democratic transition and consolidation, external factors did play a very important role (much more than in terms of democratic breakdown).

In the search for a more balanced position, the debate over external factors must take into account the dynamics of the Cold War, the confrontation between the United States and the USSR, and its repercussions in Latin America, especially after the Cuban Revolution in 1959. If there is one external factor that can undoubtedly be considered an intervening variable in the processes of democratic breakdown in Latin America in the 1960s and 1970s, it was the Cuban Revolution and its lasting effects in the region. The revolution polarized the region's political scene. No one remained neutral in the face of this new political dynamic. On one hand, the Cuban Revolution demonstrated that it was possible to leapfrog in the process of the construction of socialism— the stageist thesis historically held by the Communist Party (based on the progression of capitalism's internal contradictions) clashed with the case of Cuba, opening up possibilities for the rest of the region. On the other hand, the internalization of what had until that moment appeared to be an external threat (communism), rapidly plunged the region into previously unknown levels of political polarization. Latin America became the stage for an intense global conflict.

Within the concrete reality of Latin America, this strong political polarization manifested around the tragic dilemma that marked the political scene of the time, that of "reform or revolution." One was for either reform or revolution. The right adopted a defensive stance, at times merely as a spectator and at times opting for the supposed lesser evil, directly involving itself in the coup-based strategies supported by the domestic elites, with some support from the United States, depending on the case. Like many other countries, Chile became a showcase of the clash between the supporters of reform (represented by the Revolution in Freedom headed by President Eduardo Frei Montalva) and the supporters of revolution (the Chilean Road to Socialism led by Salvador Allende). The forces of reform and revolution—that is, the forces advocating social change—were locked in a struggle strongly influenced by the Cuban Revolution. An extreme left was emerging, based on guerilla warfare, *foquismo*, and the subversion of the democratic-bourgeois order. Meanwhile, the right launched a counteroffensive to get rid of both forces, often with the direct or indirect support of the United States. The USSR, in turn, had serious reservations about Allende's experience of socialism, built on "democracy, pluralism, and freedom," and gave its support to the Cuban Revolution, which it considered a beachhead in the region. Despite some ideological reservations, the USSR supported the extreme left, which is perhaps the closest Latin America has come to the "revolutionary infantilism" that Lenin denounced in the early twentieth century.

Similarly, political variables more than economic variables decidedly influenced the processes of economic breakdown. Structural factors were important in the long term. It is no mere coincidence that the most brutal and emblematic cases of democratic breakdown in Latin America, such as those in Brazil, Chile, Uruguay, and Argentina, corresponded to the most emblematic cases of state-directed ISI, especially since the 1940s. This was O'Donnell's great theoretical contribution. By the end of the 1960s, the ISI model was experiencing a profound crisis and showing clear signs of exhaustion, as we saw in the previous chapter. Furthermore, the crisis of this development model was one aspect of the appeal of the Cuban Revolution in the 1960s and 1970s. According to this view, just as the most emblematic supporters of dependency theory had maintained, the attempt to consolidate a national capitalism based on the idea of a second independence and inward-oriented growth (that is, ISI) had only reinforced the bonds of dependence on developed countries, especially the United States. Thus, the only solution was a socialist, anti-imperialist revolution—a thesis that gained strength after the triumph of the Cuban Revolution.

Without ignoring the external factors or the structural variables linked to the political processes, we can see that democratic breakdown was triggered more by political and internal factors than by economic and external ones. The responsibility of the ruling elites, the role of political actors, certain characteristics of the presidentialist form of government and their relation to party and electoral systems, the levels of political polarization, the deterioration of the levels of legitimacy, efficiency, and effectiveness of the political systems—all of these led to the erosion of the very foundation of democratic political regimes, leading to democratic breakdown in various countries in the region. There was nothing inevitable about these processes; indeed, Colombia and Venezuela did not suffer the same authoritarian outcome. This did not stop many from expressing the feeling of being caught in a veritable Greek tragedy, as Chilean Radomiro Tomic, former senator and presidential candidate of the Christian Democratic Party, expressed. In a letter addressed to General Carlos Prats, the commander-in-chief of the Chilean army, in August 1973 (a month before the military coup), Tomic wrote, "Just like in the tragedies of classical Greek theater, everyone knows what will happen. No one wishes for it to occur, but everyone does exactly what is needed to bring about the misfortune that they are attempting to avoid" (quoted by Alfredo Jocelyn-Holt in *Qué Pasa* magazine, November 2008, 20).

It is clear that the multiple manifestations of the economic crisis—inflation and hyperinflation, chronic fiscal deficits, and the recurring crises of the balance of payments, among so many other signs of macroeconomic instability—worsened matters while alienating the middle classes, which became one of the principal sources of support for the new authoritarian regimes. None of this, however, sufficiently explains the causes behind democratic breakdown. The weight of political factors was more influential than all of the above. The Cold War, the tension between the East and West, the decisive impact of the Cuban Revolution, and the strong political polarization in the region greatly affected the processes of democratic breakdown. It was also undeniable that the United States played a part, directly or indirectly, in the majority of the military interventions. Nonetheless, our focus has been to underscore the salience of internal and political factors over external and economic ones in the processes of democratic breakdown in Latin America.

## DEMOCRATIC TRANSITION

We are still surprised by the magnitude and depth of the third wave of democratization that began in southern Europe (Spain, Portugal, and Greece) in the mid-1970s and in Latin America in the late 1970s and early 1980s. In 1969, 19 percent of the Latin American population lived under democratic regimes, compared with 96 percent in 1999—that is, the population of every country of the region, except Cuba (Mainwaring and Pérez-Liñán 2003). Such was the case despite the considerable weaknesses and shortcomings of these new democracies, especially in terms of the challenge of democratic governability, as we will see in chapter 5.

How did the processes of transition to democracy take form in Latin America? How can we explain the recent third wave of democratization in the region? Where do we currently stand, confronted by the challenges of democratic transition and consolidation? What is the context in the region at the beginning of the new millennium? I will address these questions in the following paragraphs.

Perhaps the starting point is the classic work of O'Donnell and Schmitter, carried out with Laurence Whitehead (1986), in a project conducted from 1979 to 1984—that is, with the first of this wave's transitions, which occurred in the Dominican Republic (1978), Ecuador (1979), and Peru (1980). It is worth noting that the study does not refer to the transition toward democracy, but rather to the transition "away from authoritarianism," as if to emphasize the uncertainty of the outcome of these processes and the precariousness of the new democracies in Latin America, concerns that endure even today. The study addresses "non-revolutionary" transitions away from authoritarian regimes (thus excluding Nicaragua and Cuba), while admitting that there is a "normative bias" in this methodology in the assumption of the intrinsic value of political democracy. The authors compare Latin America to the democratic transitions that took place in southern Europe, concluding that in Latin America, unlike in Europe, the processes of transition were caused by internal factors rather than external ones.

O'Donnell and Schmitter claim that it is impossible to formulate a general theory about these transitions and that there can be only tentative conclusions about the so-called uncertain democracies. At most, we can identify certain pieces of the map on the basis of the instruments of navigation in the hands of key political and social actors. At the center of these transitions are processes of liberalization that precede the processes of democratization themselves. While stating that the processes of democratization are reversible and that regression to authoritarianism is possible, the authors argue that it is the process of "opening" or "liberalization" that leads the way to democratization.

According to O'Donnell and Schmitter, the Achilles' heel of the bureaucratic-authoritarian regimes was their initial promise to reestablish democracy and freedom, along with the permanent conflict between hardliners and softliners within the regime. All this facilitates the shift from "soft dictatorship," or *dictablanda* (liberalized authoritarianism) to limited democracy, or *democradura*. In this process, it is desirable that the transition takes place without violence or dramatic discontinuities, lest the outcome be revolution rather than democracy (as was the case of Nicaragua in 1979). The predominant paradigm of the third wave of democratization is negotiation by means of pacts ("pacted democracy"), more so than defeat in a foreign war or a revolution more likely to lead to an authoritarian regime than democracy. Since military regimes no longer conform to the traditional form based on the leadership of caudillos, but rather are led by the armed forces themselves, it is the threats perceived in the higher ranks of the military with regard to their own institutional or professional integrity, the fear of further politicization of the armed forces, and in some cases the issue of corruption, that work in favor of democratization.

Although these processes of transition through pact negotiation generally focus on the role of the ruling civil and military elites, in both the government and the opposition, it is the so-called resurrection of civil society that triggers liberalization as a prelude to democratization. Liberalization remains essentially a military moment, while democratization is a political moment. The call for elections tends to be the event that triggers transition and has a profound impact on political actors, especially in terms of political parties and the interaction between the softliners of the authoritarian regime and the moderates of the opposition. The maximalists or voluntarists on both sides tend to obstruct the transition process, even though they are part of the political game. To use the metaphor of a multilayered chess game, there are two generalizations that can be made about the transition from liberalization to democracy: the players are forbidden to threaten or take the king (the inviolable property rights of the bourgeoisie) or the queen (the existence and institutional integrity of the armed forces).

Transitions to democracy are by no means a linear process. There are advances and regressions throughout the course of this political game. This is the position adopted by Frances Hagopian and Scott Mainwaring (2005) in their study of the third wave of democratization begun in Latin America in 1978. Writing twenty years after O'Donnell and Schmitter's classic work, both authors question the theories that focus on modernization (economic development), class structure (for example, the necessity of a strong bourgeoisie or working class), or economic performance to explain the durability of democracy in the region. According to Hagopian and Mainwaring, in this recent process of democratization, the new (and not-so-new) democracies have survived critical levels of poverty and inequality. Likewise, democracy of the masses has begun to replace the elite democracies historically present in the region, including growing levels of electoral participation.

Hagopian and Mainwaring explain the changes in political regimes between 1946 and 1999 (fifty-three regime changes in total, including thirty-two transitions to democracy and twenty-one cases of democratic breakdown) as the combined effect of a series of variables, including the level of economic development (income per capita), class structure (the percent of the workforce in the manufacturing sector), economic performance (growth and inflation), the regional political environment, political fragmentation (number of parties), and partisan polarization. The authors conclude that political factors—principally contingency and agency—help to explain the regime changes in Latin America more than structural factors do. Of all these factors in democratic transition or breakdown, the regional political environment is especially influential.

If the advances are worth highlighting, the regressions cannot be ignored. According to the authors, these are observed principally in the dismal government performance during the third wave of democratization. In the majority of the countries, democratic regimes have failed to promote economic growth and to reduce poverty, crime, and inequality (Hagopian and Mainwaring 2005, 10). Despite these difficulties and their poor economic performance, the new democracies survived. The impact of poor economic performance is mediated by political factors, which have had the most influence. Among these, external factors such as the existence of a favorable international (regional and global) environment for democracy and generally favorable attitudes of the elite and the masses have contributed to sustaining new democracies. Despite the polarization, fragmentation, and mediocre economic growth, these third-wave democracies accounted for better conditions and survivability than the previous wave of democratization from 1944 to 1964. It is here, precisely, that external factors gain decisive influence. For instance, the interventions of the Organization of American States (OAS) in Paraguay, Guatemala, and Peru, and of the United States in El Salvador and Guatemala in the 1980s, greatly influenced the processes of democratization in these countries.

The contrast between the advances and regressions contributed to the large gap between expectations and reality. The marked weakness of the states (according to Mainwaring) and the vulnerability of institutions (according to Hagopian) led to the citizens' growing disenchantment with these new democracies. If these democracies have indeed surmounted various obstacles, they have done so in conditions of vulnerability. Although structural and economic factors are not the primary explanation for the changes in political regimes, they are important in terms of the quality and solidity of new democracies (a theme we will explore further in chapter 5).

One of the most notable features of this recent wave of democratization in Latin America is the way it questions core aspects of the principal theories that had been developed in the social sciences, especially since the 1950s. Adam Przeworski (1991), for instance, referring to the 1989 fall of the Berlin Wall as one of the most visible signs of this recent wave of democratization, points out that this process of recent democratization represents a dismal failure of political science. His affirmation refers principally to the distinction made in political science—primarily by Juan Linz, reflecting on the case of Spain—between totalitarian and authoritarian regimes. One of the most important differences between these types of regimes is the supposedly irreversible character of totalitarian regimes, in contrast to authoritarian regimes, which are generally reversible. We are not referring here to the political use and abuse that came about through this distinction on the part of the Reagan administration—especially by Secretary of State Alexander Haig and Jeane Kirkpatrick, ambassador to the United Nations—who justified their enmity with "totalitarian" (communist) regimes and greater flexibility (if not closeness or outright complicity) with the merely "authoritarian" regimes in Latin America, based on the supposedly reversible character and the staunch anticommunist stance of the latter.

The "dismal failure" of political science refers to literature that indicated the need for a set of economic, social, and cultural requisites, prerequisites, or structural conditions in order to establish and consolidate democracy in Latin America. Democracy seemed to be reserved to countries that were developed or had certain economic, social, or cultural characteristics. In this way, for example, in his classic work, "Some Social Requisites of Democracy: Economic Development and Political Legitimacy" (1959, 86), Seymour Martin Lipset argues that "in the modern world . . . economic development involving industrialization, urbanization, high education standards, and a steady increase in the overall wealth of the society, is a basic condition sustaining democracy." Lipset also refers to Max Weber, who argued that modern democracy can only be developed under a system of capitalist industrialization (73). Legitimacy, based on the political system's capacity to generate and maintain the belief that certain institutions are the most adequate ones, is fundamental to the stability of a political and social system. Likewise, effectiveness comes out of the degree of economic development, outfitted with the characteristics mentioned above. Lipset argues that the economic and social structure that Latin America inherited from colonialism prevented the region from following the path of the former British colonies to the north. This meant that the new republics never developed the symbols and the "aura" of legitimacy necessary for social and political stability.

There is ample literature following the same line of thought as Weber and Lipset, maintaining that the level of economic development (which usually refers to the level of income per capita) is a good predictor of democracy. In a study of twenty-one democracies that have continued uninterrupted since World War II, Arend Lijphart (1984) claims that democracy corresponds to the countries with the greatest level of well-being (characterized by high levels of economic development, industrialization, and urbanization) and that the majority of these are concentrated in the North Atlantic region. Needless to say, even in the eyes of the critics of these theories, a certain type of relationship between the levels of economic development and democratic stability does exist. However, in the case of Latin America, in the face of this third wave of democratization, these arguments about requisites, prerequisites, or conditions for democracy can hardly be sustained.

As I indicated above, the classic work of O'Donnell (1979) was one of the first to question the claims of Lipset's optimist equation that economic development would likely lead to democracy. In the same vein, Mainwaring and Pérez-Liñán (2003) revisit the relationship between modernization and democracy, referring openly to Latin America's "exceptionalism" in the comparative perspective. Looking to the results of an empirical, quantitative study, they maintain that, in the period of 1945 to 1996, there is clear evidence that (1) the level of development had a rather modest impact on the prospect of democracy in the region; (2) income per capita, and the level of economic development in general, is not a good predictor of democracy in Latin America, at least when compared to other countries with the same range of income per capita; and (3) the exceptionalism of Latin America brings into question the structural explanations for the relationship between the level of economic development and the type of political regime. Contrary to what comparative studies usually show, the survival of democracy in Latin America has been possible even under low levels of economic development, discarding any sort of proposed linear relationship between both variables.

If the characteristics and the resilience of this recent wave of democratization seem to question the theories that stressed economic development and the modernization of economic and social structures as a condition for democracy, the same can be said about the ample literature that emphasized certain characteristics of Latin American political culture to explain the difficulties of establishing and consolidating democracy in the region. In short, the presence of a Catholic, centralist, corporatist, clientelistic, patrimonialistic, elitist, hierarchical, and vertical (among other terms) political culture—ultimately, a rather authoritarian political culture—is at the root of the difficulty in establishing democracy in the region. Just as Lipset (and Weber) can be considered the pioneers of those theories based on economic development, Howard Wiarda is an important proponent of the theory based on the characteristics of Latin American political culture. "For the fact is," Wiarda (2001, viii) writes, "that Latin America was founded on a feudal, oligarchic, authoritarian, and elite basis. Latin America was a product of the Counter-Reformation, of medieval scholasticism and Catholicism, of the Inquisition, and of frankly non-egalitarian, nonpluralist, and nondemocratic principles. Many of these early characteristics, now modified, updated or 'modernized,' are still present today, embedded in cultural, social, and political behavior and in the area's main institutions." Some years earlier, Wiarda (along with Harvey Kline) asserted that, "Whereas the political culture of the United States is mainly democratic, liberal (believing in the classic freedoms of the Bill of Rights), and committed to representative government, that of Latin America has historically been more elitist, authoritarian, hierarchical, corporatist, and patrimonial" (Wiarda and Kline 1979, 11).

These characteristics, which the author associates with the existence of a particular and distinct culture and civilization, have their origin in the experience of colonialism, conquest, and the feudal, medieval, and Thomist roots of Spanish and Portuguese historical development, based on religious orthodoxy and political authoritarianism. Three centuries of colonialism, on a path diametrically opposed to that of North America, left a deep imprint on the structures of Ibero-America, which helps to explain the region's difficulties with establishing and consolidating democracy. Unlike in the United States, liberalism never became the dominant ideology in the region, nor did it ever reach a majority status or replace traditionalism. Rousseau more than Locke, and the positivism of Comte and the corporatism of the medieval Catholic Church more than liberalism, pluralism, and tolerance, were the principal influences on Latin American political development. In the early years following independence, conservative authoritarianism overtook the incipient liberalism that some of the forerunners of independence had promoted. The new political regimes showed at most traces of republicanism, but never democracy.

In his book *The Centralist Tradition in Latin America*, Claudio Véliz (1980) argues that one of the characteristic traits that differentiates Latin America from Western Europe and the United States is centralism. Writing during the period of bureaucratic-authoritarian regimes, Véliz postulates that the most recent authoritarian wave, like past waves, was rooted in Latin America's centralist tradition and corresponded to the "secular disposition of Latin American society" that differentiated it from the industrialized countries of northwestern Europe (1). This centralism can be explained by means of four lacks: (1) the lack of a feudal experience—what was present instead was Spanish absolutism at the hands of a regalistic centralism, with the exception of the "liberal pause" at the end of the nineteenth century; (2) the lack of religious nonconformity like that which accompanied the Protestant Reformation, resulting in the strong centralism of the Catholic Church; (3) the lack of anything similar to the Industrial Revolution in Europe, which resulted in a complex class structure that was in turn absent in Latin America; and (4) the lack of the ideological, social, and political developments associated with the French Revolution, which dramatically transformed the nature of European society (Véliz 1980, 3). In contrast to all these factors, Latin America had evolved along a different course, one based on preindustrial societies, premodern thinking, and centralist-oriented bureaucratization.

The simple statement of these absences is a starting point for Véliz's critics, to the extent that the economic, political, social, and cultural development of a region (in this case, Latin America) is difficult to explain simply due to "lacks" like the ones described above, using as a model the European and North American countries, the majority of which were products of feudalism, the Protestant Reformation, the French and Industrial Revolutions, and all the changes associated with these. What Wiarda, Kline, Véliz, and others hold in common is a belief that cultural characteristics can explain political processes and the difficulties of establishing democracy in Latin America.

Some theories that arose in the 1950s went even farther in speaking of certain "pathologies" that afflicted Latin American countries in the social, economic, political, or cultural realms (e.g. Pierson's 1950 "The Pathology of Democracy in Latin America"). These included, among other afflictions, the thousands of ways in which Latin America differed from the liberal, Anglo-Saxon, Protestant, decentralized, and democratic model. After three centuries of isolation from the outside world, submersion in the darkness of colonial times and structures, and the flash of the midday sun that revealed the leaders of Hispanoamerican independence, Latin America suffered a sudden blindness when faced with the brightness of revolutionary thought in France, England, and the United States (the "outside world"). The region fell again into darkness, this time one of anarchy and despotism. Only in the twentieth century did Latin America reencounter the outside world, tuning in to some of the liberal ideas present in the more "advanced" countries (Pierson 1950, 102; see also Griffith, Plamenatz, and Pennock 1956).

The above is a rather extreme explanation (perhaps even a caricature) of the political culture in Latin America and the way that this culture affects political processes like democratization. Nonetheless, there is a certain economic, social, or cultural determinism behind these explanations that prevents us from gaining a worthy understanding of such phenomena as the recent democratization in Latin America.

Along similar lines, an interesting body of literature has emerged recently that attempts to explain some of the problems related to democratic stability in Latin America, based not on economic structures or certain features of political culture, but on the presidential form of government adopted by all the countries in the region since independence (excluding the Caribbean). Although this particular focus resonates with my personal view, I must warn against determinism here as well, for it fails to explain how the new—and not-so-new—democracies in the region survive despite their common presidential form of government. Perhaps the persistence of democracy in Latin America leads us to question not only the majority of structural theories, but also the determinism that tends to appear in theories surrounding presidentialism and its relationship with democratic political stability.

Some of the primary proponents of this school, such as Juan Linz and Arturo Valenzuela (1994), hold that the majority of stable democracies in the world have been parliamentary, with a few semipresidential or semiparliamentary. The presidentialism of the United States, which was adopted by every nation in Latin America, is an exceptional case. Some of the advantages of parliamentarism over presidentialism include the dual democratic legitimacy found in presidential systems (by which the selection of president of the republic, like parliament, is based on popular vote, with the potential conflict between powers that this implies); the rigidity of presidential systems when faced with crisis (due to fixed terms); the advantages of a vote of no confidence in parliamentary governments compared with the extreme measure of constitutional impeachment in presidential systems; the winner-takes-all game of a presidential government; the implicit plebiscite component of a presidential government; the tendency toward polarization, personalism, populism, and the presence of "outsiders" in the political arena (unlike in parliamentary governments, which are based on a system of institutionalized parties). Lijphart (1984) adds to this list the advantage of "consensus democracy," with its tendency to share, limit, and disperse power, over the "majoritarian democracy" that is inherent to a presidential form of government.

This analysis implies that in trying to explain the political instability found in Latin America and its difficulties in establishing political democracy, rather than focusing on economic, social, or cultural structures or variables, one must point at the political and institutional arrangements—such as presidentialism—that underlie the political process. From this perspective, what Linz (in Linz and Valenzuela 1994, 69) terms the "structural problems inherent to presidentialism" explain a large part of the difficulties of consolidating stable democracy in the region. The fact remains that the third wave of democratization has shown that it is also possible to advance toward democratic consolidation under a presidential form of government. In fact, the "coalition presidentialism" (*presidencialismo de coalición*) that we will consider in chapter 4 appears as one of the possible political arrangements within the region's recent processes of democratization that attempts to combine presidentialism and a multiparty system.

I hold the view that the recent wave of democratization, as well as the previous ones, shows that Latin America is not condemned to authoritarian political regimes. Rather, the depth of this third wave of democratization, despite its shortcomings, questions the deterministic and structural explanations that have prevailed in the social sciences since the 1950s. Throughout this book, I argue that institutions, political actors, and public policies, more so than structural (economic, social, or cultural) factors, help to explain the possibilities as well as the limitations of democracy in Latin America, including changes in political regimes. This is not to disregard the importance of structural factors that underlie political processes in the long term. In other words, it is a question of recognizing the place of agency in terms of the role of political actors, institutions, and public policies in these processes. Having said this, I will argue in the following section that economic and social factors, especially as they relate to the role of the state and the question of performance, do matter in terms of democratic consolidation.

## DEMOCRATIC CONSOLIDATION

In the 1990s, the focus of political and social leaders, and the literature itself, began to shift from the challenges of transition to the challenges of democratic consolidation. Like the countries of southern and central Europe, Asia, and Africa, the countries of Latin America began to progress

from the processes of transition to the greater complexities of democratic consolidation and governability.

It is important to note that these are not linear, stage-based processes. Rather, they are full of contradictions and gray areas. This is precisely what leads Thomas Carothers (2002) to speak of the "End of the
Transition Paradigm." According to the author, none of the five suppositions behind the "paradigm of transition" (and a good deal of the literature surrounding it, including the work of O'Donnell and Schmitter)
have been confirmed in the much more complex reality of the processes
of democratization that have occurred in a hundred countries. These are,
namely, (1) that countries that were able to transition away from dictatorship would most likely transition toward democracy (in reality, many
have transitioned to nondemocratic regimes); (2) that democratization
processes tend to follow an ordered sequence of stages that move from
liberalization to the collapse of authoritarian regimes and democratic
consolidation (instead, the process is quite chaotic); (3) that the realization of elections was the clearest indicator of a democratic regime (rather,
many competitive regimes took on an authoritarian form); (4) that the
underlying conditions or structural factors were not fundamental in the
processes of democratization, and that "anyone" could establish a democratic form of government—the reality shows that these structural factors
are indeed important in consolidating stable democracy; and (5) that the
processes of transition to democracy occurred over a base of coherent and
well-constituted states, assuming that the construction of democracy and
the construction of the state reinforced each other (we now know that the
opposite has occurred in many cases).

Thus, Carothers argues, all this literature about the "paradigm of
transition" is wishful thinking when confronted with the reality that, out
of one hundred transitions to democracy from the 1970s to the 1990s, no
more than twenty have adopted truly democratic regimes. The vast majority of these transitions fall into a gray area—neither democracies nor
dictatorships, strictly speaking—including the majority of developing
countries and those of the former USSR. Various names for the different
types of democracy have emerged—semidemocracies, pseudodemocracies, façade democracies, illiberal democracies, and delegative democra-

cies, among other adjectives—while many trajectories have been even less clear.

With this in mind, it is worth asking whether it is possible to speak of "complete" transitions. As we will see in the following lines, O'Donnell believes it is an "illusion" to speak of democratic consolidation as such. Juan Linz and Alfred Stepan, in contrast, in *Problems of Democratic Transition and Consolidation* (1996), hold that it is possible to speak of complete democratic transitions. They hold the view that democratic breakdowns, transitions, and consolidations correspond to perfectly defined categories. For example, one can say that a democratic transition is complete when "sufficient agreement has been reached about political procedures to produce an elected government, when a government comes to power that is the direct result of a free and popular vote, when this government *de facto* has the authority to generate new policies, and when the executive, legislative and judicial power generated by the new democracy does not have to share power with other bodies *de jure*" (3). The fact remains that, analytically and in a comparative perspective, it is certainly not easy to draw a clear dividing line between the processes of democratic transition and consolidation.

On August 9, 1991, President Patricio Aylwin of Chile publicly declared that the country's transition to democracy had ended: "The transition is over" was his concise and emphatic statement. In Chile, this controversy has lasted until today. Obviously, President Aylwin's statement was not an academic statement but a political one. A democratic transition, by definition, carries with it an important degree of uncertainty. The above-mentioned presidential statement had a clear political objective in terms of bringing about political and democratic stability in a particularly complex transition in which, only as a way of an example, General Pinochet remained as commander in chief of the army until 1998. The statement was aimed at producing predictability and stability, dealing with the uncertainties of a democratic transition process.

Thus the questions emerge about how and when a transition to democracy starts and ends; which is the dividing line between a process of transition and democratic consolidation; whether there even exists such a dividing line; and how to characterize both political processes.

O'Donnell (in Mainwaring, O'Donnell, and Valenzuela 1992) points out that, in reality, there is not one but rather two transitions to democracy: the transition away from an authoritarian *government* to a democratic one (reflected in the process of liberalization and political openness, as well as the guarantee of certain basic rights, culminating in elections that decide the future democratic government), and the transition from an authoritarian *regime* to a democratic one (in which it is assumed that an authoritarian regression is not possible, backed by the rejection by a great part of the population of an authoritarian political form, along with the establishment of institutions of representative democracy). In the first case, we are speaking of a "transition" to democracy as such (a transition from an authoritarian *government* to a democratic one), while in the second case, we refer to democratic "consolidation" (transition from an authoritarian *regime* to a democratic one). Therefore, there is a qualitative difference between a process of transition and one of democratic consolidation, despite the fact that there are many complex and uncertain cases in which it is challenging to draw a decisive line between the two.

In the book mentioned above, Mainwaring writes that a clear distinction between democratic transition and consolidation is impossible, and that the form and features of transition significantly blur with the form and features of democratic consolidation. In some cases, transition takes place after the defeat or collapse of the old regime, as in Germany, Italy, and Japan after World War II, and in Argentina, Portugal, Greece, and Eastern Europe after the fall of the Berlin Wall in 1989. In other cases, by contrast, transition takes place through a complex network of transactions, pacts, and negotiations (pact transition), as in Spain, Brazil, and South Korea. Meanwhile, in other cases, transition occurs through "extraction" as the military negotiates the terms of its own situation before abandoning power. The outcomes of each type of transition have significant repercussions for the resulting type of democratic regime.

In the same volume, Samuel Valenzuela claims that democratic consolidation also requires the removal of "authoritarian enclaves," of the "tutelary powers" of the military, of "reserved dominion"—especially at the level of public policies, which limit the possibilities of the new democratic government and regime—and, finally, of the de facto powers, as it appears in the case of Chile through the authoritarian Constitution of

1980. These characteristics of democratic transition often overlap, expressing elements of continuity and change in the process toward democratic consolidation, which vary from one country to another. In this manner, processes of democratic consolidation account for the shift from what Valenzuela calls the "perverse" forms that institutions take on under authoritarian regimes to a "virtuous" form of institutionalization, linked to the existence of minimum procedural standards commonly associated with the holding of free and democratic elections.

Linz and Stepan (1996) assert that, although one can indeed speak of democratic consolidation, in terms of the quality of democracy, in a stricter way democratic consolidation takes place when democracy has become the only game in town. This implies that no significant group attempts to remove or undermine the democratic regime or promote a secession from the state, that the vast majority of the population believes that any political change must come from within the parameters of democracy, and that everyone agrees that political conflict can be resolved within the established norms. In summary, one can speak of democratic consolidation when "democracy becomes routinized and deeply internalized in social, institutional, and even psychological life, as well as in calculations for achieving success" (Linz and Stepan 1996, 5). The routinization and habituation of certain conducts and practices are characteristic of democratic consolidation.

According to Linz and Stepan, in both democratic transition and consolidation it is necessary to consider two variables that designate "macropolitics": namely, the existence of a sovereign state ("stateness") as a prerequisite to democracy as well as to citizenship, and the consideration of the type of preexisting regime, to the extent that the road to transition and consolidation has a bearing on the features of the latter (in other words, that the process is "path dependent"). Preexisting regimes are classified as totalitarian, post-totalitarian (USSR), authoritarian, and sultanistic—the last being an "extreme form of patrimonialism," according to Weber's definition, such as that in Haiti under Duvalier (1957–1971) or in the Dominican Republic under Trujillo (1930–1961). In addition to these two macropolitical variables, there are five "interacting arenas" in the sphere of development that play a part in transition and consolidation: (1) a vigorous civil society that is mainly autonomous from the state; (2) a properly valued political society that is mainly autonomous of the de facto powers and that has control of the state apparatus and political power; (3) a rule of law that transforms a simple electoral democracy into a liberal or representative one; (4) a properly established state bureaucracy; and (5) an institutionalized economic society with norms, institutions, and regulations that establish the rules of the game.

Linz and Stepan's typology is even more demanding when applied to the case of Latin America, which is characterized by rather weak states and weak political and civil societies that lack sufficient autonomy, in a context of "(un)rule of law" (to quote O'Donnell), state bureaucracies that often resemble patrimonialistic systems with a weak separation of the public and private spheres, and economic institutions that, rather than leveling the field for all players, give rise to high levels of discretionary powers among public authorities.

The shift from an electoral democracy to an authentic liberal or representative democracy is one of the greatest difficulties in terms of democratic consolidation. Larry Diamond (1999) asserts that there was in the 1990s a growing gap between electoral democracy (in terms of the realization and universalizing of free, transparent, and democratic elections) and liberal or representative democracy (which assumes both the realization of free and democratic elections and certain characteristics commonly associated with constitutional democracy, including an effective rule of law.) Of the 117 democracies in the 1990s (as opposed to the 39 democracies in the 1970s), only 81 could be labeled liberal democracies. The question in terms of democratic consolidation, then, is the quality of democracy, which extends beyond the realization of free and democratic elections.

Along with Linz and Stepan, Diamond agrees that, in order to speak of democratic consolidation, the majority of actors must perceive democracy as the "only game in town." He adds that there are three important tasks, namely: democratic "deepening," or transforming the formal structures of democracy into liberal and representative democracy, especially in terms of accountability; political institutionalization, referring to the rules and procedures of democracy; and the key question of the "performance" of the democratic regime, referring to the role of public policy and its ability to cope with the social demands. Democracy thus corresponds more to a constantly developing political process than to any given political system. In turn, the quality of a democracy can be measured by the degree of respect for political rights and civil liberties. This means that the absence of a rule of law correlates with cases of "illiberal democracy," which differs from liberal, representative, or constitutional democracy.

In a sort of counterpoint to the logic behind the theories of Diamond (and all those who emphasize democratic consolidation as a long list of problems and demands that end up forming a thick conceptual fog), Andreas Schedler (1998) proposes that we "return to the origins." Here, he refers to the initial concern for democratic survival. This implies that the probability (or lack thereof) of an authoritarian regression defines democratic consolidation, whether in the form of democratic breakdown or, as was seen in many countries in the 1990s, an erosion of democracy. Schedler's critique is directed at certain literature that, in an extreme form of conceptual inflation, has gone so far as to identify 550 types and subtypes of democratic regimes, thereby losing both value and utility. At the end of the day, Schedler argues, the classification of political regimes is reduced to four categories: authoritarian regimes, electoral democracies or "semidemocracies" (those which have clean and competitive elections but do not adequately respect civil and political liberties), liberal democracies or "polyarchies" (those in which there are free and democratic elections as well as the due respect for civil and political rights), and finally, "advanced" democracies (those which go beyond the minimalist concept of democracy). These four categories present diverse trajectories, not necessarily in linear progression. According to Schedler, the quality or deepening of democracy (important to "complete" the democracy, following the standards of the so-called advanced nations) is unclear, controversial, and problematic. The perspective of liberal democracy, which has been well defined by Robert Dahl and others, would be a much better option.

Along similar lines, O'Donnell (in Diamond and Plattner 2001) asserts that the possibility of defining the democratic consolidation in terms of the model of democracy that works for the advanced countries (or the "old polyarchies") of the United States and Europe is an illusion. In Latin America, democratic institutionalization occurs not only in terms of the formal institutions of classical polyarchies or of the more advanced countries, but also with informal institutions including clientelism, nepotism, corruption, and other nonuniversal practices. In Latin America, we find ourselves facing a form of delegative democracy, which O'Donnell defines by the existence of "a caesaristic, plebiscitarian executive that once elected sees itself as empowered to govern the country as it deems fit" (123). We lack the very controls of representative democracy that are characteristic of the old polyarchies.

In short, O'Donnell claims that it is the institutionalization of free and democratic elections—the institution of democracy par excellence, according to Dahl's focus on competitiveness and transparency—that characterizes democratic consolidation. There is no one single, exclusive form of institutionalization. Nor is there "complete" institutionalization. In fact, it would be impossible to specify when a democracy has been consolidated definitively. The truth of the matter is that we find ourselves in a true theoretical limbo. Therefore, we must discard that teleological illusion of trying to define democratic consolidation by holding as our only model that of the advanced democracies and formal institutionalization of Europe and the United States. This also implies a critique of Linz and Stepan's understanding of democratic consolidation as the only game in town. In reality, there are several games in play and a great variety of democracies or polyarchies. There *is* democratic consolidation in Latin America, although it may be weak and may not correspond, strictly speaking, to the liberal concept of the rule of law and fundamental freedoms, or to the republican concept of a clear separation between public and private spheres. In short, democratic consolidation must be understood in terms of the institutionalization of free and fair elections.

In order to capture the essence of the intellectual debate that has been waged these past twenty years, I will conclude this chapter by referencing two theoretical approaches that attempt to form a more general and systematic vision of democratization in Latin America by seeking to escape the narrow (and artificial?) categories of democratic breakdown, transition, and consolidation. I refer here to the works of Rueschemeyer, Stephens, and Stephens (1992) and Garretón (2003), which attempt to explain, from the perspectives of political science and sociology, respectively, the characteristics, possibilities, limitations, and dynamic of democratization in Latin America.

Garretón acknowledges that there existed historically a merely instrumental valorization of democracy in Latin America. Democracy was considered a "dependent" variable—dependent on economic, social, and cultural structures. The emphasis was more on the social, in the broad sense of the word, than on the institutional. This raised the question of democracy as a mere reflection of certain economic, social, and cultural structures. The impact of the recent dictatorships and the question of human rights has had a positive double effect: on one hand, the recognition of the intrinsic value of democracy, and on the other hand, the recognition of democracy as an object of study, beyond any deterministic understanding. Thus, there has arisen in the region a new approach to democracy as a political regime understood as "a system of institutional mediation" between the state and society. With that in mind, Garretón warns that we must not fall prey to the other extreme of considering democracy solely as a self-explanatory paradigm, or as the only factor to be addressed, ignoring other economic, social, political, or cultural considerations.

Garretón questions the paradigm of transition to democracy and speaks instead of "political democratization," intending this term to apply just as much to the "founding" of new democracies such as those in Central America (which actually correspond to transitions from civil wars and peace processes) as to transitions, properly speaking, such as those of the Southern Cone, and finally, to political reform or regime change, such as in the case of Mexico. In Latin America, we are dealing with "incomplete" democracies. Garretón emphasizes the need to address the unresolved problems of democratic transitions and consolidations, principally in terms of the authoritarian enclaves that still survive today and the de facto powers that limit democracy. Furthermore, he claims that Latin America's greatest challenge is to adequately establish the "deepening, relevance, and quality" of the new democratic regimes. The challenge is to establish strong parties and social actors that are both autonomous and complementary (50). The shift from a "national-state-industrial" society, like that of Latin America from the 1930s to the 1970s, to today's postindustrial, globalized society, with its lack of fusion between society and the state, necessitates a new articulation between the state, party system, and civil society. This new articulation must promote both the autonomy and the complementarity of these spheres.

Rueschemeyer, Stephens, and Stephens also address this relationship between the state, political parties, and civil society in their book, *Capitalist Development and Democracy* (1992). Along with maintaining that there is a close and positive (though imperfect) connection between economic development and democracy and between capitalism and democracy, they claim that "industrialization transformed society in a fashion that empowered subordinate classes and made it difficult to politically exclude them" (vii). They add, "capitalist development is associated with democracy because it transforms the class structure, strengthening the working and middle classes and weakening the landed upper class" (7). Thus, it is not the case (as some on the left and right have claimed) that democracy is the political form of capitalism—in fact, there have been several cases of authoritarian capitalism (Taiwan, South Korea, Brazil, and Chile, among others). Nor is the Marxist assertion true that the bourgeoisie and/or the middle classes have historically been the ones to push for democratization. Nor has capitalism on its own created the conditions for democracy—rather, it is "the contradictions of capitalism that advanced the cause of democracy" (115). The interaction between social classes, the state, and transnational structures of power is what explains the development (and breakdown) of democracies in the process of capitalist development. In terms of the role of the state, one must especially consider its relationship to civil society and the role of mediation that is performed by the political parties.

Historically, the authors claim, the working classes have been the most consistently democratic, while the owning classes have been the most antidemocratic. The bourgeoisie, in turn, have generally favored a constitutional and representative government, but have opposed the extension of political inclusion to the lower classes, while the middle classes have played an ambivalent role in the installation and consolidation of democracy. Finally, the peasantry and rural workers have played more diverse roles, ranging from the independent families (farmers) of the United States, which have favored democratization, to the more subordinate or dependent workers on the large estates (latifundios).

How does the above theory apply to Latin America? The working classes in Latin America have been smaller and weaker when compared to the working classes in other contexts, and the agrarian classes have been stronger, leading to a balance of power that has been less favorable to democratization. If the middle classes have indeed shown a certain leadership in the process of democratization, they have done so with the intent of creating a democracy more restricted than a complete one. The consolidation of the power of the state—often considered an essential prerequisite for democratization—has been difficult and complex, even though the state has evolved in the direction of relative autonomy from the dominant classes and has had a growing involvement in the promotion of economic development (shown especially from the 1940s to the 1970s), while contributing to political articulation in favor of the subordinate classes. In the context of economic dependence, the transnational structures of power have contributed to shaping the class structure in a direction contrary to democratization. Finally, political parties have played a fundamental role, constructing various types of mediations and alliances in favor of both installation and democratic consolidation. They have played a crucial part in the institutionalization of the power of the opposition, the mobilization of forces from below in order to open up the political system, and mediation in relation to perceptions of threat that might be held by the ruling elites, facilitating various concessions in the direction of democratization.

Although Rueschemeyer, Stephens, and Stephens point out that their focus is based on the "interaction of structural and institutional variables" (159), we must conclude this chapter by once again cautioning against this type of analysis, based on "structural" considerations and "requisites" and "determinant" conditions—terms that abound in their book. Although they make one of the most lucid attempts to explain democratization in Latin America by means of the balance of power between social classes and their interaction with the state, civil society, political parties, and transnational forces, there are always limitations in this type of analysis of political phenomena. Even though the authors deliberately distance themselves from abstract and deterministic approaches and highlight the importance of historical processes and the role of actors, there remains the sense that economic and social structures are what definitively determine political processes. In fact, in the conclusion of their book, the authors claim that it is the combination and interaction of these three factors (social classes, the state, and transnational power structures) that "determine political developments" (269) by concentrating on "structural factors favoring or undercutting democratization and the stability of democratic politics" (291). The balance of power among the social classes is what helps to explain the type of relationship between capitalist development and democracy, as well as the advances and regressions in democratization. Of all the classes, the organized working class is the most apt to support a complete democracy. Given the relatively minor impact of the organized working class in Latin America, the resulting democracy has generally been more limited than complete. This same factor promotes a rather pessimistic outlook toward the future possibilities of establishing stable democratic regimes in the region.

# CHAPTER 4

# TOWARD A NEW STRATEGY OF DEVELOPMENT

In our recent history, one could say that there are at least three basic approaches to economic development in Latin America: neoliberalism, neopopulism, and what we have referred to in the case of the Concertación governments (1990–2010) in Chile as "growth with equity."

More than a model, we prefer to speak of a "strategy" of development in order to emphasize the large dose of pragmatism in our own approach to economics—related to what former President Patricio Aylwin has labeled "*la política de lo posible*" (the politics—and the economics, one could say—of the possible). This is consistent with Albert Hirschman's possibilism and his warnings against the phenomena of ideological inflation and structural determinism, which have been so pervasive in Latin America.

In this chapter, I analyze how we arrived at the Washington Consensus of the 1990s, including a critical approach to it. In the next chapter, I will analyze the emergence of neopopulism, first on the right (with Carlos Menem and Alberto Fujimori), and later on the left (with Hugo Chávez, Evo Morales, and Rafael Correa)—in the latter case, as a response to the neoliberal approach of the Washington Consensus. I argue that the apparent dilemma of neoliberalism versus neopopulism is a false one in Latin America, and that the reality is much more complex, giving rise to diverse alternatives and strategies. These are "Hirschmanian" moments, if I may be allowed the expression.

"If the Great Depression and the Second World War finally crippled the export-led growth model, the debt crisis of the 1980s ended the inward-looking phase" (Bulmer-Thomas 2003, 401). The latter strategy was replaced by a new one—though not necessarily a new model— based on external openness and trade liberalization, in a process of gradual but sustained integration into the global economy. Responses to external shocks and the debt crisis of the 1980s led to "a profound shift in development strategy, away from state-led, inward-oriented models of growth toward emphasis on the market, private ownership, and greater openness to trade and foreign investment" (Haggard and Kaufman 1995, 3). The recurring foreign shocks of the 1970s (the oil crisis), 1980s (the debt crisis), and 1990s (the Tequila Crisis and Asian financial crisis) exposed the structural deficiencies of the model of import substitution industrialization (ISI), which had been in effect since the 1940s. This revelation led to a new strategy of development. The shortcomings, insufficiencies, and mistakes of the policies surrounding ISI were already apparent by the 1950s and 1960s. The foreign crises of the 1970s, 1980s, and 1990s confirmed the vulnerability of Latin American economies in the face of external shocks, putting a new emphasis on macroeconomic stability. Furthermore, these crises confirmed the impossibility of a development strategy based on inward-oriented growth in the new era of globalization.

Some authors have claimed that this new model corresponds to one belonging to a "neoliberal order" (Ffrench-Davis 2005; Ocampo 2007) or to a "neoliberal democracy" (Drake 2009). I will argue here that the process is actually much more complex, rich, and diverse than this label suggests. I hold that this process is still in the "decantation" phase and that it has transitioned from a highly ideological stage (represented by the experiment of the Chicago Boys under Pinochet and the economic reforms of the Washington Consensus, all of which are certainly neoliberal) to a more pragmatic stage in the 2000s, which Javier Santiso (2006) has called a "political economy of the possible," referring to countries such as Brazil, Chile, and Mexico. In contrast to the broad consensus established around state-led ISI, the recent process of insertion into the global economy is surrounded by an intense ideological debate, which has intensified further in the wake of the financial and international economic crisis of 2008 to 2009. Having concluded the process of transition to democracy, Latin America (excluding Cuba) remains in the process of consolidation of this new development strategy, which focuses principally on external openness, export effort, and outward-oriented growth.

Latin America's arduous trajectory from the 1970s to the 1990s was marked by political and economic crises, cycles of booms and busts, devastating external shocks, policies of economic adjustment promoted by international financial institutions, and somewhat successful attempts to carry out economic reforms in various countries. During this time there were two transitions: a political transition from authoritarianism to democracy, and a transition from import substitution industrialization to external openness and free trade. The processes of democratic breakdown, transition, and consolidation have a complex relationship with the question of development and take place in the context of the profound political, economic, and social changes throughout the world.

The search for a new equilibrium between democracy and development underlies this process, an equilibrium intended to overcome the political and economic instability that has marked Latin America in recent decades and for most of the last century during its historical struggle to replace the oligarchic order with a new, democratic one. In the following chapters, I will address both the possibilities of and the obstacles to these efforts, which strive to reconcile political democracy with economic growth despite the ongoing problems of poverty and inequality in the region. In this chapter, I will focus on the new development strategy recently implemented in the region amid the dramatic changes that have taken place, with all their possibilities and obstacles.

As I have already discussed in chapter 2, the 1960s brought with them a profound revision of the ISI model, against the background of a period in the 1950s and 1960s of unprecedented growth in the global economy. The 1970s witnessed a timid (and unsuccessful) attempt to advance to a new phase of exports, generally occurring under authoritarian regimes, in the midst of strong tensions around the oil crisis and its negative consequences for the region. The 1980s brought hope, with the promising emergence of democratizing processes in the region, but also the enormous and devastating impact of the external debt crisis and hyperinflation, culminating in the so-called lost decade. Finally, in the 1990s, a new development strategy was outlined, one based on external openness, free trade, and export effort, representing a shift from an ideological phase to a pragmatic one. There is no doubt that "the tumultuous events and changes in Latin America over the past quarter century," both external and internal, brought with them "a radical shift in paradigm," but not necessarily a "new model," in the sense that what occurred was a succession of economic reforms of varying intensity, profundity, and forms (Thorp 1998, 241). I agree with Thorp's analysis. Although the development strategy was subject to Latin America's heterogeneity, it was a new strategy nonetheless, qualitatively different from what had been in effect since the 1940s. In fact, one of the distinguishing traits of the 1990s was that the region appeared to bounce back from the models attempted in previous decades.

"The period between 1960 and 1973 constituted the most dynamic phase yet witnessed in the history of both developed markets and less developed countries" (Ffrench-Davis, Muñoz, and Palma 1997, 99). In Latin America, the production of manufactured goods grew at an annual rate of 6.8 percent, and its participation in the GDP rose from 21 percent to 26 percent. Meanwhile, gross domestic investment grew at 9 percent annually; the level of investment in 1973 was more than triple that of 1960 (102). It is in this context that the decline of ISI began, as the self-imposed exile that characterized ISI also deprived Latin America of benefiting from the boom of the global economy in the 1950s and 1960s (in addition to the model's other shortcomings, which we analyzed in chapter 2). Using regional integration as a way to supplement deficiencies and broaden markets from the perspective of intraregional trade had favorable repercussions in the export of manufactured goods in countries such as Brazil, Mexico, and, to a lesser degree, Argentina. However, this method was also based on the same structural features that had characterized ISI—that is, import substitution and protectionism. "By the 1970s, it had become evident that economic integration had failed to fulfill its initial promises" (Ffrench-Davis, Muñoz, and Palma 1997, 136). Furthermore, Latin America failed to take advantage of the favorable foreign environment in the 1960s. The Alliance for Progress, launched by the United States in 1960, and the program for economic assistance introduced by the region's leaders in Punta del Este, Uruguay, in August of 1961—which was supposed to reach a sum of two billion dollars in one decade—were "too little and too late" (Edwards 2007b).

Meanwhile, problems with the balance of payments and foreign and macroeconomic imbalances had become the "Achilles' heel" of the ISI model (Bulmer-Thomas 2003, 313), influenced by an anti-export bias that had characterized commercial policies in the region since the 1940s. This attitude stood in contrast to the booming economies of eastern and southeastern (and later southern) Asia, which had burst onto the international markets. A search emerged for new alternatives to the development model exercised since the 1940s, which had produced partial and irregular results with greater benefits for economies such as those of Brazil and Mexico (partially due to their larger internal markets), and with fewer benefits for smaller economies, including those of Chile and Uruguay. Bolivia, Ecuador, Venezuela, and the countries of Central America persisted in the export of basic goods but found themselves subject to the great volatility of international prices on raw materials, which raised a series of questions about the future.

The need to move toward a new phase of exportation became even more pronounced in the 1970s. This decade was marked by a boom in exports of raw materials and the emergence of newly industrialized countries (NICs)—those based on active international insertion and the export of manufactured goods. This was primarily the case in the countries of eastern and southeastern Asia, such as Hong Kong, Singapore, South Korea, and Taiwan, whose experience was closely followed by ECLA and economists such as Fernando Fajnzylber, who identified the enormous potential of this strategy and the virtual exhaustion of the developmentalist model used until that point in Latin America. This old model was characterized by import substitution and protectionism, with a strong presence of the state—for instance, until the late 1970s, there were 654 public companies in Brazil (Bulmer-Thomas 2003, 344). The authoritarian regimes in the Southern Cone tentatively explored a new phase of export-driven economic growth and a greater role for the private sector in the 1970s, with more consistency and a stronger ideological base in some cases (such as Chile), and in a more irregular and contradictory form in other cases (such as Uruguay and Argentina), without clear objectives and means. These countries reproduced and modernized the old formula seen in Latin America since the late nineteenth century, that of political authoritarianism and economic liberalism. Brazil tended to deepen rather than replace the state–industrialization–import substitution triad, taking advantage of its enormous internal market and the possibilities for intraregional trade, with a new push for the export of manufactured goods. The significant presence of multinational firms in Brazil contributed not just to the introduction of new technology and capital, but also to strengthening manufacturing exports.

The brutality of the authoritarian and military regimes of the 1970s went hand in hand with free trade and a market economy. Chile became a showcase for the new neoliberal imprint undertaken in the region, due to both its radicalness and its strong ideological bias. As I have already explained, from the *Científicos* in late nineteenth-century Mexico under Porfirio Díaz to the Chicago Boys in Pinochet's Chile, there was an ongoing difficulty in articulating political and economic freedom. Although it occurred in a context of strong ideological dogmatism and brutal political repression, the neoliberal experiment conducted in Chile anticipated some of the profound social and economic changes that would take place in Latin America. At a time when the world was led by figures like Margaret Thatcher and Ronald Reagan, the free-market and monetarist ideas of Friedrich Hayek and Milton Friedman found fertile ground for growth in Pinochet's Chile.

"In the 1960s, there was an upsurge of interest in ideologies and utopian visions. . . . There was much enthusiasm, as well as heated and highbrow conceptual debates, and an excess of voluntarism. . . . 'Revolution was a rallying cry shared by nearly everyone. Imagination had to achieve power'" (Meller 2000, 68). This was the reality in Chile in the 1960s and 1970s. The Revolution in Freedom of the Christian Democrat Eduardo Frei Montalva (1964–1970); the socialist revolution "in democracy, pluralism, and liberty" of Salvador Allende (1970–1973); the neoliberal revolution under the Pinochet dictatorship (1973–1990)—all motivated by the idea of carrying out supposedly irreversible processes— were three radical experiments in a context of high confrontation and polarization. The need to address the crisis of the model of import substitution and protectionism formed the background of these revolutions.

The neoliberal model carried out by the Chicago Boys (the majority of whom had been students at the University of Chicago in the monetarist school of Milton Friedman) had all the ingredients needed to transform the economic and social structures of Chile: a political dictatorship that provided a climate of social peace, maintained and enforced by might and arms, and a supposedly ideological and political neutrality attributed to technical or scientific rationality, like that of the Chicago economists (Valdés 1995). In a country that had been split between forces for reform (Christian democracy) and revolution (socialism), there was no better scene in which to carry out the neoliberal structural revolution. The political forces for social change were busy disputing history, believing they were its owners, while adopting irreconcilable positions among themselves. Meanwhile, the military, business, and technocratic right—the classic triad of bureaucratic-authoritarian regimes, according to O'Donnell—prepared themselves and seized power in the September 11, 1973, coup. It sought a path radically different from what the country had witnessed up to that point, one based on external openness, trade liberalization, deregulation of the economy, the privatization of the means of production, and the withdrawal of the state from almost every area of economic life. All of this took place along with a radical attack on protectionism, statism, import substitution, and an industrialization that had been conducted (according to the rationale of the Chicago Boys) in an artificial manner, sacrificing Chile's export and agricultural potential.

This is neither the time nor the place for a critical analysis of the neoliberal experiment of the Chicago Boys under the Pinochet dictatorship. However, in retrospect, there is a salvageable element of this experiment in its emphasis on external openness as a new structural dimension of the development strategy that would be adopted throughout almost all of Latin America in the 1990s and 2000s. It was a model of outward-oriented growth based on export expansion, the reduction of tariffs, trade liberalization, and external openness. The Chilean experience anticipated these tendencies, though in an extremely ideological form, within a highly repressive political regime. The Washington Consensus attempted something similar in the 1990s, as we will see later, but under democracy.

Both the experience of the Southern Cone under the authoritarian regimes of the 1970s and that of the Washington Consensus stained this new model of development based on external openness and a strongly neoliberal ideology. Nevertheless, in the first decade of the 2000s, a greater pragmatism arose in the midst of a heavily critical analysis of the legacy of the neoliberal reforms of the 1970s, 1980s, and 1990s. For the first time in Latin America's history, there appeared a more balanced formula for reconciling democracy, growth, and social equity.

The experiments of financial and trade liberalization carried out under the military dictatorships of the Southern Cone had ended in disaster by the late 1970s and early 1980s. At the center of this failure, aside from political errors, was the oil crisis—or, rather, the two oil crises of 1973 and 1979—and the international liquidity that plunged many countries in the region into a frenzy of consumerism (the era of *plata dulce,* "easy money"). Trade liberalization, along with policies that over-appreciated the exchange rate, tipped the scales in favor of imports and generated a boom in imports of consumer goods. The deregulation of financial markets, waves of privatization, and the ongoing process of de-industrialization also shaped these changes. Meanwhile, the region sank more and more into debt.

The price of petroleum quadrupled between 1973 and 1974. The current accounts of developed market economies had moved from US$10 billion surplus to a US$15 billion deficit, while the less developed countries had sunk from a US$9 billion deficit to one of US$21 billion. In Latin America, the net export of petroleum increased from US$7 billion in 1973 to US$23 billion in 1981. During that same period, the import of goods grew from US$44 billion to US$93 billion, while the deficit of the current account grew from US$10 billion to US$40 billion (Ffrench-Davis, Muñoz, and Palma 1997, 103). These figures indicate the tremendous effects of the 1973 petroleum crisis on the international economy and on Latin America in particular.

Growth based on debt, a product of the enormous international liquidity of petrodollars, was the trend of the 1970s. Even those petroleum-exporting Latin American countries that benefited from these price increases were subject to huge increases in foreign debt and involved in megaprojects meant to strengthen the public sector and state-owned businesses, which required more and more foreign financing (Edwards 2007b). Though it was not a petroleum-exporting country, Brazil also found itself in this situation. Despite the global shock provoked by the 1979 petroleum crisis, the prevalence of loans in Latin America—given practically unconditionally—continued uninterrupted, to the point that the region's debt grew from US$184 billion in 1979 to US$314 billion in 1982, further fueling a boom of imports (principally consumer goods). In the early 1980s, Latin America had the highest foreign debt in the Third World: between 1973 and 1981, the region had absorbed more than half of the world's private debt, primarily in the short term (Ocampo 2007), resulting in the negative transfer of resources abroad. Without the proper institutions and supervision, the financial liberalization at the center of the crisis led to astronomical levels of debt. In the absence of these safeguards, "Latin America's extreme openness in capital accounts allowed for an acute accentuation of the degrees of exposure by the end of the decade" (Thorp 1998, 216).

The bill racked up by the consumer binge of the 1970s came due for payment in the 1980s. The GDP per capita in Latin America in the 1980s fell by 8.3 percent, sharply contrasting with the Asian countries, whose income per capita increased at an annual rate of more than 5 percent during that same period (Cardoso and Fishlow 1992, 197). According to ECLA, during the 1980s rates of poverty in Latin America increased from 40.5 percent to 48.3 percent (about two hundred million people). This was the "lost decade." The 1982 financial crisis followed the second petroleum crisis of 1979. That year, Mexico announced that it would cease payments on its accumulated foreign debt and nationalize its banks. At the time, the transfer of financial resources in the region had become negative. Foreign financial flow stopped abruptly. From then on, bad news began to eclipse the hopeful transitions to democracy begun in the late 1970s in the Dominican Republic, Peru, and Ecuador and in the early 1980s in Argentina, Brazil, and Uruguay. The Baker Plan (1985) and the Brady Plan (1989) arrived, and the International Monetary Fund introduced programs for economic adjustment and stabilization, with demanding conditionality clauses for the region's countries. By the second half of the 1980s, these plans had restructured a total of US$179 billion of the region's foreign debt, based on various methods of "structural adjustment"

(Ffrench-Davis, Muñoz and Palma 1997, 151). The Brady Plan offered the chance to transform bank debt in the short term into bonds in the long term, in exchange for certain adjustments to the recipient economies. Various countries in the region eagerly accepted these benefits in hopes of relieving the burden of accumulated foreign debt and returning to a period of growth.

These plans and programs were related to the critical macroeconomic instability that had once again gripped Latin America, with its well-known and widespread reality of inflation, chronic fiscal deficits, and serious problems with the balance of payments. This was the other side of the democratization processes carried out in Brazil (under José Sarney), Argentina (under Raúl Alfonsín), Peru (under Alan García), Bolivia (under Víctor Paz Estenssoro), and other countries. In the 1980s, the inflation of previous decades evolved into a dangerous process of hyperinflation. Bolivia suffered an annual rate of inflation of 12,339 percent in 1985; Argentina, 3,058 percent in 1989; Peru, 6,837 percent in 1990; and Brazil, 2,735 percent, also in 1990 (data from the World Bank). The various plans that attempted to address this disaster and recover some macroeconomic stability—Brazil's Cruzado Plan, Argentina's Austral Plan, and Peru's Inti Plan, among others—produced mixed results, often more negative than positive. Only in 1993, under President Itamar Franco of Brazil, was Fernando Henrique Cardoso (the minister of finance at the time) able to implement a successful plan. The Real Plan led Brazil to a new path of "order and progress," living up to the motto on the country's flag. Inflation and hyperinflation aside, the resilience of chronic macroeconomic instability that had characterized Latin America in previous decades and the need to promote drastic changes in development strategy remained evident.

The 1990s, especially the first half of the decade, witnessed a process of economic recovery. The region's countries regained access to voluntary financial markets, foreign investment grew significantly, and prices on raw materials recuperated. By 1992, the net transfer of resources was working in Latin America's favor for the first time since 1981 (Thorp 1998, 226). The decade's economic reforms and the favorable foreign environment promoted Latin America's further integration into the global economy to the point that, from 1990 to 2000, the region experienced an annual growth rate (in volumes of exports) of 9 percent—the fastest in its history (Ocampo 2007). There was an increase not only in the volume of exports, but also in their diversification and the promotion of nontraditional exports. Furthermore, the fall of the Berlin Wall in 1989 and the collapse of the communist regimes meant a new set of conditions for the world in terms of the establishment of freedom and democracy. In Latin America, political freedom began to align itself with economic freedom, and democracy with development. Meanwhile, the high levels of debt that had been seen in previous decades reappeared, with a new push for processes of liberalization, privatization, and deregulation, such as that in Brazil under Fernando Collor de Mello (1990–1992), Argentina under Carlos Menem (1989–1999), and Peru under Alberto Fujimori (1990–2000). Fujimori reverted the democratization trend in the region by carrying out a self-coup in 1992.

New speculative and financial ventures accompanied the boom of the early 1990s, to the point that the debt crisis flared up again for some countries. The 1994 Tequila Crisis in Mexico led to a bailout by the United States and the IMF. Financial crises sprang up, one after another, in a chain that extended throughout Asia (1997) and Russia (1998) to finally arrive in Argentina in 2001 and 2002. The foreign financial shocks associated with cycles of booms and busts, along with the awful handling of macroeconomic matters on the domestic level, created a nightmare for the region. It is worth pointing out here the curious combination of a fixed exchange rate and a strong (even out-of-control) financial liberalization, as seen in the Chile of Sergio de Castro and the Chicago Boys in the late 1970s and early 1980s, in Mexico in the years leading up to the 1994 crisis, and in Argentina in the 1990s, under the leadership of Domingo Cavallo. Some of the above policies were at the center of the crises in these three countries. A more flexible exchange rate, such as the "crawling peg" (periodic mini-devaluations) introduced in Chile in the 1990s, more controlled financial liberalization, and the introduction of a reserve for short-term financing, helped to create a more balanced and predictable trajectory as well as a solid defense against recurring external shocks.

The sequence of economic crises in the 1970s, 1980s, and 1990s caused a series of changes in the spatial mobility of people and workers as they searched for new employment opportunities. The number of immigrants of Latin American and Caribbean origin living in the United States grew from 4.4 million in 1980, to 8.4 million in 1990, to 14.5 million in 2000. This had a strong impact on Latin America through the financial remittances sent to the region, which increased from US$1.9 billion in 1980, to US$5.7 billion in 1990, to US$19.2 billion in 2000, constituting more than 1 percent of the regional GDP (Ocampo 2007). The Inter-American Development Bank estimates that remittances to the region reached US$69.2 billion in 2008, more than the total of direct foreign investment in Latin America.

The cycle of upheaval that the region experienced between 1970 and 1990 reopened several questions: Was it possible to achieve, once and for all, political and economic stability in Latin America? Was it possible to move simultaneously toward democracy and development without causing turmoil? Was there a way to protect Latin American economies from foreign shocks without committing the same errors of the past? Could democracy exist without inflation, or were we condemned to perverse combinations of macropolitical and macroeconomic imbalances? Could these goals be achieved through sensible policies, without the intervention or imposition of a third party like the United States or an international financial organization like the IMF? These were some of the questions in the minds of the ruling elites in the late 1980s and early 1990s.

Neoliberalism thus got a second chance in Latin America, this time under democracy. The Washington Consensus was one attempt to respond to these and other questions that arose repeatedly in the region, principally among the ruling elites who needed a new type of insertion into the international economy, one that could combat the chronic macroeconomic imbalances of the 1980s. It was clear that the region had learned to export—and that the countries that had not yet learned understood the need to integrate themselves into an increasingly globalized economy—on the basis of the new prominence of the private sector, confronted with a hyperinflation that principally hit the pockets of workers and wage earners. Conscious of the favorable climate for Latin American economies in the early 1990s and the disasters of the previous decade, John Williamson called together a select group of economists in 1990 and prescribed a program of ten measures to address the region's problems in an attempt to recover its trajectory of economic growth. Behind all of these proposed measures stood the affirmation that truly groundbreaking structural change in the region consisted of moving from previous development strategies to one based on external openness, trade liberalization, and a new type of insertion into the global economy.

The ten measures that Williamson (2004) proposed were the following: fiscal discipline; prioritization and reduction of public spending, focus on basic education (rather than the university level) and primary health care (rather than hospitals), eliminating subsidies and allowing private investment in areas traditionally reserved for the public sector; fiscal reform through tax reduction; interest rate liberalization so that the market determined interest rates; competitive exchange rates determined by the market; trade liberalization through the casting off of protectionism; the liberalization and promotion of direct foreign investment; the privatization of businesses under the belief that they were better administrated by the private sector than the public sector; deregulation of the economy to combat corruption; and finally, a strengthening of property rights, especially considering the magnitude of the informal economy in Latin America. These ten economic measures could be grouped into the spheres of macroeconomic discipline, market policies, and free trade. These measures reflected the consensus of various agencies of economists (public and private, domestic and international), think tanks, and policymakers based in Washington, DC—thus forming the Washington Consensus. In short, the measures emphasized the liberalization and competitiveness of the region's economies to remedy the lost decade of the 1980s, which was marked by macroeconomic imbalances and a lack of economic growth.

As Williamson explained years after he presented his ideas in Washington, DC, in 1989, the original plan had been to review the economic policies conducted in Latin America since the 1950s in light of the policies of the Organization for Economic Cooperation and Development (OECD). When Williamson testified before Congress in 1989 on the Brady Plan passed that year (intended to alleviate the region's foreign debt), he noted a marked pessimism about Latin America's ability to make real changes to its economic policies. Williamson never predicted the tremendous ideological controversy that the proposed measures would generate, although he recognizes that the term "Washington Consensus" was behind the tone and intensity of the debate, becoming "easy propaganda material for the old left" (131).

In the collective imagination of elites and the popular classes in the 1990s, the Washington Consensus, neoliberalism, economic adjustments, conditionality, market fundamentalism, the IMF, imperialism, and the United States all became equivalent terms. Similarly, the "recipe" idea was seen as an imposition of Washington and the international financial organizations on Latin American countries. The 2001 economic crisis in Argentina was considered the last straw in a conspiracy of international financial institutions and the United States government against the developing world in general and Latin America in particular.

Beyond the caricatures, good or bad intentions, and countless interpretations of the Washington Consensus, justified or not, there are four principal critiques that can be made of the proposal. First, one must admit its marked economistic reductionism. Ultimately, it is a question of ten economic measures that have been associated with neoliberalism, a perspective that reduces everything to the level of the economy and the market. Thus arises the second critique: the neglect of the social and sociopolitical spheres, as if everything could be reduced to economics and the markets and all the rest would fall into place—much like the logic of trickle-down economics, commonly associated with neoliberalism.

The third critique is another derivation of the first and has to do with the neglect of political and institutional variables. If there's one thing we can be sure of, it is that economic forces and markets do not operate in a political and institutional vacuum, and that it is impossible to understand the complex economic, social, and political reality of Latin America (or any region) by reducing it to a question of the market alone (Payne, Zovatto, and Mateo Díaz 2007).

The fourth and final critique of the economic measures proposed in 1990 is the weakness of a one-size-fits-all formula that fails to take into account Latin America's diversity and heterogeneity. In the early 1960s, Albert Hirschman (1963, 313) warned against "*la Rage de Vouloir Conclure*," referring to the search for one solution that could be applied to every situation. At a time when the region was apparently moving beyond the ideologies, utopias, and "global planning" of the 1960s and 1970s, the

Washington Consensus created a sort of straitjacket in a region that had seen too many ideological experiments, causing new turmoil.

The book *After the Washington Consensus*, by Pedro Pablo Kuczynski and John Williamson (2003), revisits in detail many of the shortcomings mentioned above. The book was published right at the end of the so-called lost half-decade (1998–2003), during which different sectors of Latin American politicians, especially Hugo Chávez and the populist left, had strongly criticized the Washington Consensus.

The authors of this book review the economic policies carried out against the backdrop of the proposals of the Washington Consensus during the 1990s, keeping in mind the Argentine crisis of 2001 to 2002 and its devastating effects. Despite the advances in fiscal discipline and inflation control, the region suffered from low growth. The authors identify the following major tasks for the future: making the region's countries less vulnerable to foreign financial shocks through budget control; responsible management of the surplus in times of prosperity (counter-cyclical fiscal policies) and an adequate exchange rate and monetary policy; completing first-generation reforms, especially around the "flexibilization" of labor markets; carrying out second-generation reforms, particularly in the provision of certain basic public goods and the strengthening of institutions (including judicial reforms, industrial reforms, and the development of new technologies); and finally, confronting the deficiencies and challenges in income distribution and social policy reforms without compromising basic macroeconomic stability and economic growth. Kuczynski assigns a special responsibility for the region's troubles to pro-cyclical fiscal policies and the expansion of public spending during economic booms without saving for future economic busts. He also calls for a strengthening of the state's role in certain fundamental areas. Different authors review various types of policies in the region's countries, emphasizing the need to transition from first- to second-generation reforms and accenting institutions and public policies in the medium and long term.

The economic measures proposed by Williamson took form in a series of market reforms implemented in Latin America in the 1980s and 1990s, at the center of which was the crisis of the ISI model and its gradual replacement with a new strategy based on external openness and free trade and focused on economic growth and macroeconomic stability. The widespread macroeconomic instability of the 1990s, stemming from old formulas that did nothing more than deepen the problems of inflation and hyperinflation, chronic fiscal deficits, and problems with the balance of payments, created a favorable bias towards these market reforms. At the same time, Chile's successful transition, the greater pragmatism of economic policies in the last stage of Pinochet's dictatorship, and elements of continuity between policies of external openness and the economic policies conducted in Chile under the center-left Concertación (1990–2010) made a strong case for these pragmatic market reforms.

The first half of the 1990s, when the Washington Consensus was proposed, can be considered auspicious compared to the previous decade. Sebastián Edwards reflects this optimism in his 1995 book, *Crisis and Reform in Latin America: From Despair to Hope.* He writes, "During the 1980s and early 1990s, there was a marked transformation in economic thinking in Latin America. The once-dominant view based on heavy state interventionism, inward orientation, and disregard for macroeconomic balance slowly gave way to a new paradigm based on competition, market orientation, and openness" (41). These changes were also reflected in the documents of ECLA (under the influence of Fernando Fajnzylber), an organization that had been central to the formulation of ISI. Beyond this new consciousness of the need for a new development strategy, the region witnessed a "consensus" around a strategy of external openness, free trade, and macroeconomic stability. In this context, Edwards concludes, "the degree of doctrinal convergence in that part of Latin America was remarkable" (42).

Although the author himself admits that it was too early to speak of the "consolidation" of pro-market reforms (with the exception of Chile), events in the late 1990s and early 2000s demonstrated that the region as a whole was far from immune to the chronic political and economic instability of the previous decades. A series of crises followed the 1994 Mexican Tequila Crisis, creating the "lost half-decade" of low economic growth and high rates of unemployment. This painful process raised questions about both the legacy of the Washington Consensus and its neoliberal reforms (Ffrench-Davis 2005; Sunkel 2007), as well as the policies of structural adjustment promoted by international financial institutions and the United States. At the same time, a new populist phenomenon emerged that was radically critical of neoliberalism, headed by the emblematic figure of Hugo Chávez.

By the 1990s and into the 2000s, Latin America had undergone a difficult transition—one from a model of development based on ISI, protectionism, and the strong role of the state, to a new strategy (more pragmatic, less ideological) based on external openness, free trade, outward-oriented growth, a strong private sector, and a greater recognition of the centrality of macroeconomic stability. Notable progress has been made in the challenge of consolidating a democracy without inflation, leading to a favorable period between 2003 and 2007, the closest the region has come to advancing simultaneously toward democracy, economic growth, and social equity. Nonetheless, various tensions and contradictions regarding the region's political and economic development remain.

The contrast between the periods of 1998 to 2003 and 2003 to 2007 is a clear reflection of the cycles of Latin American economies, which are related to the cycles of the global economy. The annual growth of the GDP increased from an average of 1.2 percent between 1998 and 2003 to an average of 5.4 percent between 2004 and 2007. Meanwhile, the annual growth of the GDP per capita rose from -0.2 percent for the five-year period from 1998 to 2003 to 4.0 percent from 2004 to 2007. At the same time, poverty in the region decreased from 44 percent in 2003 to 34 percent in 2007 (all figures from ECLA). This virtuous cycle of growth with poverty reduction, especially from 2003 to 2007, gave rise to intense democratic and electoral activity, such that Latin America witnessed eighteen free democratic presidential elections from 2005 to 2010.

An assessment of the years between 1970 and 2004 is distressing when we consider that the annual average of growth of income per capita in Latin America was 1.01 percent, in sharp contrast to the growth of the Asian economies that reached 2.95 percent in the same period (Edwards 2007a). Many of the market reforms implemented in the 1980s and 1990s were there to stay. At the center of these reforms stood the reality of Latin America's new international insertion into the era of globalization. The degree of external openness in Latin America and the Caribbean, expressed in terms of the sum of exports and imports (foreign trade) as a percentage of the GDP, increased from 28 percent in 1985 to 49 percent in 2006 (figures from the World Bank), evidence of the region's new reality. Meanwhile, direct foreign investment in Latin America and the Caribbean increased from an annual average of US$27.536 billion between 1992 and 1996 to US$72.440 billion in 2006 (figures from ECLA). In addition, we have to consider the proliferation of free-trade agreements, especially in countries such as Mexico and Chile, and various regional and subregional initiatives to that effect (APEC, NAFTA, and the Summits of the Americas, among others), with varying degrees of progress.

If the neoliberal reforms linked to the Washington Consensus indeed revived a certain ideological climate, reinforced by the emergence of a new populism in the last decade, we must also consider the rise of new progressive, pragmatic, gradualist, and nonpopulist alternatives that have emerged in recent years, to which we shall refer in the following chapter. In the background of the populist and nonpopulist responses to the neoliberal reforms of the 1990s there is a tension between the "political economy of impatience" associated with populist responses and the "political economy of the possible" associated with nonpopulist responses, to borrow Santiso's (2006) terminology. We will direct our attention to this analysis also in the following chapter.

For now, we must point out, as Rosemary Thorp (1998, 279) writes, that "Gradually, the initial swing of the pendulum in favor of market-friendly policies began to moderate into a more mature appreciation of the role of the state, public institutions and the political base for policies." Indeed, the new democracies that arose in the region in the late 1970s and early 1980s, in the context of the fall of the Berlin Wall in 1989, led the region's progressive, nonpopulist political actors to call for renewed efforts to integrate economic and social development, taking advantage of the opportunities offered by the "new consensus" around a strategy of development that includes external opening and trade liberalization. I argue in the last chapter that in the new context of the 2000s, there is a sort of Hirschmanian moment in Latin America that takes into account the very "perceptible progress in the political economy of Latin America" (Thorp 1998, 280). Advances in fiscal policy, monetary policy, and inflation control (and in general, the need to secure macroeconomic stability), along with the looming challenges of addressing widespread poverty and inequality in the consolidation of democracy, are all examples of the new political economy at play in the region.

One of the implications of this new political economy is the way of understanding the relation between the market and the state. In this way, for example, Alejandro Foxley (in Mainwaring and Scully, 2009), strongly influenced by Hirschman's thought, argues that while great hopes for economic growth were pinned on the first half of the 1990s, pessimism had returned by the end of the decade (following the Asian crisis). These mood fluctuations led to two opposite positions: on one side, those who claimed the failure of the pro-market, neoliberal reforms of the 1980s and 1990s and advocated a stronger role for the state, and on the other side, those who believed the reforms were too weak and had to be followed by second- and third-generation reforms. More state and less market were the formula for one group, and more market and less state the formula for the other. Foxley argues that the debate is badly focused and not conducive to the economic and social development of Latin America. What the region needs is a more balanced and integrated vision, a different type of state, and consideration of the region's new insertion into the global economy and the new reality of middle-income countries.

According to the Chilean economist and politician, Latin America requires a new type of state (especially when we examine the type of state predominant in the 1950s) that is adjusted to the new reality of the global economy: "It is not about more state or less state, but rather a different state than the one we have known in the past" (Foxley, in Mainwaring and Scully, 2009). The region needs a new welfare state (or society), one that protects not only those inside the system (unionized workers, for example) but also those who are excluded from the system (such as unemployed youth and women), and all the adjustments that this would require. More of a better state is needed, including the establishment of a social safety net to account for emerging sectors in economies such as those of Latin America, which have transitioned from one model of development to another, in entirely new and different international conditions. Under these conditions and in consonance with the World Bank, the state should act as a catalyst for development, taking into account the new circumstances of the international economy. All of this would require a restructuring rather than a dismantling of the state.

What we find in the difficult period between the 1970s and 2000s is not the emergence of a new "neoliberal order" along ideological lines, but rather the search for a new development strategy that addresses the need to adapt the region's economy to the new reality of globalization, along a more pragmatic basis. This demands the introduction of economic reforms that allow the region to recover the path of economic growth while taking into account the "new social question" that emerges in Latin America in our recent history, which we shall discuss in chapter 7. This recent process differs from the contributions of ECLA and Raúl Prebisch in 1948 in terms of the introduction of a model of development that, in spite of undeniable achievements, also introduced a set of rigidities that prevented the region from accounting for its tremendous diversity and heterogeneity and from taking advantage of the great dynamism of the global economy in the 1950s and 1960s. This new development strategy has left behind the fundamental features of the development model adopted by the region from the 1940s to the 1970s.

# CHAPTER 5

# DEMOCRACY, GOVERNABILITY, AND NEOPOPULISM

I began to write this chapter—not thinking that it would become part of a book—while listening to a speech that Hugo Chávez gave in Lima, Peru, in 2005. The speech was given at one of the many summits for South American heads of state—I don't remember if it was for the Andean Community or the South American Community of Nations (later renamed UNASUR). I had accompanied President Ricardo Lagos to the summit as the Chilean minister of foreign relations. While listening to President Chávez speak, I began, pen in hand, to try to unravel some of the keys to understanding neopopulism in Latin America.

Chávez's speech was like music to my ears, icing on the cake, call it what you like. It was as if reality could be transformed, created and recreated, purely through the tone and rhythm of words. Populism, both old and new, has used and abused discourse, especially in order to achieve total emotional harmony between the leader and the masses of the people. This meeting did not include the masses, but I understood that it was being televised. The effect was the same: attempting to transmit emotion through discourse, even if it did not contain any substantive ideas.

While listening to Chávez's long and improvised lecture, I wrote ten pages that contained some of the central ideas of this chapter. As we will see, I develop in this book a critical vision of populism, principally due to the tensions and contradictions that I see between populism and representative democracy. I equate the latter, in the last chapter, to "democracy of institutions," the opposite of the personalist, *caudillista*, populist, plebiscitary democracy that has been so pervasive throughout Latin American history.

"Democracy is stronger"—such is the argument I developed in chapter 3 with regard to the new wave of democratization in Latin America. The persistence of this new democratic wave in the region is surprising, and that persistence puts into question a good part of the body of work developed on the subject in the social sciences since the 1950s. Electoral democracy (free and competitive elections) thrives in the region and enjoys new legitimacy. In addition, with few exceptions such as Fujimori's 1992 self-coup and the military intervention in Honduras in June of 2009, there have not been any authoritarian regressions or coups d'état in a region that, over the course of its history, has been characterized by recurring military interventions. This process is certainly not irreversible, but it is impossible not to recognize the progress that has been made.

"Not all that glitters is gold"—thus I could summarize the argument I develop in this chapter, against the background of the profound political and economic changes that have taken place in the region over the last two decades, some of which I have reviewed in the last two chapters. What type of democracy has emerged in Latin America? We have seen the highlights; in this chapter I analyze the lowlights of the new democracies that have emerged in the region. What kind of democracy is the most desirable? This question is related to the previous one. In the lines that follow, I examine new contributions in the field of political science, related principally to the central question of the quality of democracy and democratic governability. As part of an analysis of representative democracy and democratic governability in the final chapter, I develop my own vision of the most desirable type of democracy for Latin America as the democracy of institutions.

There is a triple process underway in Latin America: a strong awareness of the precariousness of new democracies, despite the advances made in establishing an electoral democracy; a greater theoretical demand to hypothesize the most desirable form of democracy, notwithstanding the theoretical and practical merits of a minimalist and procedural definition of democracy; and, finally, perhaps a product of the gap between the two previous questions, between reality and aspirations, there is a certain frustration, disenchantment, or malaise moving through the region.

I begin with the last point. One could say that it is almost a matter of common sense to warn against the insufficiencies of these new democracies and the disenchantment that surrounds them: "Democracy appears to be consolidated, but it is not the democracy that the people hoped for" (Sorj 2007, 8). Beyond this assessment, the reality of disenchantment in Latin America is sufficiently documented. For example, Latinobarómetro (2008) reports that, despite the evident economic advances of the "virtuous half-decade" (2003–2007), support for democracy is, on average, only 57 percent. Also according to that report, there is a clear relationship between economic growth and support for democracy, with the understanding that the economy produces more costs in times of crisis than rewards in times of plenty. Support for democracy reached a peak of 63 percent in 1997, when growth in the region was 6.6 percent, with support falling conspicuously to 48 percent in 2001 due to the Asian economic crisis and the "lost half-decade" (1998–2003). Support for democracy went through a recovery phase from 2004 to 2008, coinciding with economic growth rates of 6.1 percent in 2004, 4.8 percent in 2005, 5.6 percent in 2006, and 5.7 percent in 2007, according to ECLA statistics. This seems to show that democracy in Latin America has an important economic component.

It is interesting to note that efficient government—for example, encouraging economic growth—has important implications for citizens' perceptions of how well democracy and democratic institutions function Latinobarómetro (2008) reports that the percentage of people who think that democracy cannot exist without congress rose from 49 percent in 2001 to 57 percent in 2008, while the percentage of people who trusted parliament rose from 17 percent in 2004 to 32 percent in 2008. The proportion of people who think that democracy cannot exist without parties rose from 49 percent in 2001 to 56 percent in 2008, while trust in parties rose from 11 percent in 2003 to 21 percent in 2008—which is, certainly, still quite low. Positive attitudes towards politics and approval of national governments increased as well, also a result of this virtuous circle of economic growth. Approval of national governments rose from 36 percent in 2002 to 53 percent in 2006, while trust in government increased from 19 percent in 2003 to 44 percent in 2008. This improved evaluation of national governments, however, does not directly or automatically translate to better assessment of democracy, as satisfaction with democracy (37 percent) was less than satisfaction with government performance (52 percent). Finally, 59 percent of people consider voting to be an effective instrument of change—by comparison, only 16 percent believe that protesting is an effective means of change.

All of these changes are encouraging signs. This is important because it demonstrates that doing things right—growing economically, lowering poverty rates, and raising electoral participation—brings concrete dividends in terms of citizens' perceptions of democracy and democratic institutions. Where is the problem, then? First, even though democracy's approval rates reached 57 percent in 2008, compared to 48 percent in 2001, the level of satisfaction with democratic performance was only 37 percent. There exists, then, an important level of support for democratic legitimacy, but also a serious deficit in terms of democratic efficacy. This is, of course, an average that hides the enormous variations that exist from one country to another. For example, the percentage of people who think that democracy functions better in their country than in other countries in the region varies from relatively high levels in Chile (44 percent), Uruguay (43 percent), and Costa Rica (42 percent) to low levels in Guatemala (8 percent), El Salvador (8 percent), Honduras (7 percent), and Peru (7 percent).

Second, there is the question of social inequality and the gap that exists in regimes that respect basic rights but ignore enormous social deficiencies: "democracy is perceived as guaranteeing civil and political rights, but not social and economic rights" (Latinobarómetro 2008, 93). For example, 79 percent believe that freedom of religion is guaranteed and 63 percent think that political participation is also protected. In contrast, however, only 25 percent believe that wealth is distributed fairly and only 28 percent think that employment opportunities are protected. To put it another way, 70 percent think that powerful groups govern their country for their own benefit, while only 25 percent think that their country is being governed for the good of the people. Despite advances in economic development, 48 percent of people believe that social inequalities have remained unchanged, and only 21 percent think social inequalities have shrunk. This relates to the "paradox of democracy" described by Sorj (2007, 10), characterized by great expectations in terms of equality but accompanied by a worsening of social inequality. The existence and endurance of social inequality across time remains one of the principal limitations of democratic governance in the region.

Third, the report shows that "although we have not seen any return to authoritarian government, authoritarian attitudes continue to haunt the region" (Latinobarómetro 2008, 83). For example, despite better economic performance toward the end of the first decade of the 2000s, 53 percent of people said in 2008 that it did not matter if a government was nondemocratic if it could solve the country's economic problems. It is noteworthy that this figure remained more or less the same over several years—51 percent in 2001, 55 percent in 2004—apparently unattached to economic cycles. Advances made in citizens' perceptions of democracy associated with a virtuous economic cycle, reduced levels of poverty, and the wave of elections in 2006 and 2007, when presidents elected with large majorities were not able to eradicate certain authoritarian attitudes that remain constant across time.

It remains to be seen what effects the world economic crisis (2008–2009) will have on Latin American democracies. The relationship between economic growth (or economic crisis) and levels of approval (or disapproval) of democracy is well documented. The region's governments know, or ought to know, that good economic performance, with all it implies in terms of macroeconomic variables, the role of public policies, and the role of the state (among other things) has an important effect on citizens' perceptions of democracy. On average, however, relatively low approval ratings of democracy continue, varying from country to country, especially in relation to its performance. Remnants of authoritarian culture exist below the surface, beyond economic cycles of boom and bust. On the positive side, a perception exists that people have elected to continue with democracy, despite everything: "Latin Americans have opted to stay with democracy, however imperfect they consider it, even though serious institutional crises have offered clear opportunities for a return to authoritarianism" (Latinobarómetro 2008, 7). A decade and a half has passed without new authoritarian breakdowns, and democracy has come to enjoy a new legitimacy. The democratic deficit lies at the level of democratic effectiveness and performance, which, as we shall see later on, does affect democratic governance. All of this takes place in the context of high expectations for the future, as evidenced by the Latinobarómetro 2008 report and the ECosociAl-2007 report (in Cardoso and Foxley 2009; Tironi 2008; Valenzuela et al 2008; and Gasparini et al 2008), as we will see in chapter 7. The revolution of expectations remains one of the principal elements we must take into account when predicting and evaluating the possibilities and limitations of democracy in Latin America.

A second aspect considered in this chapter relates to the type of democracy adopted in the region. The tension between the democratic transitions of the 1980s and the economic difficulties of the debt crisis, macroeconomic imbalances, and null growth of the so-called lost decade did not disappear, despite the newly favorable economic conditions of the 1990s. Just the opposite: Alberto Fujimori's self-coup in Peru in 1992 clearly marked the first authoritarian reversal of the auspicious third wave of democratization initiated in Peru in the late 1970s. The economic reforms promoted by Fujimori in Peru and by Carlos Menem in Argentina since the early 1990s, described by some as neoliberal neopopulism, along with similar reforms such as those carried out by Fernando Collor de Mello in Brazil, are evidence of the precariousness of new democracies in Latin America, especially in regard to the role of institutions. Institutional weakness and the great strength of the executive, in the context of the economic crises that swept across most of the countries in the region, led Guillermo O'Donnell (1994) to coin the expression "delegative democracy" in order to distinguish it from representative democracy.

O'Donnell's thesis is that, unlike what is commonly referred to as representative democracy, which is principally found in the developed world and is characterized by high levels of political institutionalization, what emerged in Latin America in the early 1990s was a delegative form of democracy characterized by weak political institutions, along with the difficulty of moving from democratic governments to democratic regimes. We must remember, as we saw in chapter 3, that, according to O'Donnell, the key feature of a democratic transition is the election of a democratic government, while the main attribute of a democratic consolidation is moving from democratic governments to democratic regimes. The reality of Latin America in the early 1990s, characterized by severe economic and social crises along with the legacies of authoritarian regimes and an adverse international context in the 1970s and 1980s, led an important part of the population to impatience. Citizens turned to messianic leaders who could reverse this adverse situation. Such were the cases of Fujimori, Menem, and Collor de Mello, among others. Under these conditions, the people "delegated" decision-making power to these new governments, elected by large national majorities and characterized by strong personalistic, plebiscitary, Ceasarist, Bonapartist, and *caudillista* features, all of which express low levels of institutionalization. Thus, delegative democracy rests "on the premise that whoever wins an election to the presidency is thereby entitled to govern as he or she sees fit, constrained only by the hard facts of existing power relations and by a constitutionally limited term of office" (O'Donnell 1994, 59).

The paternal figure associated with this new type of democratic regime has allowed these messianic leaders to govern above parties and organized interest groups, ignoring or bypassing institutions of representative democracy, such as parties or parliaments, and using presidential decrees to govern without any accountability. Rather, they have imposed a manner of connecting directly with the people, supported by strong electoral legitimacy but with a weak institutionalization of power that relies on clientelistic, patrimonial, and corrupt practices, resulting in serious difficulties in distinguishing between the public and private sphere—a distinction that is essential to a republican concept of democracy. Behind this delegated power lies the severe economic and social crisis that characterized Latin America in the 1980s and the need for someone to impose order and enact economic reforms—neoliberal reforms in the three cases mentioned above—that could control inflation (or hyperinflation) and at the same time put economic growth back on track. The paradox is that, in a formal way, these new political regimes had many of the characteristics of polyarchy, following Robert Dahl's (1971) definition, but also represented a new type of democracy that is distinct from representative democracy. Neither the institutionalization of power nor government effectiveness are characteristics of delegative democracy. This form of democracy was not present in Uruguay and Chile, whose high political institutionalization, a product of their long history of creating institutions and the fact that they are both cases of political *re*democratization, prevented them from adopting the delegative form of democracy. Both countries are the closest to representative democracy in the region, according to the author.

In a similar vein as O'Donnell, who already noted the distance between delegative democracy and representative democracy (which comes out of the liberal tradition), Fareed Zakaria, editor of *Foreign Affairs* and *Newsweek*, maintains that many third-wave democracies in Asia, Africa, and Latin America are "illiberal democracies," that is, democracies of a type at odds with what is commonly called liberal democracy. Zakaria's (1997) thesis is that many new democracies are effectively electoral democracies, in that authority comes from free and fair elections, but these democracies have broken away from liberal constitutionalism, which includes the rule of law, the checks and balances inherent in constitutional or liberal democracy, the protection of certain fundamental rights, and constitutional limits set on the executive. While democracy refers to the use and process of accumulation of political power, liberal constitutionalism, which is characteristic of Western countries, refers to the limits placed on the exercise of power in order to reconcile freedom and democracy, in the tradition of Alexis de Tocqueville and John Stuart Mill. In this tradition, constitutionalism would be "liberal" in relation to the exercise of individual freedoms and "constitutional" in the effective enforcement of the rule of law.

With this recent wave of democratization, democracy has arisen everywhere, but it has not necessarily come out of the tradition of liberal constitutionalism. In fact, if we distinguish between the "political rights" of democracy and the "civil rights" of liberal constitutionalism, we see that half of the countries in the process of democratization are so-called illiberal democracies with more emphasis on political rights than civil rights. Zakaria is aware that he adopts a perspective that goes beyond a minimalist or procedural definition of democracy in the tradition of Dahl, but he does this precisely with the intention of raising the standards of democracy while uncovering the situation that many democracies face—in that they are democracies in certain respects (electoral democracy) but not in others (liberal constitutionalism). We must understand his work as a normative defense of constitutional or liberal democracy. Thus, many of the recently emerged democracies originated in the model of the French Revolution, a majoritarian democracy without checks and balances, with centralized, strong states and a presidential system, as have the majority of democracies that emerged in the so-called Third World. In Latin America, such are the cases of Peru's Fujimori and Argentina's Menem, both of whom represent a real usurpation of power.

O'Donnell confirms the deficiencies of the new democracies—and the old ones, for that matter—in Latin America, in terms of the rule of law, understood as the bedrock of liberal or constitutional democracy. In a very straightforward way, he calls out the reality of the *(Un)rule of Law* in the region—that is, the absence or negation of the rule of law. According to O'Donnell (in Méndez, O'Donnell, and Pinheiro 1999, 305), there is a demand for equality among individuals not only as individuals, "but as legal persons, and consequently as citizens—i.e., as carriers of rights and obligations that derive from their membership in a polity." This citizenship ought to be understood in a broad sense, referring to the ability to exercise civil, political, and social rights. Latin American polyarchies have undergone an expansion of political rights, especially during the recent wave of democratization, but at the same time there has been an incomplete expansion of civil and social rights in highly unequal societies marked by discrimination and exclusion (O'Donnell 2001). In this sense, the scope of the "legal state"—and democracy corresponds not only to a political regime but also to a type of state, according to the author—is very limited and incomplete. The poor are poor not only in terms of material goods—that is, in being deprived of goods and services—but also in the legal sense, in terms of being deprived of rights (see also O'Donnell, in Diamond and Morlino 2005). In Latin America, the existing democracies have the characteristics of a polyarchy under a minimalist and procedural concept of democracy, but they are barely democracies based on the rule of law as part of the legal state that is an inherent part of liberal democracy and, ultimately, of a republican understanding of democracy. Such democracies are of low quality and low intensity citizenship (see O'Donnell, Vargas, and Iazetta 2004). The difference between the democratization processes in Latin America and the huge gaps in terms of the rule of law is the focal point of the afore-mentioned book. The illegal and arbitrary use of power is fairly wide-spread in the region, a reality that affects the implementation of full citizenship characterized by the ability to exercise civil, political, and social rights and, ultimately, human rights. Latin America faces the reality of "democracy without citizenship" characterized by extralegal violence, especially in the experience of the poor and excluded (who happen to be the majority of the population).

In the 1990s and 2000s, the numerous shortcomings and insuffi-ciencies—the shadows, not just the lights—of the new Latin American democracies became the object of analyses that went beyond the region. Scholars began to notice that many of the so-called democracies that emerged in the recent wave of democratization worldwide had enormous deficiencies. The early enthusiasm that grew around the transitions to democracy of the 1970s and 1980s gave way to a more balanced and real-istic vision of the newly emerging democracies in Latin America, Central and Eastern Europe, the former USSR, Asia, Africa, and the Middle East. The objective here is not to reproduce the vast literature that emerged around the question of democratic transition or consolidation, but rather to look at the question of the "quality" of these new, emerging democra-cies. A good example of this critical analysis comes from the April 2002 issue of the *Journal of Democracy* dedicated to this theme, titled "Elec-tions without Democracy." As the title indicates, the mere existence of elections—including free and fair elections—does not necessarily de-termine the existence of a true democracy.

In that issue, Larry Diamond (2002), one of the biggest advocates of theories of the quality of democracy, refers to what he describes as "hy-brid" regimes that appeared in various corners of the world. He asks if countries such as Russia, Ukraine, Nigeria, Indonesia, Turkey, and Vene-zuela should be considered examples of democracy. Elections take place in each of these countries, but are they democracies? Diamond notes that Freedom House scores these six cases as democracies, understood as electoral democracies. However, he disagrees and prefers to identify cases such as these as something less than electoral democracy, labeling them "competitive authoritarian systems," "hegemonic party systems," "pseudo-democracies," "semi-democracies," or, simply, "hybrid regimes." These regimes combine democratic and authoritarian elements and can be generally included under the label "competitive authoritarianism" (elections without democracy). In summary, since 2001 there have been 104 democracies in the world—34 more than had existed at the beginning of the third wave of democratization—of which 73 (38 percent) were liberal democracies and 31 (16.1 percent) were electoral democracies (following Freedom House's distinction between civil liberties and political freedom), confirming that not all electoral democracies correspond with liberal democracies. At the other extreme, there have been 50 cases (26 percent) of authoritarian regimes in various forms. Between these two extremes there are 38 cases (19.8 percent) of regimes that could be considered hybrid, including those that could be called "ambiguous" (17 cases, 8.9 percent) and those that could be labeled "competitive authoritarian" (21 cases, 10.9 percent). Diamond concludes that, although military regimes have disappeared, we should not ignore the new reality of pseudodemocracies, hybrid regimes that mix together democracy and authoritarianism. In the case of Latin America and the Caribbean, Cuba is the only example of a closed authoritarian regime, with Antigua, Barbados, and Haiti as examples of competitive authoritarian regimes and Venezuela, Paraguay, and Colombia as cases of ambiguous regimes. In turn, Argentina, El Salvador, Jamaica, Mexico, Brazil, Ecuador, Honduras, Nicaragua, Trinidad and Tobago, and Guatemala qualify as electoral democracies, while only Uruguay, Costa Rica, Panama, Surinam, Bolivia, Peru, Chile, the Dominican Republic, and Guyana—plus eight Caribbean countries that he mentions separately—are classified as liberal democracies. Unlike sub-Saharan Africa, the Middle East, and North Africa, the majority of Latin American and Caribbean countries can be classified as electoral or liberal democracies (with the exception of the six cases mentioned above).

In the same series of articles published in the *Journal of Democracy*, Schedler (2002) maintains that since the beginning of the 2000s, the majority of existing regimes belong to a "nebulous zone" that lies between liberal democracies and closed authoritarian regimes. These regimes can be labeled as exemplifying either electoral democracy or electoral authoritarianism, based on seven criteria used to distinguish between the two. Following Przeworski's (1991) definition of democracy as a system "in which parties lose elections," Schedler points out that electoral authoritarianism is a system "where opposition parties lose elections" (2002, 47). Finally, Levitsky and Way (2002) argue that, when referring to hybrid regimes, it is possible to talk about regimes that are both competitive and authoritarian. Such is the logic of competitive authoritarianism, a type of hybrid regime characterized by the existence of formal democratic institutions—elections, principally—that does not meet the minimum standards for democracy. These minimum standards include free, fair, and transparent elections of the executive and of parliament, the practically universal right to vote for all adults, the ample protection of political rights and civil liberties, and the existence of an authority elected by the public that governs effectively without being subject to the control of military or religious leaders. The majority of cases of competitive authoritarianism, according to the authors, are in Africa and the former USSR. In the case of Latin America, Peru under Fujimori during the 1990s, Haiti after 1995, Mexico before the 2000 elections, and Venezuela in recent years are examples of this type of regime. If some forms of authoritarianism, such as the totalitarian or bureaucratic-authoritarian regimes of the past, have retreated, a new, subtler type of regime—competitive authoritarianism—has appeared.

Innumerable articles and books refer to the darker side of the recent wave of democratization from the perspective of the quality of democracy. A sense that "not all that glitters is gold" seems to underpin this literature, which is more cautious and less triumphal when analyzing this recent process of democratization. All of this is reflected in what Diamond calls "The Democratic Rollback" (2008a), a sort of "democratic recession," in the center of which lies the resurgence of the "predatory state." Diamond's message is that we should not declare victory. Problems related to weak governance and the widespread reality of weak institutions is at the heart of this recession. Spread across fifty countries, this recession brings with it serious risks from the perspective of certain basic characteristics of democracy. In the context of clientelism and corruption, good governance and the establishment of adequate accountability appear to be necessary and fundamental antidotes. Even though ninety countries experienced transitions to democracy since 1974, and 60 percent of independent states can be considered democratic at the beginning of the twenty-first century, certain authoritarian currents in new predatory states have led to a democratic recession. As Freedom House warns in its January 2008 report, for the first time since 1994, freedom in the world has experienced a clear decline. The poor performance of many of these new democracies stands at the center of the aforementioned problems. The 2008 Index of Democracy published by *The Economist* confirms that, "following a decades-long global trend in democratization, the spread of democracy has come to a halt," adding that, "the dominant pattern in the past two years has been stagnation." In the light of various reports to this effect, it may be noted that the main problem faced by new democracies in the world is not so much a question of legitimacy as it is a question of performance, related primarily to the issue of democratic governance.

Democratic governance is precisely the theme taken up by Mainwaring and Scully (2008; 2009), based on the argument that the facts have overtaken the literature on democratic transition and consolidation and that there is a need for new avenues of investigation into the new challenges that Latin American democracies face at the end of the 2000s. The authors distance themselves from the literature on the quality of democracy—linked to Larry Diamond and others, some of whom are mentioned above—because it continues to prioritize procedural aspects of democracy instead of worrying about not only the democraticness of a political regime, but also the effectiveness of new democracies. The greatest deficiencies of the region's new democracies can be found at the level of democratic governance. I will discuss this in the final chapter as it relates to electoral and representative democracy. According to Mainwaring and Scully, we must address not only challenges to the effectiveness of political institutions, as argued by the neo-institutionalists, but also the effectiveness of state performance, in terms of state-sponsored public policies. These challenges inspire disenchantment and frustration with the functioning of new Latin American democracies. Along with revealing the role of political institutions, which is a central aspect of the quality of democracy, and questioning the excessive optimism about neoliberal economic reforms of the 1990s, which ignored the central role of politics and institutions, the authors highlight the role of the state, public policies, and state performance in certain areas fundamental to citizens' perceptions of democracy. They do not question the content of many of these economic reforms, which, in general, pointed in the right direction. Nor do they question the irreplaceable role of political institutions, which are fundamental to democratic governance. Instead, they suggest that adequate levels of governance are impossible without adequate state performance at the level of public policies. It is a question of governing democratically, but also effectively. This mixture is the foundation of democratic governance, and it is here that the principal deficiencies and shortcomings of the new Latin American democracies lie.

State and institutional weakness are some of the central issues behind the crisis of democratic representation characteristic of South American countries, particularly in the Andean region. This is the hypothesis that Mainwaring, Bejarano, and Pizarro Leongómez (2006) develop to explain the disenchantment and frustration within vast sections of the population in relation to the region's new democracies. This disenchantment and frustration manifests in low trust in political parties and parliaments, two of the most important political institutions in a representative democracy. Behind these low levels of trust, however, lies what the authors refer to as a true "crisis of democratic representation," which can be explained either through inadequacies in the institutional arrangements of democracy (principally important political institutions such as parties and parliaments) or by deficiencies on the level of state performance, to the extent that the state is unable to execute its basic functions in terms of security and social and economic performance, among other things. Ample electoral participation exists in the region—in fact, in recent years many Andean countries have seen record levels of electoral participation—but low trust in the traditional institutions of representative democracy, such as parties and parliaments, has deeper roots in this crisis of democratic representation, a product of institutions and/or state weakness. Out of this crisis emerge populist leaders, or "outsiders," whose antiestablishment discourse comes to embody social protests against traditional elites and institutions. Rather than being the cause of the problem—without ignoring that populism has a disruptive effect on representative democracy and its institutions—the rise of this type of leadership is a symptom of a deeper crisis. Populists fill a void, so to speak, coming out of this crisis of democratic representation that carries with it a crisis of the traditional, emblematic institutions of representative democracy. High electoral volatility, the collapse of the party system—typical of countries such as Venezuela, Bolivia, and Ecuador—and the emergence of populist, outsider leaders are symptoms of the crisis.

## DEMOCRACY AND NEOPOPULISM IN SOUTH AMERICA

As I stated in chapter 1, in the quest for de-oligarchization following the crisis of oligarchic rule at the beginning of the twentieth century, populism appeared as the paradigmatic response to economic, social, and political challenges in Latin America. In this section I will argue that neopopulism's recent emergence in Latin America, particularly in South America, reveals that we are still in the process of dismantling oligarchic rule. One of the central features of populism is precisely its antioligarchic character. I argue that the ambiguity of populism towards representative democracy lies at the center of the relationship between the two. This ambiguity is a continuous, intrinsic characteristic of Latin American populism, both old and new, especially in relation to representative democracy and its institutions.

One way to analyze Latin America's history and attempts to substitute a new democratic order for the old oligarchic order in the last century is by examining the dilemmas that developed at different times, at varying degrees of intensity, and defined political processes. I argue that Latin American politics have revolved around four principal dilemmas that appeared in the region over the course of the last century. I am referring to the dilemmas of the people versus oligarchy; development versus dependence; reform versus revolution; and democracy versus dictatorship. Finally, I maintain that in recent years, along with the dilemma between inclusion and exclusion (made more visible by globalization), one of the principal dilemmas that Latin America faces is that between democracy and populism.

Tensions between the people and oligarchy shaped the first dilemma that Latin America faced when confronting the "social question" and the oligarchic crisis that took place in the first third of the twentieth century. The national and popular component of the old populism, which I analyzed in chapter 1, came to express this dilemma in an anti-imperial, antioligarchic sense. Responses to this dilemma—state-directed import substitution industrialization and the inward-oriented growth model of the populist coalition—drove both the modernization and democratization of economic, social, and political structures, creating a clear tension between populism and democracy.

A second dilemma—that between development and dependence—appeared at the end of the 1950s and continued through the 1970s. It was related to certain characteristics of the development model promoted since the 1940s. The radical left, strongly influenced by the Cuban Revolution, noted that instead of achieving a second national independence as they had hoped, this development model had deepened the region's dependence, affirming the subordinate relationship between the center and the periphery. The nationalization of basic goods, structural reforms, and, ultimately, revolution seemed to be the only way to break the chains of dependence and subordination. In retrospect, the dilemma between development and dependence was a false dichotomy. This development model represented a great qualitative leap for countries in eastern, southeastern, and southern Asia. This leap forward shows that by boosting exports, especially manufacturing exports, and actively incorporating itself into the international economy, a country could break away from a subordinate and dependent position. Latin America has followed its own path in this direction, with all of the difficulties, tensions, and contradictions noted above, a lengthy process that has meant moving from the ISI development model based on strong protectionism to a different strategy based on external opening and trade liberalization. This demonstrates that we are not condemned to underdevelopment based on our real or perceived dependence. The most recent attempts to raise the anti-imperialist flag in the era of globalization, especially when faced with the global financial and capitalist crisis from 2008 to 2009, have failed to give substance to the precarious, underhanded, and contradictory efforts to revive the theories of dependence and imperialism popular in the 1960s.

On the positive side, dependency theory made an important contribution to social science in general and to development theory more specifically in that it taught us to look at Latin America from the perspective of a more systematic and comprehensive insertion into the international economy. In this sense, despite its obvious shortcomings, the theory first developed by Cardoso and Faletto (1979), which became the core of various dependency theories as discussed in chapter 2, may have been the greatest contribution to these theories. They provoked in their time the most intense intellectual passion.

Latin America faced a third dilemma between reform and revolution in the 1960s and the early 1970s. This was one of the most important dilemmas in Latin American history, especially given the tremendous impact of the Cuban Revolution during the Cold War, when the world was divided between the United States and the USSR, with no room for nuance or subtlety. It was a bad time for politics and for democracy, to the extent that the art of politics (based on the difficult but necessary work of coordinating governments, parties, parliaments, and social movements through negotiation and compromise) and the radical critiques of formal or bourgeois democracy created a polarized and confrontational setting that hosted, tragically (but not inevitably), the processes of democratic breakdown that I analyzed earlier, especially in South America. Neither the revolutionaries nor the reformers triumphed in this confrontation, which ended with the installation in the 1970s and 1980s of bureaucratic-authoritarian regimes based on the triple alliance between the military, the business elite, and the technocrats.

The fourth dilemma was between dictatorship and democracy. It was, indeed, a real and tragic dilemma—perhaps the most tragic and real in our history. Beyond their efforts to modernize economic and social structures (which were more successful in some cases than in others), the new dictatorships that emerged in the Southern Cone brutally repressed their citizens, systematically violating human rights. This dilemma did not center around the question of ownership of the means of production—as the two previous dilemmas in some way had—but instead revolved around the question of political regime (democracy or dictatorship). The struggle for human rights, social, political, and electoral mobilization, and the liberalization processes that preceded democratization characterized this period. On the positive side, as I will analyze in the final chapter, a new ethical, legal, and political awareness concerning human rights and a new substantive valorization of political, representative democracy (or polyarchy) emerged in the region, all of which support and affirm the fragile democracies that emerged in this new and most recent wave of democratization.

This leads to the question of what dilemma Latin America is confronting now. When analyzing the region's situation, an obvious answer is the dilemma between those included and excluded in new development strategies based on external opening, trade liberalization, and new international insertion in the era of globalization. Such is the perspective, for example, expressed in the title of a report by the Inter-American Development Bank (IDB), *Outsiders? The Changing Pattern of Exclusion in Latin America and the Caribbean* (2007). According to the report, the "social exclusion" of large sectors of society that are more urban and more visible than in the past is not the result of being "outside" society, but is instead due to the type of interactions within society. These societies are prosperous and in many ways modern, but they have another side, that of exclusion. In chapter 7 I will analyze in more depth the new social question that emerges in Latin America's more recent history, focusing on the concept of social cohesion. For now, it is enough to note that many forms of exclusion still exist and that Latin America faces a serious socioeconomic dilemma between exclusion and inclusion.

In the next paragraphs I analyze the so-called neopopulism of the region in an effort to uncover its true nature and characteristics, including the elements of continuity and discontinuity with the old form of populism. What I want to stress, ultimately, are the tensions and contradictions that emerge between neopopulism and representative democracy and its institutions. Here lies another "new" dilemma in the region, that between democracy and populism. Instead of blaming neopopulism for the problems in the region, I want to emphasize that the emergence of this new phenomenon demonstrates that Latin America is still in the process of dismantling oligarchic rule (*desoligarquización*) against a backdrop of poverty and inequality. In the shift from the old oligarchic order to the new democratic order, democracy is making significant headway, but it is not exempt from its own tensions and contradictions.

One could say that the emergence and development of neopopulism in the recent history of Latin America is a play with four acts. I will now describe and analyze each one of them.

## ACT 1: THE POPULIST CYCLE

In some of his writings of the 1980s and 1990s, Alejandro Foxley, the Chilean finance minister from 1990 to 1994, refers to the emergence of a "populist cycle" in Latin America during the democratic transitions of the 1980s. He is principally referring to the type of economic policies promoted by the governments of Alan García in Peru, José Sarney in Brazil, and Raúl Alfonsín in Argentina—among the most notable—that led to the so-called lost decade. This populist cycle should not be confused with a populist regime, which I will address below; rather, it refers to the economic policies carried out by these governments during the democratization process.

In sum, the logic behind the economic policies promoted by those three governments and others is based on the need to activate the economy and raise the level of salaries through a sort of fiscal shock. These economic policies center on the old argument of the idle capacity of the economy, perhaps a variation of the argument about the "elasticity" of the economy that I have referred to when discussing the sayings of Juan Domingo Perón. These economic policies contributed to these presidents' popularity, at least during the first years of their administrations. Think, for example, of the enormous popularity President Alan García initially achieved due to the fact that things appeared to be going very well in Peru. In the second year, however, these administrations had to pay their dues in the form of the inflation and hyperinflation that started to appear on the horizon—the first signs of an economic crisis. In the third year, the economic crisis transformed into a social crisis as the popular sectors and workers led massive street protests and presidential popularity fell (such is the logic of the populist cycle). Finally, in the fourth year, the economic and social crisis became a political crisis. In Argentina's case, it became a constitutional crisis that led President Alfonsín to hand over power to his successor, Carlos Menem, six months earlier than called for by the constitution.

This populist cycle corresponds to what Patricio Meller (2000) defines as a set of populist macroeconomic policies with a strong redistributive component aimed at rapid economic recovery. According to Meller, this paradigm is characterized by an initial phase that seems to produce successful results. However, in the second phase, a strong rise in demand generates unequal growth, while the third phase ends in desperate attempts at economic adjustment meant to contain inflationary pressures through a strong, orthodox stabilization plan. Aside from the fact that this populist paradigm inflicted a terrible cost on the same social sectors that it claimed to favor, during the process of democratic transition in the 1980s it had a clear destabilizing effect, paradoxically paving the way for the neoliberal economic reforms of the 1990s.

Perhaps the best theoretical and comparative work on populism in terms of the economic policies associated with it is Rudiger Dornbusch and Sebastián Edwards's book *The Macroeconomics of Populism in Latin America* (1991). Basing their analysis on the macroeconomic policies implemented in the 1980s in countries such as Argentina, Chile, Brazil, Nicaragua, Mexico, and Peru, the authors introduce the concept of the populist paradigm. More specifically, they coin the phrase "the macroeconomics of populism" to refer to the populist regimes that historically attempted to tackle income inequality through the use (and abuse) of extremely expansive macroeconomic policies that led to almost inevitable economic crises. According to Dornbusch and Edwards, "the use of macroeconomic policy to achieve distributive goals has historically led to failure, sorrow, and frustration" (2). Ultimately, these policies failed to benefit the poorest segments of society, resulting, for example, in real wages that were lower after their implementation than before. This self-destructive feature of populism, the result of mismanagement and persistent macroeconomic instability, has led to the complete failure of the macroeconomics of populism in Latin America.

It is not a simple coincidence that the first approximation of neopopulism—referring to the cycle of populism, with its emphasis on economic policy and the macroeconomics of populism—comes from economists like Dornbusch, Edwards, Foxley, and Meller. I argue below that, in the years that followed, neopopulism came to combine certain traditional characteristics of the economics or macroeconomics of populism with political and institutional aspects that have to do with the crisis of democratic representation in Latin America and the adoption of personalistic and plebiscitary democracy. In this way, I contend that this is not just about economic policy or the economics or macroeconomics of populism, but also about the politics of populism (or neopopulism).

## ACT II: NEOLIBERAL NEOPOPULISM

In recent years, neopopulism in Latin America has come not from the left, but from the right, in the form of neoliberal reforms implemented in the 1990s. Collor de Mello in Brazil, Menem in Argentina, and Fujimori in Peru introduced not only the neoliberal economic reforms characteristic of the Washington Consensus, which I discussed in chapter 4, but also a highly personalistic, plebiscitary, populist, and delegative type of democracy that is a central feature of the neopopulism that emerged in the early 2000s in Latin America. Governing by presidential decree, direct appeals to the masses (public opinion), the popularity of populist leaders, at least in the initial phase—which led to the reelection of Menem and Fujimori—and a radical neoliberal economic reform program are some of the most salient characteristics of these governments and the policies they promoted.

Kurt Weyland (2003) coined the concept of neoliberal neopopulism when trying to unravel some of the central characteristics of these processes. In the mid-1990s, Kenneth Roberts, using the Peruvian experience under Fujimori as an example, refers to a "novel paradox" consisting of "the rise of personalist leaders with broad-based support who follow neoliberal prescriptions for economic austerity and market-oriented structural adjustment programs" (Roberts 1996). Weyland argues that, although the literature usually considers the terms "neoliberal" and "neopopulist" as opposites, a synergy between the two existed in the 1990s to the extent that neoliberal reforms needed a free hand to push through reforms and policies that sought to use state action to introduce stability or predictability into daily life. All of this, conceived as a response to the inflation and hyperinflation so characteristic of the democratization process in the 1980s, had economically devastating effects, particularly for the popular sectors, but also, in turn, explain the initial popularity of Menem and Fujimori. A strong personalistic and plebiscitary component was added to this neoliberal neopopulism in the context of low levels of institutionalization that, in turn, appear as distinct characteristics of the old and new populist phenomenon in Latin America. Following the initial phase, typified by the radicalism and audacity of these neoliberal reforms, the need for some type of institutional rules emerged with the goal of offering some level of predictability to foreign investors and other economic actors. The need for institutional rules led, almost by definition, to a gradual erosion of the neoliberal neopopulist model. With this erosion, the initial synergies that helped explain an apparently contradictory relationship also vanished.

As we well know, and as we saw in chapter 4, the neoliberal economic reforms in Latin America (populist or not) ended badly. In Argentina, the story ended with the dramatic 2001 crisis. Fujimori went into exile in Chile and was eventually extradited back to Peru. In sum, from the Caracazo in Venezuela in 1989—a popular reaction in Caracas with large street demonstrations against the austerity package and neoliberal reforms adopted by Carlos Andrés Pérez, ending in riots and killings— to the bloody events of October 2003 in Bolivia, which concluded with the downfall of Gonzalo Sánchez de Lozada and hundreds of deaths in the streets of La Paz, the neoliberal economic reforms of the 1990s, backed by the Washington Consensus, ended in disaster. One could debate forever whether this failure was due to the design or the implementation of these reforms, or a combination of both, but what is certain is that they ended badly. Nevertheless, populism survived. In fact, populism emerged once again as an answer and alternative to the neoliberal reforms of the 1990s, especially in Venezuela, Bolivia, and Ecuador.

## ACT III: NEOPOPULISM AND THE LEFT

Three interrelated processes that took place at the end of the 1990s and beginning of the 2000s help to explain populism's survival in Latin America, now in the form of leftist neopopulism. On one hand, the profound elite crisis and breakdown of traditional political institutions in countries such as Venezuela, Bolivia, and Ecuador led to the collapse of party systems—Bolivia had six governments in six years, Ecuador had seven governments in ten years, and the 1998 crisis in Venezuela led to the election of Hugo Chávez, who was reelected in 2000 and 2006. On the other hand, what we could call the "cry of the people" emerged, a desperate demand from diverse sectors of society, especially young people and new social and indigenous movements (as in Bolivia), concerning urban unemployment and expressing severe discontent and frustration, particularly with elites and traditional institutions. The intention throughout this process was to achieve recognition of the most deeply felt social demands of these emerging sectors.

The type of democracy that characterized neoliberal neopopulism in the 1990s and the neopopulism of the left represents an element of continuity between the two, a democracy that is strongly personalistic, plebiscitary, and delegative. Whether coming from the right or the left, the form democracy has assumed in the last two decades appears to be a distinctive feature of neopopulism in Latin America and one of the most serious obstacles and principal challenges to democratic consolidation— a question I will analyze in more depth in the last chapter. I define contemporary populism, or neopopulism, following René Mayorga (in Mainwaring, Bejarno, and Pizarro Leongómez 2006, 134), in terms of "a patron of personalist and anti-institutionalist policies, rooted mainly in the appeal to, or from, the mobilization of the marginalized masses." Similarly, Weyland (2001, 14) defines populism as "a political strategy through which a personalistic leader seeks or exercises government power based on direct, unmediated, uninstitutionalized support from large numbers of mostly unorganized followers." This definition is similar to the definition provided by Roberts (2007, 5), who describes populism as "the top-down political mobilization of mass constituencies by personalistic leaders who challenge elite groups on behalf of an ill-defined *pueblo*, or 'the people'."

There is no doubt that there was a high social cost associated with the neoliberal reforms of the 1990s, which provoked the emergence of strong and deeply felt social demands in vast sectors of society. Perhaps nothing more eloquently expressed the magnitude and intensity of these demands and the frustration and disenchantment with the neoliberal economic reforms of the previous decade as this phrase written in graffiti—an expression of popular culture, especially youth culture—on a wall in Lima, Peru, some years ago: "No more realities. We want promises" (reported to me by political scientist Arturo Valenzuela).

The three elements outlined above—that is, the failure of neoliberal economic reforms in the 1990s, the process of decomposition of elites and traditional institutions, and new social demands associated with emerging sectors—led to the emergence of actors who better represented the neopopulism of the left, such as Hugo Chávez in Venezuela, Evo Morales in Bolivia, and Rafael Correa in Ecuador. One could also perhaps include Néstor Kirchner and Cristina Fernández in Argentina after the deafening failure of the economic reforms implemented by Menem in the previous decade, although the characteristics and context of this case requires a distinct type of analysis. What unites the case of Argentina with the other cases, however, is the strong personalization of power and the marked institutional weakness that have become the center of permanent instability typical of Argentina over the last few decades (Levitsky and Murillo 2005). Additionally, "Kirchnerism" pertains to a Peronist tradition and a political culture that is one of the most paradigmatic expressions of populism in Latin America.

The emergence of this neopopulism of the left ought to be seen principally as the result of a process. That is, it should be seen as an answer to the failure of neoliberal economic reforms and the breakdown of elites and traditional political institutions incapable of responding to the social demands of emerging sectors, especially in certain regions. (We have to avoid generalizations: this did not happen in most countries, or in the majority of them, but it did occur in some.) In any case, in referring to the relationship between populism and democracy, it must be stated clearly that this neopopulism of the left confirms the intrinsic tensions and contradictions that exist between populism and democracy. I argue that populist regimes hide the reality of personalist and plebiscitary democracy behind appeals for direct or participatory democracy. Michael Coppedge (in Domínguez and Shifter 2003, 165), when defining the Chávez regime, describes this as "an extreme case of delegative democracy." In a 2007 interview with the Caracas newspaper *Últimas Noticias,* José Vicente Rangel, one of Hugo Chávez's closest advisors in successive terms as minister of defense, minister of foreign affairs, and vice president, defined the Chávez regime as follows: "If Chávez does represent any political power, it is the power of the people, which means that Chávez is above institutions because he is the embodiment of the people" (11 February 2007, reproduced in *La Tercera*, Santiago, 13 February 2007).

At the core of the tensions between democracy and populism we find the contradictions between the strength of institutions and the emergence of personalist leadership that generally flourishes in the context of low institutionalization (Navia and Walker 2006). Stronger institutions mean more limited personalist leadership. When democratic institutions are solid and strong, personalist leaders develop in a limited context that can be conducive to further strengthening of democratic institutions. These institutions are weights and counterweights that delimit, curtail, and restrict, but also facilitate and legitimize the exercise of power by elected democratic representatives. In this way, institutions in general, and political parties in particular, can become the strongest antidote to populism in Latin America.

We know that charismatic leadership is an essential part of winning elections. Good candidates must be capable of successfully communicating their proposals. Because the mass media has turned into the principal vehicle for delivering messages, and because the most effective campaigns use precise and inspiring messages, the candidate's personal attractiveness is essential to electoral success. However, where democratic institutions are weak, attractive leaders tend to become strongly personalistic and populist. As candidates, these leaders come to hold their electorate's trust, and when they assume power they tend to concentrate that power in their own hands. Independent of the economic policies they adopt, mandates that concentrate power in the context of weak democratic institutions tend to fall to the temptation of populism. On the other hand, when solid democratic institutions exist, the winning candidate's popularity becomes a force that generates support and loyalty for institutions that can exercise veto power over public policy. When more popular, the president has a greater ability to advance his or her own legislative agenda. In the context of strong democratic institutions, candidates with popular mandates do not fall victim to the temptation of

*Table 1.* Interaction between Presidential Popularity and Institutional Strength

|  | *Strong Democratic Institutions* | *Weak Democratic Institutions* |
| --- | --- | --- |
| Popular President | Government successfully implements campaign promises | Government faces populist temptation |
| Unpopular President | Government fails to implement campaign promises | Risk of ungovernability |

*Source:* Navia and Walker 2006, 16

populism. One of the biggest problems of the recent wave of democratization in Latin America is that the process of democratic consolidation has provided favorable contexts for the appearance of populist leaders.

Table 1 demonstrates the interaction between the popularity of a presidential mandate and the strength of democratic institutions. Popular politicians can become successful presidents in the context of strong democratic institutions or can yield to the populist temptation in the context of weak democratic institutions. Unpopular presidents are unable to push through their own agendas and fulfill their campaign promises when democratic institutions are strong. The worst of all possible worlds is when democratic institutions are weak and the president is unpopular. Under these conditions, a country runs the risk of ungovernability.

One final note about another synergy between neoliberalism and neopopulism, taken from Weyland: the neopopulism of the left does not monopolize ambiguity in relation to representative democracy and its institutions, nor is ambiguity the sole and exclusive characteristic of old or new populism in Latin America. This is a significant point of convergence between neoliberalism and neopopulism. As I outlined in chapter 1, actually existing liberalism in Latin America has historically developed in closer relation to authoritarianism than to democracy. This was the reality for a significant part of the old liberalism in the region and is also part of the new liberalism that emerged in the 1970s, associated with the new bureaucratic-authoritarian regimes that pushed forward an important set of neoliberal economic reforms. In the democratic, postauthoritarian era, the economic reforms of Fujimori's neoliberal neopopulism were possible due to his 1992 self-coup. In light of this history, both the old and new liberalism, in the concrete way that it appears in Latin America, seem to have been more of a detriment than an asset to representative democracy and its institutions.

When we speak of neoliberalism, we should distinguish it from classical liberalism. There are three principal differences between classical liberalism and neoliberalism that show the clear superiority of the former over the latter, especially from the point of view of democracy. First, the most characteristic aspect of neoliberalism in the recent history of Latin America is its strong economic reductionism, in contrast to the old liberalism, which was simultaneously philosophical, ethical, political, economic, and social. Second, as a consequence of this first difference, neoliberalism has a sort of contempt for the public sphere, politics, and the state, while classical liberalism developed a complete system of ideas that encompassed not only economics and the market but also politics and the state. A third feature of neoliberalism comes out of the two previously stated characteristics, that of a certain ambiguity towards representative democracy and its institutions, which would have been scandalous to the proponents of classical liberalism, such as John Locke, John Stuart Mill, and Alexis de Tocqueville.

In sum, neoliberals—and unfortunately many of the old liberals in the region—have been ambiguous towards representative democracy and its institutions. Encounters between liberalism and democracy have not been easy, and neither have encounters between populism and democracy. Rather, it is a story of disagreement.

### ACT IV: POPULIST AND NONPOPULIST RESPONSES
### TO NEOLIBERAL ECONOMIC REFORMS OF THE 1990S
### (THE EMERGENCE OF A NEW SOCIAL DEMOCRATIC MOVEMENT)

In the last part of the previous section I argued that Hugo Chávez could be seen as the most visible and strident political figure in Latin America but should not be considered the most representative example of the complex, rich, and diverse realities of the region. This may seem counterintuitive, as

Chávez usually monopolizes headlines and editorial pages outside the region and within it. Nevertheless, this does not transform him into the most representative political figure in Latin America. Instead, I argue that Chávez is the exception rather than the rule in the region.

Something similar can be said about Evo Morales. True, foreign headlines and editorials have increasingly aimed to expose the indigenous Bolivian leader. Although there are elements common to both cases, Bolivia is not Venezuela, and Morales is not Chávez, in the same way that Latin America is not Chávez and Chávez is not Latin America. The Venezuelan and Bolivian cases are distinct, each with its own specific context. The indigenous issue was important in Bolivia, but it was not an important factor in Venezuela. Although the Bolivian Constitution was approved in a dubious process (from many distinct points of view), it is important to note that the opposition—or oppositions—has had a majority in the senate and control over five of the nine departments in the country, at least until very recently. In Venezuela, the opposition had practically no representatives in parliament, at least until 2010. It is still early for a definitive analysis, but the cases of Ecuador, Argentina, and Nicaragua have their own specifics that make it hard to make generalizations. What is certain is that the neopopulism of the left is still developing.

The central point I want to make in the following lines is that there is not one single type of response to the neoliberal reforms of the 1990s. There are instead several types, both populist and nonpopulist (Navia and Walker 2006). These reforms and their subsequent outcomes paved the way for the emergence of the neopopulist left, but we should not forget that there was also a group of countries that implemented other, nonpopulist solutions. I will argue below that this is the reality for the majority of the countries in the region.

We should not lose sight of the fact that there have been governments of the right or center-right in different countries throughout recent years. Such has been the case for ARENA (the Nationalist Republican Alliance) in El Salvador under the presidencies of Alfredo Cristiani (1989–1994), Armando Calderón (1994–1999), Francisco Flores (1999–2004), and Elías Antonio Saca (2004–2009). The March 2009 election placed a leftist president, independent journalist and FMLN candidate Mauricio Funes, in the presidency for the first time in the history of El Salvador, which confirms a leftist tendency in the region. (It must be said, however, that in public speeches President Funes has said that he identifies with former President Lula da Silva of Brazil and aspires to strengthen ties with the United States, even if this means acting independently of the FMLN.) The case of President Álvaro Uribe of Colombia, who was elected and reelected with more than 60 percent of the votes, also represents a case of a government of the right and center-right, as it is the case with his successor, Juan Manuel Santos. A third example of a center-right government is Mexico and the two National Action Party (PAN) governments headed by Vicente Fox (2000–2006) and Felipe Calderón (2006–2012). We must also keep in mind that both Mexico's Andrés Manuel López Obrador (of the Party of the Democratic Revolution [PRD]) and Peru's Ollanta Humala, typical proponents of the neopopulism of the left, lost their elections to Felipe Calderón and Alan García, respectively—although Humala did win the 2011 presidential election. In addition, a right-wing government, led by Sebastián Piñera, was elected in Chile, in 2010. This only confirms that we cannot talk about the uncontested dominance of the populist left in Latin America.

Going beyond these cases, I argue that there is no unified left in the region, nor two lefts, as has been argued by Jorge Castañeda (2006) and Patricio Navia (2006). I hold that there are at least three lefts in Latin America and that this makes a big difference in terms of democracy. I am referring to the existence of a Marxist left, a populist left, and a social-democratic left (Walker 2008). The first two have converged and built alliances together, leaving aside old ideological and political disputes. This new convergence can be seen in the ties between Fidel and Raúl Castro, Hugo Chávez, and Evo Morales. A new social-democratic left that should not be Ignored emerged along with these two lefts in various countries in the region. The "social-democratization" of a significant portion of the left is a relatively recent phenomenon, a process that does not have many antecedents in the history of the left in Latin America, which has looked on the (principally European) social-democratic left with a certain disdain.

I approach the term "social-democratic" as a reformist position, in the tradition of Edward Bernstein, father of European social democracy, who stressed the need for a "democratic, socialist party of reform" that was not ambiguous in its approach to the institutions of representative democracy. This left emerged from the enormous gap (which already existed at the beginning of the twentieth century) that it saw between the premises of Marxism and the reality of capitalist development, which has demonstrated a capacity for adaptation that far outstripped what theories of Marxism and revolution predicted. "Social-democratic" specifically refers to the social reforms that have been introduced to capitalism, which in the concrete case of Europe has pointed in the direction of the welfare state—if you will, social democracy refers to the construction of capitalism with a human face. In our time, social democracy has adopted a friendlier stance towards the market economy and the process of globalization, dealing not just with threats, but also with opportunities as part of a more universal tendency that extends to diverse countries and regions.

Referring to the experiences of Brazil and Chile, former President Fernando H. Cardoso—who, along with former President Ricardo Lagos, may be one of the most representative figures of this new Latin American social-democratic left—directly refers to the existence of a political model that he calls "globalized social democracy." This model "does not fear foreign markets, values institutions and citizen responsibility, and is aware that the stability of the democratic process depends to a significant degree on economic progress but also on political initiatives directed towards reducing poverty and extending social welfare" (Cardoso 2008). The emergence of this new social-democratic left in Latin America has much to do with the existence of a post–Cold War, post-Marxist, post-authoritarian, and postrevolutionary era, which explains its reformist, moderate, center-left character. This surely explains the clear line of division that exists between the Marxist and populist left and this new social democratic left, especially when referring to the question of representative democracy and its institutions.

It is clear that, along with the populist left, there is also a left rooted in the Marxist tradition that cannot be ignored. It is part of the political landscape and culture of Latin America, with its own specific nature. Such is the case of Fidel and Raúl Castro's Cuba, the Communist Party in Chile, important sectors of the FMLN in EL Salvador and the FSLN in Nicaragua, parties and factions to the left of the Workers' Party (PT) in Brazil, as well as small sectors of PT itself. This Marxist left is not what it was in the 1960s following the Cuban Revolution or even in the 1970s and 1980s during the Nicaraguan Revolution, but it has its own specificity and its own historical roots.

The new social-democratic left emerged alongside the Marxist and populist left. Previously, although in a different context, I argued that in the 1970s and 1980s, social-democratization already existed under the Pinochet dictatorship within an important sector of the Chilean left (Walker 1990). This process led to a new valorization of political democracy, which had previously been pejoratively classified as formal or bourgeois, due to a discovery of the democratic and reformist credentials of the European left and a rediscovery of the democratic roots of Chilean socialism. In the Chilean case, this renewal process led to the formation of the Concertación, a political and strategic coming-together of Christian democrats and social democrats that resulted in four center-left governments between 1990 and 2010. This period included the administrations of Ricardo Lagos (2000–2006) and Michelle Bachelet (2006–2010), both of which represent the new democratic socialism that emerged in Chile since 1990.

The social-democratization of the left goes well beyond the case of Chile. Such is also the case of Presidents Cardoso (1994–2002) and Lula da Silva (2002–2010) in Brazil. Despite the differences between the two presidents and the parties that they led (the Brazilian Social Democrat Party [PSDB] and the PT, respectively), both represent the Latin American social-democratization of the left—to the point that some minority sectors on the left have abandoned the PT, denouncing the "neoliberal" policies of then-President Lula de Silva. The case of Brazil is even more emblematic when we remember the ghosts raised by Lula's election in 2002, a politician accused of being a faithful advocate of Latin American populism, perhaps as a result of his social origins and his record (and that of his party) of taking radical positions in the 1980s and 1990s. What is certain is that these ghosts quickly dissipated. The stability achieved by the Concertación in Chile and by Cardoso and Lula in Brazil are good examples of the existence of a new nonpopulist, democratic, and reformist left and demonstrate the differences between this new left and the Marxist and populist left.

Other cases in the region that are representative of this recent political phenomenon of renewal and change within the Latin American left include President Tabaré Vásquez, José Mujica and the Broad Front (Frente Amplio) in Uruguay, Martín Torrijos in Panama, Óscar Arias in Costa Rica, and in the Dominican Republic Leonel Fernández, who succeeded the populist leader Hipólito Mejía. More recently, in Guatemala, a moderate from the center-left, Álvaro Colom, defeated former general Otto Pérez Molina, who campaigned under the slogan "iron fist" in the context of serious public security problems and who appeared, according to opinion polls, to be certain to win. (Pérez Molina finally took revenge by winning the 2011 elections.) I could also mention other cases, such as the majority of countries in the Caribbean under the leadership of social-democratic (Labor) governments. All of this indicates that, although we are dealing with a less visible or strident reality when compared to the Castros in Cuba, Chávez in Venezuela, or Morales in Bolivia, there is a moderate, social-democratic left that coexists alongside the Marxist and populist left. At the center of this process sits the unambiguous valorization of representative democracy and its institutions.

In an attempt to unravel the true meaning and scope of populist and nonpopulist responses to the neoliberal reforms of the 1990s, Michael Reid (2007), Latin American editor of *The Economist*, maintains that in the preceding decade two contenders with very different views have fought for the soul of Latin America: "populist autocracy," personified by Hugo Chávez, and the "democratic reformism" found in countries such as Brazil, Chile, and Mexico. According to the author, although the former has received much more attention from international public opinion, it is the latter that has won the battle. While Reid recognizes that the neopopulists capitalized (at least in appearance) on the shift from excessive optimism in economic matters in the mid-1990s to the marked pessimism at the end of the decade, and while the region is far from achieving true democratic consolidation with acceptable conditions of governability, it is democratic reformism that has the best chance to achieve stable democratic consolidation in Latin America. This pragmatism, with its clear preference for reform, search for a certain basic consensus, and friendlier view of globalization, places democratic reformism in a better position to achieve true democracy accompanied by growth and equality. Beyond a general discrediting of the neoliberal reforms associated with the Washington Consensus—clearly a bad point, according to Reid—the most important disaster of the 1990s had to do not with economic reforms themselves, but rather with the lack of state and institutional reforms and errors and deficiencies in public policy.

Even though there were serious flaws not only in the conception but also the implementation of these neoliberal reforms, as I argued above, and even though Reid's classification tends to ignore the formal democratic legitimacy enjoyed by the populist autocrats who have recently emerged in the region (despite their authoritarian inclinations), I think it is important to emphasize the reality and the possibilities of democratic reformism as a nonpopulist response to the neoliberal reforms of the 1990s. In the final chapter I argue in favor of reformism as a quality inherent to democracy of institutions, which emerges as an alternative to the personalist democracy typically associated with Latin American populism and neopopulism.

In addition to having an unambiguous dedication to representative democracy and its institutions, the nonpopulist responses to neoliberal reforms that emerged in Latin America in the last decade exercised restraint when proposing economic and social reforms. Many of the cases, such as Brazil and Chile, are the titular examples of Javier Santiso's *Latin America's Political Economy of the Possible* (2006). Far from the utopias that have littered Latin America's history since the time of the conquest and the uncountable experiments attempted since the 1950s, Latin America—the land of magical realism, as Santiso reminds us, with its grand theories and paradigms—has recently adopted a greater pragmatism or possibilism (in the Hirschmanian sense) expressed in more realistic economic policies, thereby making a qualitative move away from the utopianism of the past. This is expressed not only in fiscal and monetary policies adopted by Chile, Brazil, and Mexico, but also in the construction of institutions that move away from the extremes of the past. Santiso writes, "The region's economies have propelled one of the most remarkable reform processes of their history, in tandem with a generalized movement toward democracy. Although incomplete and imperfect, this synchronized dual movement of economic reforms and a transition to democracy is very encouraging. To a large extent, this political and economic shift has been accompanied by an epistemic change. The reformist policies enacted reflect a more pragmatic approach, a political economy of the possible" (4).

According to Santiso, the political economy of the possible, driven by moderate parties and coalitions (generally from the center-left), and the nonpopulist responses to the Washington Consensus and the neoliberal economic reforms of the 1990s differ from the political economy of the impossible (the majority of experiments of the 1960s and 1970s that tended towards ideological inflation) and the political economy of impatience (populism). The age of "good revolutionaries," inspired by Marxism and the Cuban Revolution, and "free-marketeers," with their neoliberal dogmatism, gave way to a more pragmatic age. A healthy combination of more orthodox fiscal policy, designed to control inflation, and progressive social policies intended to fight poverty and inequality stands at the center of new efforts towards the economics of the possible. It is a true epistemological change from utopianism to possibilism, from the state and revolution to democracy and the market, from the rhetoric of intransigence to the greater pragmatism of a new era of collaboration that leaves behind the era of politics conceived as a zero-sum game. The "ethics of consequences" (and of responsibility) strongly influence this change, as opposed to the "ethics of convictions" around which a large part of past policies have turned (a distinction outlined by Max Weber). Although he continues to warn against the neopopulist and neoliberal siren song that still hovers over the region, and despite the fact that the possibilist momentum is both fragile and incomplete, Santiso gives a positive interpretation of this recent process, in the spirit of Albert Hirschman and his classic *A Bias for Hope* (1971).

I hope to have demonstrated with these arguments that Latin America is not condemned to choose between neoliberalism and neopopulism. This is a false dilemma. There are other, real dilemmas of the last century and the recent past that I have presented here. The reality of the region, however, is much richer, complex, and diverse than the false dilemma suggests, as the populist and nonpopulist responses to the neoliberal reforms of the 1990s prove.

# CHAPTER 6

# PRESIDENTIALISM AND PARLIAMENTARISM

I have been a member of the Chamber of Deputies and a senator, worked in the executive and the legislative branches of government, been part of the governing administration and, most recently, been part of the opposition. One could say that, through personal experience in the political system, I have reached some understanding of the relationship between the president and parliament.

This means that my approach to the issue is not just theoretical, but also practical. I cannot fail to recognize, however, that throughout my career I have found the debate over the issue of presidentialism and parliamentarism truly fascinating. If we justify this debate from a theoretical and comparative perspective, we must also recognize its indubitable practical implications.

This debate has me turning somersaults. Sometimes I support parliamentarism, sometimes presidentialism. Finally, I discovered that we are not condemned to pick between one and the other; there are other, intermediary paths that should be explored. These paths include not only the case of semipresidentialism, about which much has been written, primarily concerning the French political system under the Fifth Republic, but also to what, in Latin America, has been most recently known as coalition presidentialism.

At the beginning of the process of democratic transition, some scholars and politicians spoke of a double transition from dictatorship to democracy and from presidentialism to parliamentarism. We held conferences and seminars and traveled to hear from experts. Sometimes, however, we were carried away by theoretical and academic tangents, not practical implications. In the end, the harsh reality of presidentialism prevailed in the region, a reality I have compared to the Andes: standing firm and immovable before us, at least in appearance.

No doubt our system is markedly presidentialist. Perhaps it is "hyper-presidentialist" or "imperial presidentialist," as it is sometimes called. However, this may be a caricature or oversimplification. On one hand, there are executive powers that I find reasonable to keep, such as exclusive legislative initiative in fiscal matters and taxation. I have seen how this executive power can operate as an antidote to demagoguery and populism, which are my sworn enemies. I have no problem with this.

On the other hand, I believe that calling the Latin American system simply hyperpresidentialist or an imperial presidency overstates the lack of power held by parliament and by parliamentarians—I heard this various times from Edgardo Boeninger, one of the main architects of the democratic transition in Chile, who was also a (designated) senator. For one thing, the ability to approve or reject a bill that originated in the executive, as occurs in the majority of cases, is not a minor issue, nor is the array of changes that parliament can introduce. In my experience, legislation never leaves parliament the same as it entered, and there is a whole field of action open to the legislature. Parliament and its parliamentarians have more power than is usually recognized.

In this chapter I go beyond taking a side in this debate and analyze the advantages and disadvantages of presidentialism and parliamentarism in light of the rich emerging theoretical and comparative literature on the subject. I turn a more critical eye on presidentialism, but with the understanding that there are intermediate possibilities worthy of exploration, such as semipresidentialism and coalition presidentialism. I try to present the complexities of the issue, its variations and possibilities, rather than take a position for one or the other.

Contrary to what some political scientists have suggested, I do not consider this debate to be over. An important part of the functioning of the political system, from the perspective of democratic governability, has to do with how the executive and legislature interact. As we know, this varies in important ways when dealing with a presidential or parliamentary government. This chapter is part of that discussion. I do not believe that Latin America is doomed to live under presidentialism, but neither do I believe that presidentialism is the root of all of our problems. We must explore intermediary alternatives. Additionally, throughout this book, I try to avoid dogmatic, one-size-fits-all prescriptions.

The debate around the issue of presidentialism and parliamentarism in Latin America—and in academic circles in the United States—is motivated principally by the work of Juan Linz (see Linz and Valenzuela 1994; Linz's initial manuscript, "Presidential or Parliamentary Democracy: Does it Make a Difference?" began circulating in 1985). It is comparable to the heated debates over modernization, democracy, and authoritarianism in the 1980s, provoked by Guillermo O'Donnell's (1979) book, to which I refer in chapter 3. What are the origins of parliamentarism and presidentialism? What characterizes both forms of government? How do they differ? To what extent can we hold the presidential form of government adopted by all of Latin America since independence responsible for the political instability—and, in the extreme, democratic breakdown—that has characterized the region for two centuries, especially in our most recent history? Is there some intrinsic quality of presidential government that can explain the recurrent political instability, or are there other elements that should be taken into account? Finally, what causal relationship exists—if there is one—between presidentialism and political instability in Latin America? Is the region doomed to presidentialism, or is adopting a parliamentary or semipresidential form of government possible? These are some of the questions that I ask in this chapter.

I take Shugart and Carey's (1992) work on the origins of parliamentarism and presidentialism as a point of departure, adapting it to my own analysis and to Latin America, arguing that the evolution of parliamentarism and presidentialism has at least five stages. Historically, the emergence of parliamentary governments has been linked to the evolution of constitutional monarchies and the shift in power relations from the monarchy to parliament throughout the nineteenth century. This evolution was related to the historical processes surrounding the English and French

Revolutions in the seventeenth and eighteenth centuries and the struggle against the absolute monarchies of the old regime. In the nineteenth century it led to the constitutional monarchies based on the central role of parliaments. Thus, emerging concepts such as parliamentary democracy, ministerial responsibility (of the cabinet to parliament), and parliamentary confidence, among others, became typically associated with parliamentarism. In many (principally European) countries, heads of state (the monarchs) already existed, thereby negating the need to replace them, although their role was much more ceremonial than real. Others, however, immediately adopted a republican rather than monarchical form of government—France definitively established its republic in 1871, and Germany did so in 1918—in which the head of state is democratically elected either directly by the people, as in the semipresidential types (like France since 1962), or indirectly by parliament, as in the parliamentary democracies (such as Germany under the 1949 Constitution). The concepts of parliamentary democracy and constitutional monarchy emerged in this first stage.

We find a second historical phase that runs diametrically opposite the previous one and that comes out of the emergence of presidential government in the United States following its independence at the end of the eighteenth century. This was an original creation, a work of political and constitutional engineering created from above, without historical precedent. As this was a new country—the United States is "the only country in which the *starting-point* of a great people has been clearly observable," according to Alexis de Tocqueville in *Democracy in America*—the Founding Fathers established a presidential form of government based on the concepts of the separation of powers, checks and balances, and presidential term limits, as recorded with singular eloquence in the *Federalist Papers,* which were influenced by Montesquieu. As part of the structure of checks and balances, the separation of powers between the executive and the legislature marked an important difference from the collaboration of powers usually identified with parliamentary democracy. Both the executive and the legislature originate in the popular will—another way it differs from parliamentary government—as expressed by the Electoral College established by President Andrew Jackson in the 1830s, which reflects popular preferences and a true popular mandate in relation to the election of the president of the republic. For obvious reasons, a monarchy that could act as an element of continuity and unity before and after the independence process never existed in the United States. The head of state is a democratically elected president of the republic, moving away from the parliamentary democracy model and the constitutional monarchy, as was adopted in Europe.

Latin America appears to be in what could be considered the third stage of democratization, which corresponds almost exactly with the presidentialist Constitution of the United States, under the direct influence of the United States. The direct election of the president of the republic for a fixed term is the concrete expression of this process and was the established form of government in the nascent Latin American republics, with no exceptions. Some countries in the region, with time, adopted a federal system, and others adopted a unitary one; some were more centralized and others more decentralized; in some cases they established a bipartisan system and in others a multiparty system, with various electoral systems, but all of the new republics adopted, almost mechanically, a presidential form of government. Like the United States, Latin America's lack of a monarchy to provide an element of continuity and unity following independence—despite the sporadic attempts in that direction—and the rupture it created with the absolute monarchy in Spain (in the case of Brazil, the republic was not established until 1889) also resulted in the election of a president of the republic for a fixed term.

Returning to Shugart and Carey's analysis, there was a second stage of democracy in Europe, which I identify here as the fourth stage in the development of presidentialism and parliamentarism. This stage took place towards the end of the Germanic and Austro-Hungarian Empires after World War 1. In general, this second wave of democratization in Europe led to a form of government that is distinct from both presidentialism and parliamentarism, assuming the form of semipresidentialism or "premier presidentialism," as in the cases of Finland, the Weimar Republic, Austria, Ireland, Iceland, and, since 1962, France under the Fifth Republic, which was installed by Charles de Gaulle in 1958. Unlike in the first democratizing wave in Europe, a monarch who could act as head of state did not exist or had not survived, and these countries opted for a democratic president of the republic who was directly elected by the people. Ultimately, all of Europe adopted, as a general rule, a parliamentary form of government, while some exceptions adopted semipresidentialism. In almost all of the countries in this second category, the head of government (usually a prime minister) and the cabinet are responsible to parliament.

Finally, there is perhaps (in my adaptation of Shugart and Carey's analysis) a fifth stage of development that has its roots in the many decolonization processes in the so-called Third World and gained momentum in the new democracies that emerged in the 1970s, 1980s, and 1990s during the third wave of democratization. The majority of these processes led to the adoption of a presidential form of government, with important exceptions in the countries of southern and eastern Europe, which should not surprise us given that the European continent was the first to establish and consolidate parliamentary democracy. Even some former British colonies within the Commonwealth, cradle of parliamentarism, such as Guyana, Nigeria, and Zimbabwe, adopted presidential forms of government.

Now that I have briefly reviewed the historical origins and evolution of parliamentarism and presidentialism, I will characterize each form of government, pointing out the principal differences between the two. There are two major differences between these two types of government. While the president of the republic is directly elected by the people—or in some exceptional cases, including the United States, by the electoral college—under presidential governments, in the case of a parliamentary government, parliament indirectly elects the government, which corresponds as a general rule to a prime minister—or a president of the Council of Ministers in the case of Spain, or a chancellor in the case of Germany. Second, under a presidential government, the president of the republic is elected for a fixed term, generally four, five, or six years, with or without the possibility of reelection depending on the country. In a parliamentary government there is no fixed term—although the government must call elections within a certain number of years—and the government can, therefore, remain in place as long as it can count on the confidence of the parliament.

Some other important differences come out of these two major differences. For example, under a presidential government, the head of state (president of the republic) is at the same time the head of government, while under a parliamentary government these are two separate posts manned by two different people. In the first case, the president of the republic cannot dissolve congress (the assembly), while in the second case, the head of state can dissolve parliament and call for new elections. In the case of presidentialism, the head of government, who is at the same time the head of state, cannot be removed from office except in the exceptional circumstances of impeachment. In a parliamentary form of government, however, the head of government, who is distinct from the head of state, can be removed from office, generally through a vote of no confidence, which can be less traumatic than an impeachment. Presidentialism is based on the separation of powers and a system of checks and balances, while parliamentarism is based on collaboration between the executive and the legislature. One can speak of mutual independence between the executive and the legislature in a presidential system, especially insofar as they are both elected by the people, while parliamentarism depends on a mutual dependence between the two, insofar as the government (the executive) emerges from the parliament (the legislature) (see Stepan and Skach, in Linz and Valenzuela 1994, 120). Finally, in the first case, the president of the republic appoints and removes cabinet ministers from office, which falls under the president's unique and exclusive powers, while in the second case it is the head of government (usually the prime minister) interacting with political parties who has the power to appoint and remove the ministerial cabinet.

Finally, under a semipresidential form of government, the president of the republic is directly elected by popular will and has political powers that include the ability to name the prime minister or head of government and to dissolve parliament. However, in contrast to a presidential form of government, the cabinet is collectively responsible to parliament. Such is the case in France, Portugal, Finland, and Iceland, among others, principally in Europe. The main critique Linz (in Linz and Valenzuela 1994) makes of this type of regime (within what is considered its "ambiguity" and great variety) is the existence of what is called the "dual" or "bipolar" executive, split between the president of the republic elected, directly or indirectly, by the people, and the prime minister who depends on the confidence of the parliament. In every case, this type of regime has emerged under "unique" and "exceptional" conditions, as is the case of the Fifth Republic in France. Many of the cases of semipresidentialism in Europe come close to being de facto parliamentarism.

All of the countries in Latin America, without exception, have a presidential form of government. There are no cases of parliamentarism or semipresidentialism. In all of America, only the British-influenced Caribbean and Canada, as part of the Commonwealth, have parliamentary systems.

Some deduce certain advantages and disadvantages of each of these distributions of power—some speak of "political regimes," "political systems," or "systems of government" in discussing parliamentarism, presidentialism, or semipresidentialism—that stem from the characteristics that I outlined above. This has been a long and intense debate. In an attempt to summarize the principal arguments put forward in favor of parliamentarism, especially those based on the work of Juan Linz, I list here some of the principal advantages of parliamentarism. First, it is simple in comparison to the complexity of presidential government. The government remains in place while it has the confidence of parliament, while under presidentialism, by virtue of the principle that Linz calls "double legitimacy" in that both the president and parliament depend on the popular will, there is, almost by definition, a permanent potential conflict between the executive and legislative powers.

Second, parliamentarism is more flexible, as opposed to the rigidity of presidentialism, which is based on a fixed term of government. What would happen if the incumbent government loses the support of public opinion, the electorate, or parliament? There is no turning back: the incumbents must finish their mandate, even if there are many years left. Third, parliamentarism fosters collaboration between the executive and the legislature due to its greater propensity for constructing coalitions and political alliances, as opposed to the zero-sum game implicit in presidentialism, where the winner of the presidential election takes all and the loser loses everything. Fourth, there is a greater coherence under the parliamentary form of government, in that the majority represented in the government (the executive) generally corresponds with the majority represented in parliament (the legislature). In contrast, a presidential form of government often has a "divided government" or a "divided majority" or minority or weak governments that can lead to immobility and paralysis inasmuch as the majorities represented in the government and the parliament do not necessarily coincide (there is, then, less coherence).

Fifth, the players in a parliamentary system generally correspond to political actors—party leaders and parliamentarians—who act within the system (insiders). Presidentialism attracts people who act from outside the system (outsiders) or against the system, which leads to the weakening of the party system and parliaments or open hostility between parties and parliament with a propensity for antisystem conduct. Latin America is full of examples of this, such as Fernando Collor de Mello in Brazil and Alberto Fujimori in Peru in the 1990s. Within the presidential system that characterizes the region—or any other region, for that matter—there is an "implicit plebiscitary component of presidential authority" that easily leads to populism or the "delegative democracy" phenomenon coined by O'Donnell (Linz, in Linz and Valenzuela 1994, 25 and 29).

Sixth, under a parliamentary form of government, a political crisis or crisis of government, by definition, does not necessarily lead to a regime crisis. This may be because under a parliamentary form of government—since a head of state who represents the entire nation is different from a head of government who, in turn, is the expression of partisan struggle—a political crisis can lead to the removal of the head of government without affecting the basic continuity of the state. Prime ministers can more easily become real fuses in that by exiting or abandoning their post they do not provoke greater disorder in the functioning of the whole political system. It must be said at this point that Linz sees many of these advantages in the Spanish transition, in which the existence of a parliamentary form of government with many of the characteristics mentioned above (simplicity, flexibility, the logic of collaboration rather than confrontation, coherence, propensity for the presence of insiders rather than outsiders) favored the transition's success. On the other side lies the case of Latin America, with its history of chronic political instability expressed in waves of authoritarianism and democracy characterized, without exception, by a presidential form of government.

A seventh advantage of parliamentarism is that it facilitates the formation of coalitions or political alliances, which is particularly relevant in multiparty systems—we must remember that one of the reasons that many attribute political stability to U.S. presidentialism is that it is a two-party system, unlike the majority of cases in Europe and Latin America, which are multiparty systems. The existence of various parties and their need for representation in the government and in parliament makes necessary the existence of institutions with incentives for the formation of stable coalitions and government majorities. This is an advantage for parliamentarism. The opposite case of presidentialism, with its logic of zero-sum, divided government, divided majority, or minority government, often leads to presidents who win the vast majority of votes but have minority representation in parliament, which leads to instability or paralysis. This is a fairly widespread reality in Latin America—think, for example, of President "Lula" in Brazil, who was elected and reelected with over 60 percent of the vote while his party, the PT, made up only 15 to 20 percent of parliamentarians. Mainwaring and Shugart (1997b, 396), who develop a critical vision of Linz's thesis, recognize that "interparty coalitions tend to be more fragile in presidential systems." One of the principal advantages of parliamentarism over presidentialism can be seen in these multiparty systems, which require greater incentives for the formation of stable coalitions and government majorities. It is because of this that Latin America has been so prone, historically, to the emergence and proliferation of minority presidentialism.

An eighth advantage of parliamentarism, following Linz, is that the leadership it builds is more institutional than personalistic. This leadership has its origins in representative democracy's own institutions, such as political parties or parliament, while personalist leaders are much more common under presidentialism. In fact, Linz goes further in order to denounce the myth that leadership, which is always needed under a democratic political regime, whether parliamentary or presidential, is more typical of the latter, while under parliamentarism there is a certain difficulty in generating political leadership. Is it not the case, Linz asks (in Linz and Valenzuela 1994), that the leadership of Winston Churchill and Margaret Thatcher in Great Britain, Konrad Adenauer and Willy Brandt in Germany, Alcide de Gasperi in Italy, Olof Palme in Sweden, and Adolfo Suárez and Felipe González in Spain demonstrate that it is a myth that only presidential governments are able to generate true leaders? This does not reveal a difference between forms of government, but rather shows that leadership is more institutional than personalistic under parliamentarism, thereby removing the danger of *caudillismo* and populism that is so typical of Latin American presidentialism.

Thus, Juan Linz and many others like him, such as Arturo Valenzuela, Arend Lijphart, and Alfred Stepan, to name a few (with the most diverse considerations that do not always coincide), are more inclined towards parliamentarism and more critical of presidentialism. To put it another way, they are critical of presidentialism, principally from the perspective of democratic stability (not necessarily considering the extreme political instability of democratic breakdowns). To summarize his point, Linz notes that his analysis focuses on "some of the structural problems inherent in presidentialism: the simultaneous democratic legitimacy of president and congress, the likelihood of conflict, the absence of obvious mechanisms to resolve it, the zero-sum character of presidential elections, the majoritiarian implication that can lead to disproportionality leaving more than 60 percent of voters without representation, the potential polarization, the rigidity of fixed terms and no-reelection rules normally associated with presidentialism, among others" (Linz and Valenzuela 1994, 69).

According to Valenzuela (2004), it should not surprise us, nor should it be seen as a simple coincidence that, in the last two decades of the twentieth century and in the middle of the recent process of democratization, fourteen presidents — in fact, fifteen if we include Honduras in 2009 — have not been able to finish their mandate (see Introduction). While it is encouraging that these cases have not turned into military interventions, as in the past, they demonstrate a greater propensity for political instability due to the "core logic of confrontation" inherent in presidentialism.

Also in Linz and Valenzuela's (1994) volume, Arend Lijphart tackles this issue from a different perspective in "Presidentialism and Majoritarian Democracy: Theoretical Observations." He maintains as his central thesis that presidentialism reveals a marked tendency towards "majoritarian democracy," primarily because it concentrates power in the hands of one person—the president of the republic, who is the head of state and the head of government—while parliamentarism, which concentrates power in the head of government (prime minister) and the ministerial cabinet, which is incorporated in a collegial electoral body, is more disposed towards consensus-building. In this way, presidentialism is by definition more inclined towards majoritarian democracy ("Presidentialism spells majoritarianism" [101]), which is inconvenient in those countries that lack basic consensus or that need a special kind of consensus, especially those in the process of redemocratization following a military dictatorship or civil war, as they pursue democratic consolidation and stability. This is a weakness of presidentialism when compared to a parliamentary form of government. Thus, following the work of Phillipe Schmitter, Lijphart finds that a consensus democracy is by definition a "defensive" democracy based on the logic that to "share, disperse, and limit" power is a much more functional objective than the democratic stability of a "majoritarian democracy," such as that associated with presidentialism, which is a more "aggressive" democracy based on a certain pretension of "superior democratic legitimacy" that makes the president less inclined towards commitment and compromise (103). Majoritarian democracy is appropriate for more homogeneous societies, while consensus democracy is better for more plural, diverse, and heterogeneous societies, in that it facilitates the formation of a coalition government and allows the principal political forces to participate in shaping and steering the government.

As I wrote at the beginning of this chapter, the storm of comments and critiques that emerged in the 1990s (and continue even today) around Juan Linz's defense of parliamentarism and his critique of presidentialism is comparable in extent and intensity to the critiques that emerged in the 1980s around O'Donnell's book on bureaucratic-authoritarian regimes and his analysis of modernization, authoritarianism, and democracy. It is no exaggeration to say that O'Donnell and Linz represent a good portion of the discussion about Latin America in the field of political science over the last three decades. If the center of the controversy over O'Donnell's book was the causal relationship he established between the degree of development, industrialization, or modernization achieved by some South American countries and the type of political regime (bureaucratic-authoritarian) that resulted, the center of the debate over Linz's work was the idea that we cannot consider presidentialism itself to be the cause of the democratic instability that has characterized Latin America. Certainly, the critics of both authors often make a veritable caricature of these valuable theoretical contributions. What these criticisms hint at, however, is that both authors tackle some of the core questions about democracy in Latin America, from the perspective of both political processes and political institutions.

Of the flurry of criticism directed towards Linz, I want to concentrate on two different critiques that I feel adequately reflect the majority of criticism of his work. These include the more moderate criticism made by Mainwaring and Shugart (1997a and 1997b) and the more radical critique made by Cheibub (2007). What is clear is that Linz's work has not left anyone indifferent, and the debate over the advantages and disadvantages of presidentialism and parliamentarism from the perspective of political stability and the survival of democracy is not over (despite what Cheibub thinks, as we will see below).

Mainwaring and Shugart's (1997a and 1997b) critique is that we cannot consider presidentialism and parliamentarism superior or inferior forms of government by themselves, and the question of political stability (or instability) and the survival (or breakdown) of democracy should be analyzed in the light of their institutional contexts, paying particular attention, according to Mainwaring, to the "difficult relationship" between presidentialism and multiparty systems. They warn that presidentialism has important variations from one country to the next that have implications and consequences for the entire political system. In addition, parliamentary democracy exists almost exclusively in European countries and functions better in high-income countries, ex-British colonies, and small countries. In Latin America, we must consider not only the interaction between presidentialism and the party system, but also socioeconomic factors and the existence (or absence) of a democratic culture when trying to explain political stability or instability. The fact that the majority of cases of failed presidentialism take place in developing countries (the so-called Third World) only strengthens the argument about levels of development.

As for the distinct forms of presidentialism experimented with in Latin America, we should consider the interaction between the president's constitutional powers and the degree of control the president has over political parties. Thus, for example, proactive powers exercised through presidential decrees that create a new status quo, reactive (veto) powers aimed at defending a particular established situation, and power of the president to be the sole initiator of certain (principally economic) laws shows us how strong or weak Latin American presidencies are. These types of variables and considerations explain levels of political stability and instability. In the case of party systems, factors such as the number of parties, the level of party fragmentation, the level of party discipline, and the form in which parties interact with the president of the republic make a difference in terms of the functioning of presidential democracy. In the case of Latin America, it is better to have less party fragmentation and a certain level of party discipline so as to avoid an overwhelming presidential majority that could affect the checks and balances within the political system. Many of the elements mentioned above, especially the existence of party discipline, facilitate the "institutionalization" of the party system (see Mainwaring and Scully 1995). On the other side, excessive party fragmentation or the absence of a certain level of party discipline easily leads to clientelism, patronage, *caudillismo*, and the ever-present temptation for the president to bypass parliament and adopt administrative measures of dubious constitutionality that could result in institutional paralysis.

Ultimately, the questions of where (what country or region) and under what conditions these forms of government are established (such as income and development levels, the size of the country, or the size of its population, among other things) better explain the continuity of democratic regimes than the intrinsic characteristics of parliamentary or presidential forms of government. On one hand, Europe, the ex-British colonies, and the Commonwealth countries are more likely to have a parliamentary form of government, and on the other, Latin America, Africa, and the exceptional case of the United States are more likely to have a presidential form of government. Depending on the country or region and the conditions under which it was established, presidentialism can have more advantages than parliamentarism (as we will see below).

Cheibub's (2007) critique, meanwhile, is based on the assertion that Linz's criticism of presidentialism has no empirical basis. On the contrary, based on data he himself collected, Cheibub argues that each and every one of the assertions and hypotheses developed by Linz are wrong and unsustainable (empirically speaking). These hypotheses include: (1) the separation of powers, or mutual independence of the executive and the legislature, as one of the principal sources of political instability; (2) the scarce or absent incentives for forming political coalitions that exist under a presidential form of government; (3) fragile coalitions, composed of undisciplined parties or prone to generating minority government, conflict, paralysis, and legislative inefficiency; and (4) the tendency of presidential democracies to produce instability. Cheibub writes, "The chain of events to be set in motion by the separation of powers that defines presidentialism (i.e., minority governments with no legislative support, deadlock, and democratic breakdown) does not materialize in the presidential systems that have actually existed since 1946" (19). Even though Cheibub admits that presidential democracies tend to be more unstable than parliamentary democracies, this is not explained by the intrinsic characteristics of presidentialism. He recognizes that the explanations based on exogenous conditions, such as the level of development or the size of the country, are not much better and that, in this sense, "the puzzle remains open."

The alternative hypothesis Cheibub posits is that it is not the intrinsic qualities of presidentialism, but rather the "military-presidential nexus" or "authoritarian legacy" that explains the fragility of Latin American presidential democracies. In general, a presidential government follows a military dictatorship (a dictatorship has almost never been followed by parliamentarism). Once activated, it is difficult to control the military. Such is the case for presidential democracies, which follow military dictatorships much more often (66 percent, according to Cheibub's model) than parliamentary democracies follow dictatorships (28 percent). Inversely, military dictatorships tend to emerge under presidential democracies rather than parliamentary democracies. It is this relationship between military dictatorships and presidentialism that explains the fragility of presidential democracies. Presidentialism tends to exist or to emerge in countries that are prone to experiment with military dictatorships. Under these conditions, practically any form of democracy is doomed. There is, therefore, no causal relationship between presidentialism and democratic breakdown.

Rather, it is the authoritarian legacy that explains the fragility of presidential democracies.

There is much to say concerning Cheibub's methodology related to the models that have been in vogue in political science for the last few years, linked to applied statistics, mathematics, and econometrics and the desire to measure and predict everything with absolute precision. Even though this is completely outside the interests of this book, I cannot help but notice the presence of a certain intellectual arrogance in some of these approaches, which Cheibub's work clearly reflects. For example, the author notes that "we need to put to rest the notion that presidential institutions are not conducive to democratic consolidation. . . . [T]his notion finds no empirical support in the data" (165), adding that "the higher instability of presidential democracies can be *entirely* attributed to their authoritarian legacy; it has *nothing to do* with their constitutional structure" (emphasis added). In other words, "*there is no question* about the military-presidential nexus, as its existence is strongly supported in the data" (23, emphasis added). The emphasized words suggest that the greater instability (or fragility) of presidential democracy is "entirely"—that is, 100 percent—explained by authoritarian legacies and has "nothing to do" with constitutional structures.

Additionally, we must look at how well Cheibub accurately reflects Linz's principal thesis. For example, Cheibub constantly refers to democratic "breakdown" (and the survival of democracy); although Linz's work raises the question of democratic breakdown in Latin America (as we saw in chapter 3), it more often refers to the question of democratic stability or instability. Also, despite its scientific claim, Cheibub's work has a bias towards presidentialism. I share with the author the idea that we should not attribute political instability to certain intrinsic or endogenous characteristics of presidentialism, which is the principal critique he directs at Linz. That said, it is still interesting, and somewhat surprising, that even Cheibub admits that "presidential democracies are more unstable than parliamentary democracies" (6) and that they "have shorter lives" (4) even though he tries to explain this with reasons other than those Linz raises.

In any case, what is clear is that the debate over presidentialism and parliamentarism and the alleged link between political instability and presidentialism is far from being settled or resolved, theoretically or empirically. It would be wrong to say that we can put to rest the notion that presidential institutions are not conducive to political stability. Such statements are not in keeping with the true nature of political science in particular and the social sciences in general, which run on the basis of necessarily tentative and preliminary hypotheses rather than definitive and conclusive statements.

Although I have tried to synthesize some of the core aspects of a vast and fascinating literature triggered by Juan Linz's interesting and pioneering work on the subject, I have yet to lay out the advantages of presidentialism as compared to a parliamentary form of government. Just as I identified the principal advantages of parliamentarism, following the work of various authors, I identify here some of the major advantages of presidential government. Based on the work of Mainwaring and Shugart (1997a, starting on 460, and 1997b, starting on 33), and Shugart and Carey (1992), the following are advantages of presidentialism.

First, the separation of powers, based on a system of checks and balances, is one of the characteristics—if not the principal characteristic—of presidentialism. This guarantees a basic equilibrium within the political system that prevents the supremacy or irresistible power of the executive over the legislature (or vice versa). Such is the genius and originality of the Founding Fathers of the United States of America when conceiving, designing, and creating a new form of government whose success, in the context of a two-party system, many link to its unprecedented and exceptional historical experiences. The constitutions adopted in the first half of the nineteenth century in Latin America were copies of the Constitution of the United States, but without the rich constitutional discussion that took place between the Founding Fathers—we will return to this below. The logic of checks and balances is particularly important when in the presence of an overwhelming majority that, by itself, could lead to inequalities within the system. Rather than creating a sort of political and institutional inertia, as some critics have noted, a presidential form of government has a set of checks and balances that operates in the interaction between the executive and the legislature through negotiation and compromise, which impedes the unilateral imposition of the will of the executive over the legislature and will of the majority over the minority.

A second advantage is the easy identification ("identifiability") under a presidential form of government, in that the electorate votes for a particular person, clearly identified by their first and last name. Unlike the parliamentary form, in which the electorate votes for a parliamentarian, a list of parliamentarians, or a closed list of candidates designated by parties, and the majority in parliament indirectly elects the executive, under presidentialism, a particular person is directly identified at the ballot box. This is an argument in favor of the popular vote, in that the people elect the head of government, who is also the head of state (president of the republic). This, in turn, facilitates accountability, in that the executive is directly responsible to the electorate—some add that the president of the republic's reelection is another way to affirm and reinforce this type of accountability.

A third advantage is the greater predictability and stability of presidentialism in relation to the existence of a fixed term of government. What is to the critics of presidentialism a disadvantage is an advantage for its supporters. It is well known beforehand that the president of the republic, who was directly elected, has a fixed term limit: that is to say, the president's mandate has an expiration date that is known in advance. This contrasts with parliamentarism, where an absence of any fixed terms can lead to frequent cabinet changes, depending on the fluctuating majorities and minorities represented in parliament that can, in the extreme, lead to conspicuous political instability.

A fourth advantage of presidentialism is that the voter, at the moment of voting, has two options rather than the single option offered under parliamentarism. In the latter case, the voter marks only one preference for a parliamentarian, list of parliamentarians, or closed party list, while under presidentialism, the voter directly chooses the executive (president of the republic) and the legislators (parliament or assembly). There exists, then, broader power to decide. Consequently, the authorities, whom voters directly choose, have greater legitimacy. Such is the logic of presidential democracy, characterized by the existence of "two agents" (presidents and assemblies elected by the people under distinct constitutional designs and electoral dynamics), unlike parliamentary democracy, which is based on the election of just one agent: the assembly or parliament (Shugart and Carey 1992).

A fifth advantage of presidentialism is that, by definition, parliament has a greater independence in legislative matters. As I outlined above, under a presidential form of government, the executive and the legislature are independent actors due to the separation of powers characteristic of this type of government. This implies that parliament independently analyzes, considers, and votes on the merit of a particular piece of legislation as soon as it is introduced. An advantage of presidentialism is the possibility of sufficient legislative independence such that support for executive initiatives is not automatic (Mainwaring and Shugart 1997b, 419). In contrast, under a parliamentary form of government, many times the study and analysis of particular pieces of legislation are related, directly or indirectly, to confidence in the government, which can even lead to the removal of the government (through a vote of no confidence).

A sixth advantage of presidentialism is the existence of a clear equilibrium between the executive and the legislature, based on the checks and balances mechanism that prevents the overwhelming majority from unilaterally imposing its will on the minority. Contrary to what the critics of presidentialism maintain, the logic of checks and balances precludes the possibility of winner-take-all. In fact, under certain forms of parliamentary democracy, such as the Westminster democracy of Great Britain, there is a greater possibility of the unilateral imposition of the government majority precisely because of the dominance of parliament and the absence of presidential democracy's checks and balances. The English parliamentary majority can make and unmake legislation with few limits or checks.

A seventh consideration in favor of presidentialism is that a parliamentary form of government has only been successful in certain countries or regions, under precise and exceptional circumstances. In truth, parliamentary democracy has had only partial success. For example, parliamentarism has been quite successful in countries or regions with a certain level of development, as in ex-British colonies, countries that are part of the Commonwealth, or in small countries. Following the same logic, many of the problems attributed to presidentialism are related not to presidentialism itself, but rather to other variables such as the relationship between presidentialism and the party system, the characteristics of the party system (more or less fragmentation or party indiscipline), the level of development, and the political culture of a particular country or region, among other factors and considerations.

Finally, it should be noted that we cannot talk about the presidential form of government as homogenous because there is a wide range of presidentialisms, as the case of Latin America demonstrates. For example, presidentialism where the president of the republic has broad and irresistible power in the context of fragile political institutions, a weak parliament, and fragmented and undisciplined parties is different from presidentialism set in a solid party system that is properly institutionalized with a small number of disciplined parties. In this manner, constitutional design, political engineering, and institution building make a difference in terms of the viability or sustainability of a certain type of government and between different types of presidentialism.

What can I add to an interesting debate that has aroused such strong passions and is so far from concluding? What follows are my own reflections and findings on this issue.

I will begin by echoing the principal critique that has been levied against Juan Linz's work, in that we cannot say that parliamentarism or presidentialism are, on their own, good or bad, inferior or superior. There are no qualities intrinsic to one or the other form of government that makes them functional or dysfunctional, conducive or not to democratic stability. The abundant empirical evidence provided by numerous authors offers arguments for both possibilities. Another aspect of Linz's very interesting work merits criticism: somehow, everything that is successful but is not parliamentary democracy is "exceptional." For example, U.S. presidentialism is successful from the point of view of democratic stability, but it is an exceptional case. Linz cannot deny the merits of the Fifth Republic's semipresidential democracy, but cases such as this only emerge in "very special and unique circumstances" (in Linz and Valenzuela 1994, 49). Thus, it appears that only parliamentary democracies have intrinsic qualities that ensure democratic stability, while any other cases, whether presidential or semipresidential democracy, have only exceptionally achieved this objective.

Second, we must not forget that in Latin America, presidentialism, which has been strongly entrenched in Latin American history and political culture, presents certain singular characteristics. As we have seen, presidentialism is not homogeneous. One of Mainwaring and Shugart's principal contributions is distinguishing between different types of presidentialism in the region. Since independence, however, people have constructed a sort of myth around presidentialism, to the point that one might ask if it is even possible to search for alternatives to presidential government and what the limits and potential for innovation might be in this regard. Some writers and historians highlight the fundamental continuity between the old Spanish monarchy and the new presidentialism of the nascent republics. For example, Simón Bolívar wrote that "the new American states, formerly Spanish, need kings with the name of president" (in Botana 2005, 80), while the Chilean essayist Alberto Edwards, referring to the Portales Republic (1830–1860) forged on the basis of the strongly presidentialist Constitution of 1833, wrote that it "seemed new but it was old: what it did was materially and morally restore the monarchy, not in its dynastic principles, which would have been ridiculous or impossible, but in its spiritual foundations as a conservative force for order and institutions" (1959, 46).

The myth, or myths, constructed around presidentialism, the strongly concentrated power deposited in the executive, and the relatively weak position held by parliament are some examples of this. Based on the reinforcement of presidential systems — even though there are those who doubt this, as we will see below — the form in which democracy re-emerged during the transitions of 1979 to 2009 only serves to highlight this foundational characteristic of Latin American nations. O'Donnell's work on delegative democracy and the many accounts of what has been called "enhanced presidentialism," "hyperpresidentialism," or "imperial presidentialism" present in the history of presidential democracy in Latin America are other examples.

Many of these findings are somewhat exaggerated and often present caricatures of actually existing presidential government in Latin America, which are much weaker and precarious than is usually stated. From the point of view of democratic stability, which is the perspective that I have adopted in this chapter, we cannot concentrate on the intrinsic qualities of presidentialism, leaving out the cluster of institutions that make up the whole political system. I think that we are faced with a three-legged table whose fundamental components are the executive, the legislature, and the party system. How these three fundamental components combine determines the stability or instability of democracy (see Smith 2005, chapter 6). We could also be dealing with a four-legged table if we include the electoral system. Based on the history and idiosyncrasies of a particular country, the characteristics of its political culture, and its level of economic and social development, we should design institutional arrangements aimed at creating democratic stability. Here, once again, there are no unique, abstract, or generally valid recipes or formulas. I have criticized such one-size-fits-all formulas in this book and will continue to do so in the final chapter.

This is precisely the focus of Payne, Zovatto, and Mateo Díaz's (2007) book. Instead of postulating this or that form of government, party system, or electoral system as abstract ideals, they point out the trade-offs that exist between the distinct institutions or institutional arrangements that vary from country to country. Their report makes clear that institutions matter and different institutional combinations or arrangements are possible within a democratic regime. The authors operate on the assumption that an adequately functioning democracy is a necessary condition for equitable and sustainable development and that economic forces, including the reforms implemented since the 1980s, do not exist in a political or institutional vacuum. What types of institutional arrangements are more conducive to political stability in the context of the presidential democracies that exist in the region? This is the question posed by the report, whose authors warn that they do not see signs of wanting to move from a presidential democracy to parliamentary or semi-presidential forms of government. In Latin America, the most frequent combination is presidentialism, a multiparty system, and proportional representation. It is not an easy combination, but neither is it an impossible combination (as I will argue below). According to Payne, Zovatto, and Mateo Díaz, the challenge, in this context, is introducing incentives for building majoritarian political alliances within a multiparty presidential democracy. Not only the form of government, but also the party system and the electoral system should point in this direction, with special attention focused on institutionalizing the party system and avoiding party fragmentation and polarization.

Of the three components that I have mentioned—the executive, the legislature, and political parties—presidentialism is the most substantial (again, like the Andes). I will argue below that we are not necessarily condemned to a presidential form of government, but we cannot ignore the fact that it has dominated the region, without exception, since independence. Party systems are another matter, as they have been experimented with over time. In fact, Latin America has had important cases of two-party systems, a formula that, according to some (the classic work on this is by Maurice Duverger), corresponds to the natural tendency of all party systems and facilitates democratic stability (as demonstrated by the United States, a classic example of two-party democracy). In effect, countries such as Colombia (Liberals and Conservatives), Venezuela (Adecos and COPEI, or social democrats and Christian democrats, respectively), Uruguay (Colorados and Blancos), Costa Rica (National Liberation Party [PLN] and Social Christian Unity Party [PUSC]), Honduras (Liberal Party and National Party), and Argentina (Peronists and Radical Civic Union [UCR]) have had two principal (effective) parties during the majority of their contemporary history, approximating the reality of a two-party system. This has generally varied in more recent history under the third wave of democratization. There has been not only a general transition from two-party systems to multiparty systems, but also a movement towards party fragmentation. Only Honduras has maintained a two-party system over the course of its long history, with the possible addition of El Salvador, with ARENA and the FMLN. All of the other Latin American countries have evolved towards multiparty systems.

The predominant relationship in Latin America is between presidentialism and a multiparty system, with electoral systems that vary from one country to the next but that principally revolve around proportional representation. Systems vary from country to country—with or without reelection, with plurality or runoff elections, with or without simultaneous presidential and parliamentary elections, with voluntary or obligatory voting, with open or closed candidate lists, with unicameral systems (like the majority of Central American countries) or bicameral systems (such as that in Mexico and the majority of South American countries)—with the understanding that the type of combination established should aim to promote the representativeness and effectiveness of the entire political system in order to ensure democratic governability. Emphasis on one (representativeness) or the other (effectiveness) varies from country to country, but we must take into account the trade-offs between the two. There is no unique formula, recipe, or prescription that works for every situation, but rather a menu of options that can be tried and, in fact, have been attempted in different countries and regions of the world.

Even though Latin America has invariably featured a presidential form of government—and nothing suggests that there is a real possibility of advancing towards a semipresidential or parliamentary form of government—each country, according to its own reality, has to choose institutional arrangements that are most conducive to democratic governability. We are not doomed to political or democratic instability because of sharing a presidential form of government. The existence of different types of presidentialism (as eloquently argued by Scott Mainwaring) and different institutional arrangements makes the difference between democratic stability and instability. The art of politics and constitutional engineering consists of designing and implementing these institutional arrangements and distinct combinations, escaping simplistic formulas. This means adopting and implementing decisions that adequately correspond to each country's social and economic problems, according to its level of development and political culture. The interaction and type of negotiation and agreements that can emerge between political actors affects the outcome. There are no straitjackets—so to speak—that we cannot escape, be it a presidential or parliamentary form of government or different institutional combinations or arrangements. Instead, there is a menu of options that should be explored in each country according to its own reality and objectives. Political science should call attention to the trade-offs that exist between these options from a theoretical and comparative perspective, as Payne, Zovatto, and Mateo Díaz rightly point out. However, nothing can substitute for the role of political actors and their own strategic decisions on this matter.

A perspective similar to my three-legged table appears in an Inter-American Development Bank report (2005, starting on 27) that focuses on public policy. According to the report, what truly matters is the type of relationship or interaction between the executive, the legislature, and political parties. Limiting its focus to public policy and the ability of the president of the republic (government) to advance his or her legislative agenda, the report assigns a fundamental role to political parties and the party system. The successful implementation of public policy (legislative agenda) will depend on these structures. For example, in a presidential system, the existence of programmatic rather than clientelistic parties within a properly institutionalized party system appears to be one of the keys to success. Fragmentation and a lack of party discipline, on the other hand, can compromise the success of the government's legislative agenda. The report concludes that "divided government" is a particularly critical situation. Like Payne, Zovatto, and Mateo Díaz, the IDB concludes that minority governments, party fragmentation, and lack of discipline create adverse conditions for democratic governability. Hence, in the context of presidential democracy, the "politics of public policy" is just as important as the content and characteristics of public policies.

Again and again, even from different academic perspectives, scholars arrive at what Mainwaring calls the "difficult relationship" between presidentialism and a multiparty system in Latin America. Truthfully, if we analyze the different countries and regions that correspond to cases of multiparty democracy—there are many empirical studies on this subject—we find that the majority of successful cases, in terms of democratic stability, are parliamentary democracies. Such is the case in Europe, including central and eastern Europe after the fall of the Berlin Wall, with some semipresidential cases (the exception rather than the rule), and also in Canada, New Zealand, and the great majority of Commonwealth countries, Japan, and India, which is nothing less than the largest and poorest democracy in the world (and which, by the way, calls into question once again the argument about the socioeconomic requisites, prerequisites, or conditions for democracy). I could mention many other examples of democratic stability in multiparty systems. Latin America, forever (or at least since independence) characterized by presidential government, is perhaps an example of the polar opposite, chronic instability: "It is significant that with the notable exception of Latin American countries, few democracies have opted for the U.S. model of presidentialism. . . . [In] Latin America, it rarely if ever produced lasting political stability. . . . The vast majority of the contemporary world's stable democracies have had parliamentary forms of government" (Linz and Valenzuela 1994, x).

Is this a mere coincidence? Is it a coincidence that the immense majority of cases of democratic stability under multiparty systems appear to correspond with parliamentary democracies, while the overwhelming majority of cases of political instability under multiparty systems appear to correspond with presidential democracies, as in Latin America? Be that as it may, we cannot forget that Latin America, with its history of chronic instability, has made important progress in the most recent wave of democratization. For the moment, there have not been any military coups d'état or authoritarian regressions, with the single exception of Honduras. Fujimori's 1992 self-coup in Peru and Hugo Chávez's authoritarian or semiauthoritarian traits in Venezuela—although we cannot deny that Chávez has formal democratic legitimacy—among other cases of dubious commitment to democracy, are the exception rather than the rule. There are certainly problems with the quality of democracy and a deficit in democratic governability, a subject I will address in the final chapter. We could say that this progress also has to do with the way in which the (apparently contradictory) relationship between presidentialism and multiparty systems is articulated.

Nohlen and Fernández (1998) made one of the first attempts to address this issue in a book that offers an explicitly stated defense of presidentialism in Latin America. The authors maintain as their thesis that presidentialism has successfully weathered the challenges posed by democratic transition, consolidation, and governability. They argue that the challenge Latin America faces has more to do with how to make democracy more efficient, participatory, and transparent in the middle of a crisis of credibility, how to "renew" democracy and "adapt" presidentialism for better-functioning governments.

A similar perspective is to be found in a book edited by Jorge Lanzaro (2001). Escaping the traditional canon and the theoretical disputes between presidentialism and parliamentarism, the authors argue that Latin America has advanced in coordinating presidentialism and multiparty systems through coalition presidentialism. Even though these terms can appear contradictory because of the "difficult relationship"—although not impossible, as we will see below—between presidentialism and multiparty systems, Latin America has had rich and varied experiences with this over the last three decades.

Jorge Lanzaro and René Antonio Mayorga (in Lanzaro 2001) point out that, given that presidential regimes continue to be the common form of government in this recent phase of democratization in Latin America, and considering the enormous diversity of types of actually existing presidentialism, there are innovative ways of dealing with this relationship that take into account the advantages and not just the disadvantages of presidential government. Under presidential democracies of a majoritarian or a pluralist type, including the populist or neopopulist varieties, under centralized or decentralized structures, or under different party or electoral systems, or with majority or minority governments, Latin America has not experienced the "perverse effects" that some authors—Juan Linz, among others—attribute to presidentialism. Along with cases of "hard" presidentialism, various cases of moderate presidential systems have appeared under different forms of cooperation, negotiation, pacts, accords, compromises, and coalition construction. In this way, incentives for constructing political alliances and coalitions that many assumed were restricted to parliamentarism have emerged under coalition presidentialism. This "neopresidentialism" that has surfaced recently in Latin America has boundaries considerably more flexible and productive than what was imagined by theories of presidentialism and parliamentarism. A rich diversity of experience exists in Latin America in this sense, demonstrating that the combination of presidentialism and multiparty systems is possible.

Deepening these ideas, Lanzaro (2001) points out that "the expansion of presidential government can also conform to the geometry of institutional equilibrium and a range of opinions by assembling the will to give rise to the separation of powers and a plurality of political representation" (20), through different schemes and efforts at compromise, alliances, and coalitions. Without ignoring that presidentialism has, for good or bad, an "innate plebiscitary" propensity, which installs itself most comfortably in "majoritarian" systems, we must not forget experiences of "moderate presidentialism," which is more prone to more "pluralistic grammar." In the same volume, Daniel Chasquetti questions the "difficult combination" of presidentialism and multiparty systems, asserting that a presidential system of government can incentivize coalition construction, which "mitigates" tensions between presidentialism and multiparty systems; that governmental "majority coalitions" facilitate democratic stability; and that "moderate" multiparty systems are preferable to "extreme" multiparty systems (defined as an excessive proliferation of political parties). The biggest problem, then, is found in multiparty presidentialism without government coalitions. On the other hand, presidentialism with coalitions, or coalition presidentialism, makes it possible to bring presidentialism and a multiparty system together.

All of these contributions remind us that multiparty presidentialism is, today, the most common combination of political institutions in Latin America and that a variety of rich and diverse experiences of different types of presidentialism have been able to coexist with a multiparty system by constructing political coalitions. These coalitions, and the incentives designed and established around them, make this coexistence possible. In this way, political coalitions are viable in presidentialism, and political stability is possible under a multiparty presidential democracy. This democratic stability is particularly viable under majoritiarian governments within a moderate multiparty system.

Various comparative political science works have addressed the relationship between the executive and the legislature, which stands at the center of the debate over presidentialism and parliamentarism from a theoretical and empirical perspective. Many of these works have demonstrated not only that democratic stability is possible under a presidential form of government, but also that in many Latin American countries, parliaments have more power than is usually recognized. Among these works, I want to mention a particularly interesting contribution from Pérez-Liñán (2005), who argues, on the basis of a study of twenty-seven instances between 1950 and 2000 in which the executive closed the legislature or the legislature removed the executive from office, that democratization of presidential systems in Latin America (especially as the region moves towards democratic consolidation) has limited the ability of presidents to challenge the legislature. In many cases, there has been a true "legislative supremacy." The small probability of military intervention, the elimination of constitutional mechanisms that have been used by the executive to dissolve congress, and, in general, the significant stability of the constitutional environment have all contributed to this supremacy. In another work, as we saw in chapter 3, Pérez-Liñán (2007) referred to the way that impeachments—one of the expressions of this legislative supremacy—have put the executive on the defensive. Impeachments have led to changes of *government* but not changes of political *regime*—a "crisis without [democratic] breakdown." In this way, a more balanced relationship between the executive and the legislature has emerged recently in Latin America. Thus, we have passed from the "moderate supremacy of the executive" in the 1960s and 1970s to a more predominant parliament under the most recent wave of democratization.

Finally, it is worth asking the question: Is Latin America condemned to presidentialism? If presidentialism is, as I suggested above, something akin to the Andes, then there is nothing to be done. If it is certain that presidentialism is in the DNA of Latin America, this should not leave us with an uncritical eye, based on the myth of presidentialism and a marked prejudice against parliamentarism—which, it should be noted, has never been seriously attempted in Latin America. The closest parliamentarism came to becoming a reality in Latin America was in the framework of Brazil's Constituent Assembly from 1987 to 1988—and, in a way, in the old republic of 1889 to 1930—where it was rejected by the electorate. In Chile, essayists and historians refer (erroneously, in my judgment) to the so-called parliamentary regime that existed between 1891 and 1920. In one work (Burgos and Walker 2003), I have argued that this was a "distorted form of presidentialism" more than a form of parliamentary government, consisting of a series of political practices that were introduced in the political process while the constitutional texts remained clearly presidential (as it has been in the 1833, 1925, and 1980 Constitutions). In this same work, we postulated the possibility of a form of parliamentary government for Chile, but there is no reason to reproduce those arguments here.

I cannot deny that over time, like many studious and political people, I have become more skeptical about this issue, not because I cannot devise good reasons to install a parliamentary government in countries like Chile, Uruguay, and Costa Rica, for example, but because I cannot see the viability of an endeavor that would be a true paradigm shift in Latin America, in terms of both institutions and political culture. Perhaps eight years in parliament and many others in the executive have contributed to this skepticism. As Shugart and Carey (1992, 3) write, the "bad news" for the defenders of parliamentarism is that "no existing presidential system has ever changed to a parliamentary system, while several have made the reverse move." Be that as it may, the possibility of innovation should not be thrown out a priori. Beyond the question of presidentialism (or parliamentarism) itself, we ought to consider the different types of relationships possible between the executive, the legislature, and the party system.

If the case in favor of parliamentarism appears to be a crazy idea in light of Latin America's political culture—although I have made an effort throughout this book to avoid all types of determinism—why not consider the possibility of introducing a prime minister alongside the president of the republic in a particular country or group of countries with certain characteristics (an acceptable level of party system institutionalization, for example, and a more deeply rooted democratic culture)? Political scientists will come to define at what point such an experience comes close to being a semipresidential form of government. With these last lines, I wanted to raise certain tentative and preliminary questions and open new avenues in terms of ideas, academic debate, and political endeavors. Rather than closing off possibilities in a given direction, I have tried to avoid prejudices, fatalism, and determinism of any kind. Despite Cheibub's assertion, this debate is not over, and I intended to analyze here the pros and cons of different options, demonstrating Latin America's complex and rich diversity.

# CHAPTER 7

# THE NEW SOCIAL QUESTION

As a senator, I represent a district of twenty-six municipalities and five provinces that stretches from Valparaíso to Aconcagua, with a predominantly poor, rural zone and another predominantly urban one. In both areas, a new middle sector is breaking through in the midst of the profound transformations that have taken place during the process of democratization carried out since the late 1980s. When attempting to summarize this in a single image, one could say that the grandchildren of the beneficiaries of the agrarian reform endorsed by President Eduardo Frei Montalva during the Revolution in Liberty (1964–1970) are now enrolled in college and university — today, seven of every ten students enrolled in higher education in Chile are the first in their families to reach that level of education. Having said this, we must not lose sight of the great diversity and heterogeneity in Latin America, which will help us avoid simplifications and generalizations.

The contrast between this new reality and the old social reality that existed only a few decades ago is significant. I remember what the twenty-six communities of the region I represent in parliament were like when I was elected as a deputy to the National Congress in 1993. The changes have been profound and obvious. This is the shift from the old to the new social question.[1]

In 1993, these communities were too close to the image of Third World or underdeveloped countries, with deficiencies in all types of basic needs, especially things like nutrition, literacy, education, health, and infrastructure. Chile is a different country now when compared to what I knew in my youth, and Latin America is a different region. This reality varies so significantly from one country to another that we must avoid the temptation of looking only at the averages in terms of poverty, inequality, and per capita income. In the constituency I represent one can still find pockets of poverty and extreme poverty, along with the social inequality that continues to be Latin America's great scandal. There are common patterns, however, that I try to unravel in this chapter. At the core of this new reality one could point to the fact that, at the beginning of the twenty-first century, Latin America seems to be more like middle-income countries—varying, of course, from one country to another—with new forms of social mobility related to the significant rise in education and profound changes in social structures.

Latin America's "social question" was at the center of the crisis of oligarchic rule and the national and popular model that aimed to substitute a new democratic order for the old oligarchic one. It was linked to the emergence of a new proletariat in the incipient process of industrialization that opened the way for the last stage of outward-looking growth, the accompanying migrations from the countryside to the city, and the urbanization associated with the modernization process. The anticlerical struggles of the "religious question" typical of the nineteenth century

1. This chapter is fundamentally based on investigations and studies carried out by CIEPLAN and the Fernando H. Cardoso Institute between 2006 and 2009. The results of these studies can be found in Cardoso and Foxley (2009) and in three volumes on "social cohesion" published under the coordination of Eugenio Tironi: Tironi (2008), Valenzuela et al (2008), and Gasparini et al (2008). The conversations, conferences, seminars, and monographs inside and outside of Chile that inspired the ideas in this chapter are innumerable. They include a seminar, Social Cohesion in Latin America (Assembling the Pieces), at the Kellogg Institute for International Studies at the University of Notre Dame on April 16, 2009. In the lines that follow, I try to bring together the essence of these reflections as they relate to what has been called Latin America's new social question.

gave rise to new social and political movements and organizations. These new organizations sought to represent the interests of the popular sector and middle sectors of society through the new, state-led import substitution industrialization development model. Sometimes this process took place under a democratic political form, while in other cases it took place under authoritarianism. I analyzed the characteristics, consequences, and economic, social, and political implications of this development model in chapters 2 and 3.

Latin America is not like it once was, even though, in some sense, we are still in the process of de-oligarchization (which has much to do with the neopopulist phenomenon that I discussed in chapter 5), and poverty and inequality remain elements of continuity in terms of its economic and social development. The new social question that has emerged recently in the region has characteristics distinct from those we have experienced in the past. This comes out of the profound economic and social changes linked to the new development strategies imposed on the region in the era of globalization. I dedicated chapter 4 to these enormous transformations. More importantly, this new social question emerges in a democratic context.

The countries of the region have little to do with the images of the underdeveloped Third World countries that we knew in the 1960s and 1970s. The new social question is more related to the reality and characteristics of middle-income countries with emerging economies that appear, in their recent history, to be the most dynamic in the world. As Alejandro Foxley (2009b) points out, middle-income countries are something like the Second World, distinct from the First and Third Worlds, but sharing characteristics of both: "these are societies characterized by conflict that can achieve significant progress during a determined period of time but that are affected by frequent falls in levels of growth, social tension, and political instability. In sum, these are economies and societies where nothing is going well at the same time, even though the predominant tendency has been towards higher levels of development." Even though Latin America is still far from achieving the great dynamism of southeastern, eastern, and southern Asian countries, we can say that we are "halfway" in the path toward economic and social development (Cardoso and Foxley 2009).

That said, we have to take into account the great heterogeneity of the region, where some countries are ahead (Brazil, Mexico, Chile, Costa Rica, Panama, Uruguay, and Argentina) and others lag behind (Nicaragua, Honduras, Guatemala, Bolivia, and Paraguay). A third group find themselves in an intermediate stage of development (Colombia, Peru, Venezuela, El Salvador, and Ecuador), according to the World Bank. It is, then, an unequal process that has traveled, and continues to travel, in a contradictory and sometimes torturous way, with advances and setbacks, from underdevelopment to development.

The virtuous five years between 2003 and 2007 are one example of the advances made in the region, when we came closer than ever to the triple objectives of democracy, growth, and social equity. This was in contrast to the "lost decade" of the 1980s and the "lost half-decade" from 1998 to 2002, following the Asian financial crisis. Today, free and democratic elections (electoral democracy) prevail, perhaps as never before in the history of Latin America (we will return to this topic in the next chapter). Along with this, the region has experienced a 5.5 percent growth rate from 2003 to 2007, with exports growing at 7 percent annually. In turn, public debt fell from 65 percent of GDP in 2003 to 35 percent in 2007, while unemployment shrunk from 11 to 7.5 percent (Foxley 2009b). According to statistics from ECLAC, poverty decreased from 44 percent in 2003 to 34 percent in 2007, which means that there are 184 million Latin Americans who still live below the poverty line (with 68 million living in extreme poverty). Nine countries in the region improved their income distribution, also according to ECLAC (Panorama Social 2008). Nora Lustig (2009) similarly points out that, since the beginning of this decade, eleven out of eighteen countries in the region improved their income distribution. Despite this, Latin America continues to be, along with sub-Saharan Africa, one of the most unequal regions in the world.

Beyond the fact that we still do not know the full implications of the 2008 to 2009 economic and financial crisis, this confirms that external shocks continue to be one of the principal obstacles on the path to development. What is certain is that Latin America is not the same as it used to be (as I will demonstrate in the lines that follow). The profound changes and great economic and social transformations that occurred in the last two or three decades, both in the region and in the world, speak of an economic and social structure very different from what we have had historically. The new reality of middle-income countries is at the heart of these changes.

In effect, within the region's great heterogeneity and following the World Bank's classification of high, upper middle, lower middle, and low income countries, we can say that "in 2007, this indicator reveals that the situation of Latin America's population is consistent with the international middle sector. There are no countries considered to be low income and almost two thirds (65 percent) are in upper middle income countries" (Medici, in Cardoso and Foxley 2009, 494). Similarly, systematizing and expanding on the available data using the World Bank criteria, which is also used by the OECD (even though now they are labeled "middle-income countries" [MICs]), a report from the Spanish Ministry of Foreign Affairs and Cooperation (Ministerio de Asuntos Exteriores y de Cooperación 2006) points out that there are 93 countries, out of a total of 208 countries and territories, that can be considered as middle-income. Along with the 54 countries designated as high-income (none of them in Latin America), and 61 countries that are labeled as low-income (from Latin America, only Nicaragua is in this category), there are 93 middle-income countries, a category that can be subdivided into 37 upper middle-income (gross national income per capita between US$3,035 and US$9,385 in 2003 dollars) and 56 lower middle-income (between US$766 and US$3,035). These are countries that have a per capita income between US$766 and US$9,385, which corresponds to 35 percent of world GDP (in purchasing power parity), 31.1 percent of imports and exports of goods and services, 23.7 percent of direct foreign investment, and 57.8 percent of foreign remittances. Forty-seven percent of the world's population and somewhere near 41 percent of the world's poor live in these countries, which make up 60 percent of the countries traditionally considered as "developing." The bulk of the MICs are concentrated in two regions: Latin America (32 percent) and Europe and central Asia (25 percent). Despite their great internal heterogeneity, these countries and regions are characterized by a high vulnerability to external shocks and internal crises. According to the report, the Latin American countries that fall into the upper-middle income category are Chile, Costa Rica, Uruguay, Mexico, Panama, Argentina, Venezuela, and Brazil. El Salvador, Peru, Ecuador, and Colombia are in the lower-middle income group, as well as, further back, Guatemala, Paraguay, Honduras, and Bolivia.

It is interesting to note that Latinobarómetro data confirm the previously mentioned tendencies from the point of view of public opinion. According to the Latinobarómetro (2006, prepared with ECLAC), 7 percent of the population of Latin America consider themselves "rich," 32 percent consider themselves "poor," and a significant 69 percent consider themselves "middle class." Argentina, Chile, and Uruguay lead the group, with more than 70 percent of respondents classifying themselves as "middle class," while in Nicaragua, El Salvador, Honduras, and Ecuador 70 percent consider themselves to be "very poor." This indicates that both objectively, on the basis of the World Bank classification, and subjectively, on the basis of the perceptions of public opinion, middle-income countries that have transitioned (and continue to transition) from underdevelopment to development drive the new social reality in Latin America, notwithstanding the great heterogeneity of the region.

This new economic and social reality has much to do with Latin America's international insertion in the age of globalization, including both its achievements and its enormous deficiencies. Indeed, according to one study (Benavente, in Cardoso and Foxley 2009), from the perspective of innovation and competitiveness, which is where the biggest gap between the developed and developing countries lies, there is a recently established third group of countries behind the "advanced" countries with per capita incomes greater than US$35,000 annually (Finland, Ireland, and some Asian countries) and a second group of advanced countries with per capita incomes between US$24,000 and US$30,000 that developed more recently (Australia, South Korea, Portugal, New Zealand, among others). This third group of developing countries, such as the Baltic countries and Malaysia, hovers much further behind and includes, at a distance, Latin American countries such as Argentina and Chile. The report's thesis is that, along with having sound macroeconomic accounts and the "perspiration" required for savings and investment, a greater amount of "inspiration" in terms of more knowledge, more productive practices, and a greater capacity for innovation is necessary for these countries to pass into the first two groups.

If what we saw in terms of the reality of middle-income countries allows Latin America to distance itself from the sixty-one low-income countries (located principally in Africa), a great divide based on innovation and competitiveness separates it from the developed countries. Latin America's growth has been based on perspiration (principally cheap and underqualified manual labor concentrated in the exploitation of natural resources) but with little advancement in terms of inspiration (knowledge). A study headed by Alejandro Foxley (2009b) asks the question of how a country moves from having a per capita GDP of US$15,000 (PPP) (like that of Chile, one of the most open countries in Latin America) to a per capita GDP of US$20,000 or US$25,000 (the level of a developed country), reinforcing the idea of a country or a region that finds itself halfway along the path towards development. Making a comparison with similar countries—that is, those of medium or small size, situated on the periphery of centers of economic power, and that are halfway on the road towards development (Australia, New Zealand, South Korea, Finland, Norway, Spain, and Portugal)—Foxley attributes great importance to the formation of human capital, especially in the field of education.

Observing World Economic Forum's Global Competitiveness Index and how Latin America lags in this area, José Miguel Benavente adds that countries such as Argentina, Chile, Costa Rica, Mexico, Panama, and Uruguay find themselves in the second (intermediate) stage of development, where the search for gains in efficiency adds to the factors of labor and capital (perspiration). The most important leap, in terms of development, takes place in the third, definitive stage, which prioritizes innovation and technological progress (only Brazil, Chile, and Costa Rica have any possibility of getting closer to this third and last stage). Latin America, which spends only 0.8 percent of GDP on research and development, lags behind when we consider, for example, that in 2005 the European countries agreed to raise spending on research and development to greater than 3 percent of GDP (a level already reached in Israel, Finland, and South Korea). Benavente concludes by pointing out that "the majority of Latin American countries are still in intermediate stages of income" (in Cardoso and Foxley 2009, 335).

Perhaps the most appropriate way to characterize the new social reality in Latin America is in relation to the profound sociodemographic changes that have taken place over the last decades. According to a study by Osvaldo Larrañaga (in Tironi 2008), the principal changes correspond first to the changes in reproductive behavior in the Latin American family, characterized by a profound and rapid fall in the fertility rate to the degree that women in the region are having half the number of children that their mothers did three or four decades ago (2.9, as compared to 6.2 children per mother). This fall in the fertility rate, along with a rise in life expectancy, has modified the structure of the household and society, including the demographic bonus (associated with a more favorable relationship between individuals who are occupationally active or passive), with potential benefits from a rise in the availability of goods per capita, the reduction of income inequality and the inequality of opportunities, and greater gender equality.

A new division of labor within the household represents a second change stemming from the progressive incorporation of women in the labor market. This is perhaps the greatest sociodemographic change in Latin America in the last few decades. This resulted in not only reduced poverty and income inequality, but also improvements in women's self-esteem and dignity, including their incorporation into the public sphere. We will see below, however, that each one of these changes brings with it diverse costs and important implications in terms of welfare systems and social policies.

An example of these costs relates to a third change that Larrañaga notes—the growth of the population comprised of older adults, to the extent that this sector requires new types of financing and health care. Like the situation of children, the increasing vulnerability of older adults is related to women's progressive absence from the household and new modalities in the relationship between the state and the family. The growth in the number of older adults is related to the decrease in fertility rates and/or the rise in life expectancy, which increased from fifty-six years in 1960 to seventy-two years in 2010.

A fourth change refers to the types of families in the region and alternative forms of marriage associated with new cultural and social patterns. The changes Latin American countries are experiencing include an increase in separations, cohabitation, single mothers, children who grow up without their biological father, and, in general, the fragmentation of the traditional nuclear family. Although there has always been a double standard in Latin American families that came out of traditional European patriarchy based on masculine domination and a woman's obedience, on the one hand, and the establishment of informal couples, extramarital births, consensual unions, and children living in single-parent homes, on the other, it tends to reinforce the sociodemographic changes that I outline above, with strong implications in terms of social policy.

Finally, according to Larrañaga, there are changes related to the role of the family in the transmission of socioeconomic inequality. The family is one of the key social institutions in the reproduction of social inequality, as evidenced, for example, by the formation of couples among peers: that is, couples that share the same socioeconomic characteristics (homogamy). This widespread practice of economic segregation in the formation of couples reproduces inequality. All of the changes mentioned above, centered on the role of the family and of women, are similar to those experienced by developed countries as an aspect of the modernization of economic and social structures. Although many of these changes point in a positive direction, especially from the perspective of social cohesion, which I will examine below, they bring with them strong modifications not only in terms of existing social and cultural patterns, but also in terms of social policies, with both positive and negative implications.

## SOCIAL WELFARE REGIMES

The economic and social changes experienced in Latin America around the end of the twentieth century, some of which I mentioned above, bring with them a new way of understanding social welfare regimes.[2] The new reality in middle-income countries that find themselves in an intermediate stage of development, with a new middle sector based on their

2. I define "welfare regime" as the set of rules, institutions, actors, and structured interests that produce results in terms of social welfare.

insertion into the global economy, has strong implications for existing social welfare regimes in Latin America. This is a very different reality than the one that exists in developed countries (principally European, in terms of the welfare state). Based on the work of Esping-Andersen, Mario Marcel (in Tironi 2008) contends that in capitalist developed countries, social welfare regimes have been established on the basis of various types of linkages between the state, the market, and businesses. Depending on what is emphasized, those welfare regimes with a heavier emphasis on the state correspond to a "social democratic" regime (Sweden, Denmark), while those with a greater emphasis on the market correspond to a "liberal" regime (United States, Canada, New Zealand, Great Britain), and those that emphasize businesses—and to a lesser extent, the state— correspond with a regime type that Esping-Andersen calls "conservative-corporatist" (Germany, Italy).

Latin America differs from the existing model in developed countries in the sense that, along with the state, the market, and businesses, the family has a strong presence—one of the critiques aimed at Esping-Andersen is that he neglected to include an analysis of the family in the southern European cases, which are much closer to the Latin American cases—as does the underground, informal economy. This corresponds to a much more complex reality that can be divided into four types of welfare regimes. At one end stand potential welfare states (PWS), which correspond to those that, historically, combined import substitution with various social security systems, counting on a more active state and greater democratic continuity and institutional solidity (Argentina, Brazil, Chile, Costa Rica, and Uruguay). At the opposite end stand "informal-privatized" regimes, characterized by a virtual absence of the state as a significant welfare provider, with informality, the market, and/or the family replacing the state, with serious internal conflicts and weak political institutions within structures that could qualify as premodern and precapitalist (El Salvador, Guatemala, Honduras, Nicaragua, Paraguay, and Peru). Between these two extremes are two intermediate levels. On one side is a type of social welfare regime that Marcel calls "conservative," in that the principal providers are businesses and the family, with a strong presence of nontributary income (oil) and a history of disparate political institutions (Ecuador, Mexico, and Venezuela). On the other side is a "dual" regime with a strong underground, informal economy and, to a lesser extent, market and state presence, with significant levels of conflict (Bolivia, Colombia, and Panama).

These four social welfare regimes show dissimilar performance levels in the socioeconomic sphere. Thus, for example, the percentage of people living below the poverty line (following the World Bank criteria of US$2 a day) in PWS countries is 8.3 percent, in contrast to the 38.7 percent living below the poverty line in the informal-privatized countries, with a GDP per capita of US$8,714 in the former and a GDP per capita of US$4,194 in the latter. While the PWS use 30 percent of their GDP for public spending, in the informal-privatized countries this figure is only 18 percent, with social spending for the former at 64.5 percent of public spending, in comparison to the social spending of the latter, which stands at 41.6 percent of total public spending. Finally, among other examples that I could cite, while the PWS countries have a tax burden of 18.8 percent of GDP, for the informal-privatized this figure is only 14.8 percent. In general, the two remaining regimes are located in intermediate positions under different parameters.

One of Marcel's conclusions when comparing social welfare regimes in Latin America "in the process of transitioning to modernity" is that "greater state participation in welfare generation and distribution is clearly beneficial from the point of view of social development and does not appear to involve a loss of competitiveness or potential for growth" (206). The contrast between PWS countries and informal-privatized countries is eloquent in this respect. All of this happens within the context of considerably dispersed social indicators, generally high poverty, and unequal income distributions. Marcel adds that despite high levels of inequality, the majority of countries in the region are considered to be in an "intermediate stage of development."

The social and economic changes that I have briefly described above, like brushstrokes painting a much more complex reality full of tensions and contradictions, have a series of implications as to how to address the issues of poverty and inequality, especially from the point of view of public and social policy. Thus, for example, according to Marcel (as he has expressed in various works and presentations), this new social reality implies passing from a static approach—a photograph capturing the number of poor people living above or below the poverty line—to a dynamic approach—a movie—in which social policies consider the situation of those sectors that go in and out of poverty, attending to the vulnerability of distinct social sectors from the broader perspective of social mobility. This entails attending to the reality of the new middle sector along with the reality of the poor and extremely poor. As the relative importance of the poor and extremely poor shrinks, it becomes necessary to move from the traditional tactic of "targeting" poverty and extreme poverty, typical of a static, or traditional, approach, to a focus on "universalizing" benefits and/or social rights—according to the approach or perspective adopted—that comes out of what in Europe is known as the welfare state or what in Latin America is generally known as a social safety net. This suggests that countries must meet the needs and demands of the whole population, especially the most vulnerable sectors, which, as I have already mentioned, are not limited to areas of poverty and extreme poverty.

What I describe above raises the question of how sustainable actual levels of social spending and the tax burden are over time, given the new reality of middle-income countries. My hypothesis is that it is not. In a region with elevated levels of poverty (34 percent, equivalent to 184 million in poverty in 2007), that is considered the most unequal in the world (with a Gini coefficient of 0.53, compared to 0.45 in Asia and sub-Saharan Africa and 0.36 in Europe, central and southern Asia, and developed countries) (Lustig 2009), that is in the process of modernization and in an intermediate stage between underdevelopment and development, questioning of the amount of fiscal effort this implies is inevitable. This assumes, of course, that we ask this at the levels of both social spending and the tax burden, as well as investigating the efficiency of both.

Average government spending in Latin America in the middle of the 2000s was 25 percent of GDP, compared to 40 percent in OECD countries. In terms of per capita public spending, the difference between Latin America and the OECD countries is 1 to 20. (The following data are taken from Marcel and Rivera and from Meller, both in Cardoso and Foxley 2009.) Social spending represents 48 percent of the average spending in OECD countries. In relation to GDP, public social spending in Latin America (on average) is 11.5 percent, varying between 5 and 23 percent depending on the country—the OECD figure in 2003 is 29 percent of GDP, almost triple. In general, this is moderately redistributive spending, with greater levels of targeting (for the most poor) on primary education and health, compared to more regressive social spending on higher education and pensions. From the point of view of these social spending components, we could say that the more developed the country—particularly in the case of PWS countries—the more it spends on pensions, and the poorer the state, the more it spends on education. From the perspective of economic cycles, social spending has been fairly procyclical, which means that in times of plenty it increases, while in times of busts it decreases, thus affecting sectors with fewer resources when they need help from the state the most. Social spending in Latin America has had a markedly welfare-oriented character (*asistencialista*), without ignoring that since 2000 we have seen interesting results in terms of conditional cash transfers, a frontal attack on poverty and extreme poverty in the short term rather than the creation of human capital in the long term (which was, at least initially, one of the declared objectives of these programs).

Lower social spending and a lower tax burden are two characteristics of social and economic development in Latin America that are entirely insufficient to account for the new social realities I have described above. The region's tax burden in 2005 was 16 percent of GDP—half of the tax burden in OECD countries—notwithstanding that total tax revenues grew by the equivalent of 4.5 percent of GDP between 1992 and 2008. These revenues are strongly supported by indirect taxes (9.8 percent of GDP), in comparison to developed countries (5.5 percent of GDP), which place emphasis on direct taxes. Some countries in the region, such as Mexico, Venezuela, and Ecuador, are dependent on natural resources (oil) and strongly rest on nontax revenues (a third of all total revenue in these three countries), thus relaxing internal taxation in terms of direct and indirect taxes.

Several theories attempt to explain the reality of a low tax burden and low social spending in Latin America, especially considering its new status as a region of middle-income countries. Among them, those that put emphasis on state inefficiency in terms of spending—and the subsequent problems of legitimacy associated with them—stand out, as do those that stress the lack of reciprocity between taxpayer contributions and state-provided services—which is critical for the middle sectors. Finally, some theories emphasize resistance from business groups with the capability of applying pressure to prevent a rise in tax levels and, consequently, social spending—in fact, in many recent attempts to carry out tax reform in Latin America, this last factor has been quite decisive (Meller, in Cardoso and Foxley 2009, 275). Be that as it may, existing tax burden and social spending levels are unsustainable when viewed from the perspective of middle-income countries.

One of the principal differences between Latin America and developed (principally European) countries is the very divergent impact of taxes and state transfers in terms of inequality and redistribution. In the case of Europe, the Gini coefficient after taxes and transfers is, on average, ten percentage points lower—that is, less unequal—than the Gini coefficient determined by market income (before taxes and transfers), while in Latin America the difference is only one or two percentage points (Lustig 2009). In other words, income inequality in Latin America before taxes and transfers (market income) is 18 percent higher than in Europe, while income inequality after taxes and transfers (disposable income) is 45 percent higher than in Europe. This means that unlike in Europe, taxes and state transfers have a very low redistributive effect in Latin America in terms of reducing market-driven income inequality. Perhaps, in the case of Latin America, social spending has a greater redistributive impact than taxes.

In more qualitative terms, one could say that government social programs, principally in terms of social spending, recently began to timidly and gradually take notice of these new middle sectors, especially insofar as targeting (of poverty and extreme poverty) continues to be the general trend. One of the principal challenges to tackle is how to direct fiscal resources to emerging middle sectors and identify the most vulnerable sectors among them in a dynamic rather than static way, focusing on universal rather than targeted benefits. According to Marcel, the signs of demographic transition that Latin America has experienced—such as the fall in fertility rates, along with reduced infant mortality rates, the rise in life expectancy, increases in education levels, and the incorporation of women into the workplace—should result in greater pressure (voice) on the political system and political actors, thereby strengthening the fiscal component of the fight against poverty and extreme poverty and at the same time redirecting these forces towards supporting the growing middle sectors that are one of the most characteristic elements of the new social question in Latin America. State and institutional weakness and low levels of social spending are incompatible with the dynamics of a region characterized by the existence of middle-income countries.

## THE SOCIAL COHESION PERSPECTIVE

The question of what prevents a "social explosion" in Latin America, given its extensive poverty and inequality—which, despite the important advances of the last five years, remains a continuous element throughout history—and the new threats that loom over the region, such as crime and corruption (new in their breadth and depth), inevitably emerges. Answers go beyond the fact of living in a democracy or the more recent experience of the virtuous half-decade of 2003 to 2007). In other words, a question arises as to what keeps us united (cohesive) as a society, beyond the ills, problems, and threats, old and new, that afflict the region. In the rest of this chapter, I suggest that perhaps the most appropriate way to approach old and new social issues is through the concept of "social cohesion," both what makes it possible and what threatens it—that is, what sustains it and what erodes it.

In a broad sense, the question about social cohesion refers to the question of modernity and its disruptive effects on traditional ties (solidarity and community ties) that have historically kept society united. Today, after the recent experience of neoliberal reforms and under the hegemony of neoclassical paradigms, with their emphasis on a supposed "spontaneous order" based on interaction between individuals, contracts, and markets (Peña and Tironi, in Tironi 2008, starting on 19), it may be even more difficult to ask what makes social cohesion possible. It is not the result of the market's invisible hand, nor does it automatically stem from human nature or emerge by divine design. Social cohesion does not exist in a natural state; it is instead either created or broken. Social cohesion is "that force or action through which individuals belonging to a society are held together" (Tironi 2008, 323). It is the glue that keeps a collective united around a certain sense of belonging.

In the interests of my analysis and from a comparative perspective, one could say that there are three principal models of social cohesion: the European model, the U.S. model, and the Latin American model (Sorj and Tironi 2007). Each one has its own specificity and accounts for various methods of understanding and approaching social cohesion, taking into account particular historical, economic, social, and cultural configurations.

The European model comes out of two great historical confrontations: the religious wars of the seventeenth century, which gave rise to the modern concept of the state ("absolutist state" in a Hobbesian sense), and the social class conflicts that emerged during the process of industrialization in the nineteenth century, which gave rise to the welfare state that developed throughout the twentieth century. Thus, the state is the key factor that binds together European society. The European social model, or welfare state, took shape around the extension of social rights, with a broad definition of citizenship that referred to the exercise of civil, political, and social rights. The 2005 Council of Europe defines social cohesion as "the capacity of a society to ensure the well-being of all its members, minimizing disparities and avoiding marginalization. A cohesive society is a mutually supportive community of free individuals pursuing these common goals by democratic means." Returning to Tironi and Sorj's analysis, it was the social-democratic tradition, with its emphasis on the state, politics, and rights, and the social-Christian tradition, with its emphasis on the family, civil society, and community life, both sharing anti-individualist sentiments, that imposed themselves on the old continent around the European social model. Said model stressed the role of the state, public policy, and social policy in creating and assuring adequate levels of social cohesion. This is what kept European society unified and cohesive. The biggest challenge today, in the context of the eruption of globalization and neoliberalism, is how to reinforce the foundations of social cohesion without losing competitiveness in the new global economy, with special concern for the issues of migration, unemployment, and urban violence.

The U.S. model is distinct from the European model. In contrast to the Old World, with its longstanding traditions and history, the New World appears as the land of opportunity, based on individual effort and upward mobility. Unlike in the European model, in the U.S. model social cohesion is not based so much on the state as on civil society, the ethic of the individual, and the market, which is the principal distribution mechanism for welfare and knowledge (Sorj and Tironi 2007). It promises not equality, but social mobility founded on merit and individual effort (the American dream). The European model revolves around a true culture of social rights, developed principally through state action, while the U.S. model moves at the hand of the individual, civil society, and its interaction with the market. It is the agreement between private parties that shapes the nation's social and political body. Such is the original spirit of the Founding Fathers, which continuously recreates itself through the multiple civil associations that keep U.S. society glued together and cohesive, as Tocqueville noted in the first half of the nineteenth century.

In the concrete reality of Latin America, the concept of social cohesion has very different foundations and characteristics when compared to the two previous models. In contrast to Europe, where the concept of social cohesion originated, Latin America did not suffer the dramatic breakdowns of the social order that Europe experienced during the religious wars and class struggles that finally resulted in the concept of the state I describe above (including the welfare state). Neither the state nor civil society explains social cohesion in Latin America. Rather, community relations and a cultural ethos have historically acted as the main factors for social cohesion in the region, making social disorder less likely (Cousiño and Valenzuela 1996). For example, *mestizaje* (ethnic mixing) helped to neutralize the differences between ethnicities and prevent tensions that could have led to segregation or apartheid and the breakdown of social cohesion. In turn, evangelization carried out by the Catholic Church ensured that religious differences did not reach critical levels, as they did in Europe in the seventeenth century. Despite the recent eruption of Evangelical churches, religious differences still have not led to social disorder. Political differentiation has been addressed on the basis of certain types of reciprocity between the governors and the governed, based on different types of authority related to the exchange of favors and loyalty, such as patronage, *caciquismo*, and populism. Finally, in terms of economic differentiation, despite the enormous differences that exist, Latin America has not historically experienced hunger, and, with the exception of the Mexican Revolution, the countryside has been relatively peaceful due to an abundance of natural (agricultural) resources, a low population density, and particular characteristics of the old agrarian order. In sum, familial and community relationships, a culture of reciprocity, *mestizaje*, evangelization, patronage, *caciquismo*, and populism, among other things, have historically supported social cohesion in Latin America. This has ensured that ethnic, social, political, and religious differences and existing polarization have not arrived at the critical levels that other regions have reached (typically in Europe).

It is worth asking the question of which factors contribute to both maintaining and eroding social cohesion in Latin America today. In this respect, the ECosociAl survey, conducted by CIEPLAN, the Fernando H. Cardoso Institute, and the Kellogg Institute for International Studies in major cities in seven Latin American countries (Mexico, Guatemala, Colombia, Brazil, Argentina, Peru, and Chile) in 2007 gives us a new and interesting background to the previous question. From a comparative perspective, we could say that in contrast to the associative Tocquevillian tradition present in U.S. society, Latin America has a weak civil society accompanied by high levels of distrust and fear, which affects cooperation and civic engagement (Valenzuela et al 2008). In turn, unlike in more egalitarian models, such as European models based on equitable resource distribution and welfare opportunities made possible by specific institutional arrangements, huge inequalities persist in Latin America, with strong levels of distrust in the state and in institutions.

There are three main phenomena that erode or threaten social cohesion in Latin America. First, social disorder and its counterparts, insecurity and fear, which are disposed to resent collective action and cooperation. Existing levels of victimization and fear indicate that crime looms as one of the main threats to social cohesion, especially in the largest cities (there is no data from rural areas in the survey). One could say that although there is no potential for macroviolence (revolution), there is still potential for urban microviolence (murder, crime, drug trafficking, organized crime, and street gangs, among others). The extent to which the micro level will affect the macro level remains to be seen. Suffice it to say that, along with being the most unequal region in the world, Latin America has the highest homicide rates in the world.

The second phenomenon is distrust of those outside one's own personal circle and the accompanying feelings of discrimination and intolerance. An elevated proportion of respondents report a lack of interpersonal trust, especially towards those outside their intimate circle (family, friends, neighbors), along with modest levels of associativity. Finally, the third phenomenon is distrust in and distance from political institutions and a strong sense of alienation towards political power, which makes democratic loyalty rates suffer. This often manifests in the degree of justification for extraconstitutional mechanisms, especially in countries such as Guatemala and Mexico. In general, one could say that insecurity and crime are the biggest threat to social cohesion in Latin America.

Considering that not only the state but also civil society are weak, unlike in Europe and the US, respectively, what are the factors that maintain social cohesion in Latin America? According to the ECosociAl survey and the work of Valenzuela et al (2008), the following are the principal factors that support social cohesion in Latin America: first, the solidarity or basic ties within the family, friendship, and the neighborhood, and, most importantly, loyalty to the nation. Interestingly, despite the existence of the typical phenomena associated with modernization, such as growing individualism, important ties to tradition and community remain. These ties include links to the family and the nation and, to a lesser extent, friends and neighbors. In the case of family, it remains to be seen to what extent the profound sociodemographic changes mentioned above, especially women's incorporation into the labor market, will affect social cohesion. Given what we know of history, this raises the need for a new relationship between the state and the family. In the case of the nation, it should be noted that this tie, which has a strong popular component, is one of the strongest elements of social cohesion in Latin America, well above regional or ethnic identity: "national identity largely prevails over any ethnic or regional identity" (59). This symbolic national strength allows the nation to survive weak state institutions, even though we still do not know what effects globalization will have in the future.

Second, in their discussion of ECosociAl, Valenzuela et al (2008) note the existence of relatively low levels of political, ethnic, socioeconomic, and religious polarization in the region; these, along with high expectations for mobility, contribute to the maintenance of social cohesion. Despite high levels of socioeconomic inequality, there are generally low levels of polarization—understood as high identification with a member group (the poor, for example)—and an equally high hostility towards the nonmember group (the rich, for example). Even though there is some religious polarization, especially in countries such as Mexico and Colombia, socioeconomic, ethnic, and political polarization is not clearly visible in Latin America. Low levels of social polarization offer a certain legitimacy to social inequality, in that the factors attributed to poverty and wealth are more associated with individual achievement than with ascriptive or systemic factors. Thus, wealth (or poverty) is an achievement that is acquired rather than ascribed (through inheritance, influence, or contacts): "although with differing intensity, the culture of achievement clearly prevails over the culture of adscription and this occurs horizontally over all social strata: not only wealth but also poverty is associated more with effort and merit than with origin, fate, or the social system" (57).

Third, the cohesive effect produced by elevated levels of educational mobility, as witnessed by significant advances in terms of primary and secondary education—including, in some countries, at the level of higher education—adds (and contributes) to optimistic expectations of mobility. It is striking how heavily social cohesion relies on the high levels of educational mobility Latin America has experienced, which tend to weaken or neutralize the effects of extremely unequal income distribution. These figures, according to Valenzuela et al, prop up an "exaggerated optimism" towards upward social mobility, as they are most likely disproportionate to objectively reported indicators of the education system and the labor market. The 2008 to 2009 financial and economic crisis may have thwarted these expectations, especially when compared to the recently experienced virtuous half-decade.

Since the end of the 1990s, when Latin America found itself in the middle of the profound structural transformations that moved principally in pro-growth and pro-market directions, various authors have argued for the need for a more dynamic focus on the relationship between poverty and inequality, taking up the issue of mobility. Graham and Pettinato (1999), for example, explore the relationship between objective measures of inequality and social mobility and subjective variables such as self-evaluations of past social mobility and expectations for future mobility in an attempt to respond to the question of why some societies peacefully tolerate high levels of inequality when others do not. They arrive at two conclusions: on the one hand, over time, opportunities and mobility are as important as actual income distribution; on the other hand, subjective evaluations of past mobility and expectations for future mobility are as important as objective trends. As for the implications of this analysis for public policy, the authors suggest that the level of macroeconomic volatility and existing social protection programs are key to understanding the differences in the relative importance individuals attribute to the market/state and growth/redistribution. Thus, for example, the data show that in countries that have experienced more recent crises and reforms, that have managed to stabilize, and that have low levels of social protection, people tend to favor pro-market, pro-growth policies and are less likely to support state redistribution. This suggests that in the context of economic volatility, citizens reward growth and stability. In turn, in countries that have more stabilizing reforms and better social protection systems, individuals adopt a more favorable position towards redistribution and the state than toward growth and the market.

One year after Graham and Pettinato, Nancy Birdsall and Carol Graham (2000) wrote a book on the effects of market reforms introduced in Latin America in the 1990s, during the process of democratization. The authors approach the topic from the angle of mobility, using both objective and subjective variables. They question whether the new trends in mobility and opportunity found in Latin America, related to pro-market and pro-growth reforms imposed by the state and associated with poverty reduction (if not inequality), could have some effect on support (legitimacy) for economic reforms. In other words, they ask if the market reforms of the times created (or did not create) new opportunities for individuals in the context of the enormous economic and social mobility in a changing world. Perhaps for the first time in history, Latin America advanced simultaneously in the directions of democracy and the market, which generated questions of legitimacy, sustainability, and what implications these changes have. Based on the fact that there were no advances in terms of inequality—in fact, it regressed—the question is whether individual (upward) mobility and the opportunities associated with these social and economic changes, based on a more meritocratic system, compensated in some way for the deficits of social inequality.

The central idea put forward by Birdsall and Graham is that mobility is a better form of measurement of the new opportunities that emerge from the social and economic changes described above than traditional ways of measuring inequality (such as the Gini index), which do not sufficiently take into account how actors either objectively or subjectively perceive these changes. Along with noting a certain satisfaction with the possibility of upward mobility on the basis of merit and individual effort, the authors warn that there is also a fairly widespread concern for the lack of an adequate social safety net for the most vulnerable sectors and a deficit of efficient state institutions. This double perception, they conclude, could come to erode the legitimacy of pro-market reforms and the democratic institutions that sustain them.

The point remains that both the foundations of and threats to social cohesion in Latin America have to be seen in a dynamic way, as an always changing, permanently moving reality. This brings us back to the central role of public policies, which can either sustain or erode social cohesion. As Tironi summarized in an April 15, 2009, speech at the University of Notre Dame, social cohesion is a "public good" that public policies should foster. Community relations and cultural foundations are not enough to sustain social cohesion in Latin America. Nor should we consider the absence of major conflicts (polarization)—at least at critical levels—to be synonymous with social cohesion, just as social inequality does not, on its own, disrupt social cohesion. Social cohesion is a much richer, more complex, and more dynamic concept that takes into consideration the profound economic, social, and cultural changes that Latin America has experienced over the last two decades. These changes suggest the need to place public policies at the center of the debate, moving away from the traditional way of addressing poverty and inequality towards a new focus related to the new social question that characterizes Latin America as a group of middle-income countries situated in an intermediate stage between underdevelopment and development.

As we have seen, the public policy approach has occupied a central role in European social cohesion. Although Latin America has its own specificities in relation to both the European model and the U.S. model, the changes described above bring with them a need for a new social contract that redefines the traditional relationships between the state, the market, businesses, the family, and the informal market, with new fiscal agreements—and public and social policies in general—that take charge of the new reality of middle-income countries, characterized by the emergence of new middle sectors that coexist with those living in poverty and extreme poverty. In countries where poverty and extreme poverty prevail, emphasis must be put on economic growth and education as absolute priorities, using traditional targeting policies. However, in countries that are becoming potential welfare states, redistributive polices intended to bring universal social benefits as well as policies aimed at growth must be stressed.

Thus, the design and implementation of pro–social cohesion public policies should take into account the region's great diversity and respond to each country's reality, avoiding one-size-fits-all formulas in an attempt that considers flexibility when responding to the profound economic and social changes that I describe above. For example, the incorporation of women into the labor market and changes within the family represent a challenge for social welfare regimes. Even now, the family is one of the biggest traditional foundations of social cohesion in Latin America, a fact that raises questions and obstacles in the sphere of public policy in terms of accompanying women in their incorporation in the social and economic (and public) sphere while at the same time supplementing, through new types of public policies, their progressive absence in the household. (Think, for example, of the solidarity and subsistence networks built around the strong presence of women in the care of children and the elderly.) In turn, the great threats posed by an extensive perception of victimization when faced with the reality of crime, especially in metropolitan areas, and the new and ominous characteristics of violence in the region presuppose new forms of action in the realm of public security. Finally, the relationship between education policies and labor markets is one of the central dimensions of this new social reality in terms of significantly rising school enrollment rates and great expectations for social mobility.

The economic and social changes that I briefly describe above should generate new demands and pressures on the state and political actors, which have repercussions as to the type of democracy that we are called to build. In the next and final chapter, I argue that a democracy of institutions is in the best condition to meet these new economic and social demands, which come out of one of the most significant dilemmas facing Latin America: the dilemma between the personalization and institutionalization of power.

# CHAPTER 8

# DEMOCRACY
# OF INSTITUTIONS

As O'Donnell explains (and as we saw in chapter 5), Latin America faces poverty both in the material sense, as a lack of goods, and in a legal sense, as a lack of rights. The implication of this fundamental idea is that the region faces the challenge of providing not only welfare, but also institutions (among other things), so that the provision of material welfare is sustainable across both time and space.

Throughout this book I have defended politics and institutions, a defense that I will systematically develop in this last chapter. Latin America's primary deficits are found at the level of institutions and the state. We need a better state and better institutions. We have elections as never before in our history, but we are still far from being able to say that we have secured representative democracy—an ideal rather than a reality for many Latin American countries—and democratic governance.

The biggest political challenge for Latin America, today and in the future, is the transition from electoral democracy to an authentic representative democracy, while addressing the broader issue of democratic governance. The present chapter revolves around three axes: electoral democracy, representative democracy (understood as democracy of institutions), and democratic governance. I argue that the path towards democratic deepening must be built on gradualism and reformism.

## ELECTORAL DEMOCRACY

Perhaps the greatest lesson that we can learn about Latin America's recent history is the intrinsic value of political democracy understood as a "universal value" (Sen 1999). As we saw in previous chapters, accustomed to a literature detailing the so-called requirements, requisites, prerequisites, or structural conditions for democracy in the social sciences, we have been surprised by the persistence of democracy in the region since the last wave of democratization initiated at the end of the 1970s. Living in a postauthoritarian age, with the decay of different totalitarian and authoritarian regimes (save for some vestiges of the old regime), must have something to do with the revalorization of political democracy and its institutions. Human rights and democracy play central roles in the globalization process that we experience in all spheres of our social, economic, political, and cultural lives. Democracy thus enjoys a new legitimacy, although grave problems and challenges still remain in regard to its practical effectiveness, institutional quality, and the broader question of governance.

It is a solid and encouraging fact that between 2005 and 2010 there were eighteen presidential elections in Latin America (as well as legislative and local elections in many countries). In nine of these eighteen elections (Costa Rica, Peru, Colombia, Brazil, Nicaragua, Venezuela, Bolivia, Dominican Republic, and Ecuador), incumbents ran for reelection, with electoral triumphs for eight (the exception being Bolivia, with the defeat of Jorge Quiroga). There were three cases of alternate reelection (Óscar Arias in Costa Rica, Daniel Ortega in Nicaragua, and Alan García in Peru) and five immediate reelections (Álvaro Uribe in Colombia, Luis Inácio Lula da Silva in Brazil, Hugo Chávez in Venezuela, Leonel Fernández in the Dominican Republic, and Rafael Correa in Ecuador). In two of the eighteen elections, candidates from the governing coalition were elected, both of whom were women: Michelle Bachelet in Chile, and Cristina Fernández in Argentina. The official party won in nine cases, while the opposition won in the other nine cases (for an analysis of the majority of these recent elections, see Zovatto 2007).

The Freedom House 2008 Freedom in the World Report, which measures levels of political freedom and respect for civil liberties, mentions that ten out of the nineteen countries in the region can be considered "free": Argentina, Brazil, Chile, Costa Rica, El Salvador, Mexico, Panama, Peru, Dominican Republic, and Uruguay. In turn, eight of the nineteen Latin American countries can be considered "partly free": Bolivia, Colombia, Ecuador, Guatemala, Honduras, Nicaragua, Paraguay, and Venezuela. Cuba is the only country in the region labeled "not free."

The Democracy Index compiled by *The Economist* includes five indicators that go beyond electoral democracy to include qualitative or substantive aspects. These indicators are: free, transparent, and competitive elections (electoral democracy); due respect for civil liberties as an aspect of liberal democracy; government functioning in accordance with the degree that governmental decisions are implemented; electoral participation as an aspect of citizen participation in public life; and the existence of a democratic political culture. The report does not consider economic and social welfare levels, based on the idea that a variety of socioeconomic levels are compatible with political democracy. The following list is adapted from this report (each country's rank among the 167 countries included is in parentheses):

**"Complete" Democracies (1–30)**
Uruguay (23)
Costa Rica (27)
Chile (32)[1]

**"Imperfect" (or "Defective") Democracies (31–80)**
Brazil (41)
Panama (43)
Mexico (55)
Argentina (56)
Colombia (60)
Paraguay (66)

1. I include Chile in this category because, although *The Economist* includes it in the category of "imperfect" democracies, the scores that separate it from Costa Rica and Uruguay are insignificant. If I did not move Chile, it would appear in the same "imperfect" or "defective" category as Paraguay (66), Peru (70), Bolivia (75), Nicaragua (78), and Guatemala (79), which are much further down the list.

El Salvador (67)
Peru (70)
Dominican Republic (73)
Honduras (74)
Bolivia (75)
Nicaragua (78)
Guatemala (79)

**"Hybrid" Regimes (81–116)**
Ecuador (85)
Venezuela (95)

**Authoritarian Regimes (117–167)**
Cuba (125)

As a region, Latin America is in third place on the Democracy Index: that is, it is below North America and Western Europe, but above the Caribbean, Eastern Europe, Asia and Australia, sub-Saharan Africa, and the Middle East and North Africa. The majority of "imperfect" democracies are found in Latin America, Eastern Europe, and, to a lesser extent, in Asia. In the case of Latin America, the report points out that despite some advances under the most recent wave of democratization, many of the region's countries remain "fragile" democracies, especially in terms of levels of political participation (relatively low) and democratic culture. Phenomena such as *caudillismo* put the region in a comparatively weak position.

Despite these insufficiencies, we should not lose sight of the fact that, from a historical perspective, the third wave of democratization in the region has brought with it an important level of political stability. There is more popular and elite support for democracy than in the past—even though there is a normative deficit in terms of value-based support for democracy—and, contrary to what has historically happened in Latin America, episodes of political instability have not been accompanied by democratic breakdown and coups d'état. Perhaps the best examples of this are cases of impeachment—an extreme form of political failure that proliferated with a singular force between 1992 and 2004—which act as institutional mechanisms for resolving political crises without resorting to military intervention. As Aníbal Pérez-Liñán (2007) writes, Latin America is experiencing new forms of political instability that are distinct from what it has known in the past: "As in previous decades, democratically elected governments continue to fall, but in contrast to previous decades, democratic regimes do not break down" (3). According to the author, this "paradox of democratic regime stability" takes place in the context of presidentialism (as impeachment only occurs under presidentialism), and the type of relationship that exists between the executive and the legislature demonstrates that the legislature is not as destitute in terms of institutional power as is commonly believed in a region known for the strong predominance of presidents and the executive.

## REPRESENTATIVE DEMOCRACY

Economic and social forces do not operate in a political and institutional vacuum. In our most recent history, one of the first to propose the importance of institutions for development was Douglas North (1990), working from the perspective of economics. The economistic reductionism associated with the economic reforms of the 1990s, especially those associated with the Washington Consensus, did nothing but reinforce the need for an institutional framework that made economic and development processes more sustainable. Furthermore, the market reforms made it necessary to rely not only on an adequate institutional framework, but also on a state capable of securing suitable conditions of governance.

Truthfully, democracy is not in crisis in Latin America. In fact, democracy is enjoying more legitimacy than ever before, despite some malaise and discontent, especially in regard to how democracy functions. It is the political systems themselves and the different combinations of presidentialism, multiparty systems, and proportional representation in the region that explain many of the difficulties in consolidating democracy as a political regime. Some of the elements that hinder democratic

consolidation and governance in Latin America include hyperpresidentialism (reinforced or "imperial" presidentialism), government by presidential decree, the deterioration and growing discrediting of legislative
action, the proliferation of constituent assemblies replacing the role of
parliaments, party fragmentation, minority governments, unlimited proportional representation and the lack of incentives for the formation of
stable and majority coalitions, the lack of correspondence between the
majorities represented in the executive and in the legislature, the proliferation of elections and nonconcurrence or simultaneity of presidential and parliamentary elections, the absence of effective checks and balances and of both horizontal and vertical accountability, the absence of a
professional civil service supported by competent technical staff, a lack of
appropriate mechanisms to ensure equity and transparency in political
and electoral financing, and political structures and a political culture
often characterized by the extensive reality of clientelism and patrimonialism, leading to corruption.

One could say that, although we have successfully traveled from dictatorship to electoral democracy, we are still far from consolidating an authentic representative democracy. This consolidation necessarily includes
securing, strengthening, and improving democratic institutions (specifically, governments and parliaments elected freely and democratically, in
strict accordance with the constitution and the law), an effective rule of
law, equality before the law, majority rule with respect for minorities, political pluralism, an independent judiciary with transparent and effective agencies capable of effectively protecting the rights of the people and
ensuring equilibrium between state powers, a properly institutionalized
party system, solid and stable political parties that act as effective vehicles
for political representation, and the respect and protection of fundamental rights and freedoms, among other elements. Merely listing these classic
characteristics of representative democracy demonstrates the enormous
gap that separates it from electoral democracy. In the Latin American context, representative democracy is more of a goal than a reality.

This ambitious goal, understood as the need to advance towards an
authentic representative democracy, is not the result of a purely theoretical, academic, or intellectual exercise. We must remember that the entire
Inter-American system is built around the idea of representative democ-

racy, from the Charter of the OAS in 1948 to the more recent Inter-American Democratic Charter of September 11, 2001. The preamble of the former describes representative democracy as "indispensable for the stability, peace, and development of the region." It continues by stating that one of the "essential purposes" and "principles" of the OAS is the promotion and consolidation of representative democracy. OAS Resolution 1080, "Representative Democracy," passed in 1991, created a series of mechanisms to make representative democracy function effectively. The Inter-American Democratic Charter defined "essential elements" of representative democracy in terms of respect for human rights and fundamental freedoms, adherence to the rule of law, the realization of periodic free and transparent elections based on the secret ballot and universal suffrage stemming from the sovereignty of the people, a pluralist system of political parties and organizations, and the separation and independence of state powers. In turn, the First Summit of the Americas, celebrated in Miami in 1994, declared that representative democracy is the "only political system" capable of guaranteeing certain rights and fundamental freedoms. Thus, adhering to representative democracy constitutes a firm commitment on the part of the thirty-four American states and the backbone of the entire Inter-American system.

Democratic governance requires a political system that enjoys both legitimacy and practical effectiveness in order to make social cohesion possible (see chapter 7). Only a truly representative system can bring these features together, a system that expresses social diversity and can design and implement public policies that balance economic growth, effective equality of opportunities, and protection of the weak. In this regard, there is no substitute for representative democracy. All democracies that can be considered successful are representative democracies. Participation mechanisms and forms of citizen empowerment should be channeled through—and not used as an alternative to—representative democratic institutions. Moving politics to the street is a serious threat to the proper functioning of institutions. Defining politics around modes of direct action by the masses, in the sense of being merely contestive, whether under the label of anarchist, fascist, or populist ideologies, is incompatible with the conception of representative democracy (Flisfisch 2008). In an important sense, a genuine notion of citizenship under a democratic and republican concept of government is based on the primacy of institutions.

From this perspective, I share with Brennan and Hamlin (1999) the view that representative democracy is a "first-best" and a "superior political alternative," especially when compared to so-called direct democracy in its diverse forms and variations. As these authors point out, there has been a certain tendency in the field of democratic theory to describe direct democracy as a superior but impractical—or, at least, difficult to implement—form of democracy. Faced with this idea, theorists accept the indirect form of mediation and decision making that is representative democracy as "second-best." The reality of actually existing democracies, however, especially those that can be considered successful, demonstrates the opposite: namely, that representative democracy is a superior form of government when compared to direct democracy. In addition, representative democracy is the least costly political regime to implement. It is possible to put other political regimes into effect, but not without an extraordinary dose of coercion—think, for example, of the experience of the so-called popular democracies (communism) or organic democracies (fascism, Nazism) throughout the twentieth century, or the more recent experiences of bureaucratic-authoritarian regimes in Latin America's Southern Cone (principally the Chilean case, built around the concept of protected democracy), as some of the proposed alternatives to representative democracy.

## DIRECT OR PARTICIPATORY DEMOCRACIES

The crisis of representation and the "democratic deficit" found in Latin America will not be resolved by replacing representative democracy and its institutions, but rather by perfecting and deepening it. During the recent wave of democratization in Latin America, we have seen many attempts to replace the normal functions of representative democracy's institutions with forms of so-called direct or participatory democracy. For example, between 1978 and 2005, there were thirty-five referendums in eleven countries in Latin America, five of them under authoritarian regimes (Zovatto, in Latinobarómetro 2006). We must recognize that the appeal of direct or participatory democracy is due to the low prestige and legitimacy that institutions such as political parties and parliaments enjoy. These forms of direct democracy supposedly tend to reinforce mechanisms of citizen participation. In practice, however, they often are reduced to manipulating public opinion and the electorate without the distortions of political mediation mechanisms unique to representative democracy, such as parties and parliaments and institutions commonly associated with the rule of law, including an independent judicial system, a supreme court that effectively ensures the enforcement of fundamental rights and freedoms, or a constitutional tribunal that ensures the validity and supremacy of the constitution and the democratic guarantees inherent to it. Appealing directly to the masses (public opinion), governing by presidential decree outside of the institutions and procedures of deliberative and representative democracy, and the use and abuse of constitutive assemblies are some of the recurring practices behind these forms.

As I wrote in chapter 5, the reality and practice of personalist, populist, plebiscitary, and delegative democracy often hides behind the appeal of a certain form of direct or participatory democracy. This form is most often presented as an alternative and superior type of democracy while, in practice, it ends up questioning and bypassing the institutions of representative democracy. Unlike the old populism that grew out of the authoritarian wave of the 1930s and 1940s, this new populism emerged not only during a democratic wave but also with the features of a formal, democratic legitimacy, as evidenced by the fact that the most emblematic populist figures have been elected and reelected at the polls. Ultimately, however, it is not the central role of institutions, but the personal characteristics of charismatic leaders and their identification with the masses that define this type of regime. As René Mayorga (in Mainwaring, Bejarano, and Leongómez 2006, 135) wrote, "unlike historical populism, neopopulism is involved in the democratic game. It accepts the rules of political competition, but at the same time resorts to the higher quality and legitimacy of the leader, who presents himself as the redeemer and embodiment of the people and the nation."

Under the fear and criticism of globalization and neoliberalism and the feelings of abandonment associated with them, people tend to seek refuge or protection in the old model of a charismatic leader and a national and popular state. They have ambivalent feelings about the emergence of democracy and a market economy (Correa 2007). When fear of abandonment dominates enthusiasm for new opportunities, people run to stand behind caudillos and their proposals of democracy "with adjectives." Such action affects, threatens, and erodes the fundamental foundations of democratic regimes. The history of *caciquismo, caudillismo*, and the exercise of personalist power have important antecedents in pre-Colombian, colonial, and postcolonial history in Latin America, in the context of patrimonial (or neopatrimonial) structures and a political culture that prevents the delineation of a clear line between the public and the private spheres. Moreover, these types of personalist regimes are the product or outcome of a complex series of events that cause distress and despair.

As I outlined in chapter 5, this new populism is based on the crisis of traditional political institutions, such as political parties and parliaments and the emergence of new demands and social movements that are not satisfied with or channeled by traditional systems. All this emerged within the context of neoliberal experiments in the 1980s and 1990s, with grave social and political implications. In this sense, the problem in Latin America is not populism itself, but the causes of populism. We cannot ignore that these types of regimes "with adjectives" have real social bases. The populist phenomenon often manages to appeal to feelings and emotions that do not resonate in and are not received by the formal procedures of representative democracy, whose institutions are sometimes seen as removed from people's daily lives, especially by the popular sectors. This new populism has symbolically filled a void left by representative democracy's institutions, which are seen as distant and merely formal, if not corrupt or decaying.

None of the above should lead us to discard the existence, under suitable conditions, of an important space for direct citizen consultation and public participation. This is, typically, the role of local government, where direct citizen participation is not only possible but also desirable and recommended for matters pertaining to municipalities and prefectures, among other forms of local government administration. Participatory budgeting, for example, has been attempted with both good and bad results, varying from place to place. It is also possible to stage plebiscites or referendums at critical junctures, such as political regime changes, or on issues of national interest that make direct consultation of the public necessary. But these mechanisms of direct or participatory democracy should complement rather than replace the normal functioning of representative democracy and its institutions. Plebiscites, referendums, and other mechanisms of direct citizen participation should be the exceptions rather than the rule.

## DEMOCRACY OF INSTITUTIONS

Institutionalization versus personalization of power: this is one of the principal dilemmas concerning democracy as a political regime in Latin America. As I argue above, there is an evident tension in the region between political democracy—either representative democracy or democracy of institutions, which I use here interchangeably—and personalistic, populist, plebiscitary, and delegative democracy. Although the latter appeals to supposedly direct or participatory democracy, it ends up threatening, ignoring, or suppressing the value and validity of the institutions of representative democracy. Invoking the old contrast between "substantive" and "formal" democracy and the idea of a democracy "of results" based on "real equality," these modalities of direct or participatory democracy end up threatening and undermining democracy's very foundations and destroy the formal equality unique to constitutional democracy.

Following Przeworski (1991, 39), I define democracy as a "system of institutions" that aspires to gain spontaneous commitment from all major political forces (principally political parties) based on political-electoral competition and the uncertainty of electoral results. According to Przeworski, democracy is "a system in which parties lose elections," a system, therefore, based on the institutionalization of uncertainty. In order to last, democracy should marshal the spontaneous support of the principal political forces by appealing to the pursuit of their own self-interest. Using game theory, the author argues that democracy should be understood in terms of the equilibrium of autonomous political forces' decentralized strategies. Democracy provides the "institutional framework" that makes competition between multiple political forces possible—in this sense it is a "system of institutions." These institutions and the free interplay of political forces that pursue their own particular interests make this equilibrium and a "system of self-government" possible. This is what characterizes democracy as a political regime. Ultimately, institutions are what make a difference.

Democracy of institutions, understood as a self-sustaining political system capable of producing concrete results for its citizens, is the most conducive to democratic governance. As I argued in chapter 5, this is particularly pertinent to democratic consolidation in a context favorable to the appearance of personalistic leaders. The consolidation of democratic political institutions is the best antidote against personalistic democracy. This implies procedures or rules of the game that level the playing field so that all players are able to participate equally. There is an obvious tension or a sort of trade-off between the strength of institutions and the appearance of the personalistic leaders that have been so distinctive of the tradition of *caciquismo* and *caudillismo* in Latin America. The previous argument is directed not against the necessary and irreplaceable role of leadership in a democracy, but instead against the idea that leadership can replace institutions. We need leaders rather than caudillos. An adequate relationship between institutions and leaders is necessary for the strengthening of democracy.

Thus, emphasizing democracy of institutions should not lead us to underestimate the irreplaceable role of leadership and political actors. Institutions act as a system of incentives for political actors who move intentionally. Political institutions correspond to institutional arrangements that affect political actors' behavior through incentives or restrictions. Institutions can doubtlessly be changed and perfected, but there are limits to institutional engineering. Actors' preferences and orientations should especially be taken into account. If institutions and institutional arrangements can make a difference for democratic stability and governance, such preferences cannot be separated from the type of leadership and the role political actors play in the democratic process.

What is certain is that, although it is a great advancement, we cannot stop at electoral democracy if we want a stable, consolidated democracy in Latin America with acceptable conditions of governance. A 2004 report from the United Nations Development Programme (UNDP) calls for the transition from electoral democracy—a significant advance in Latin America's recent history—to a "citizens' democracy." The report shows the latter as superior to a purely minimalist or procedural conception of democracy. It maintains that democracy is more than a simple method for electing rulers. It is the old and ever-present question of the person defined as the subject of rights and responsibilities seen from the broader perspective of "full citizenship," understood as the effective exercise of political, civil, and social rights. Democracy is seen as an integral part of this broader definition of rights, in which the key player is a citizen rather than simply a voter. Without ignoring the results electoral democracy obtained in terms of the exercise of political rights, this proposal aims to effectively extend "social citizenship." Democracy should be seen in terms of its capacity to enforce citizens' rights, including the broad range of political, civil, and social rights. Thus, electoral democracy should not be considered outside the persistence of poverty and inequality, which constitute the most pressing problems in Latin America. The democratic deficit covers not only institutional insufficiencies, which require more or better democracy, but also the challenges of greater equality in terms of economic and social development. There is a contradiction between the formal equality of political democracy, on the one hand, and the de facto social and economic inequality present in the region on the other hand. In this context, the "political crisis" refers not only to parties and representative institutions, but also to the state's inability to address citizens' demands. In sum, "democracy of citizenship is more comprehensive than the political system and the mere exercise of political rights. Democracy must be extended into the realm of civil and social rights" (62). Weak states and fragile democracies in Latin America, in which legal equality and de facto inequality contradictorily remain, make it necessary to move in the suggested direction.

I believe that the contents of the UNDP report briefly summarized above are perfectly compatible with the concept of democracy of institutions that I present here. This concept of citizenship cannot be seen separately from the central concern of institutions (as citizenship itself is an institution, conforming to the republican understanding of democracy).

The citizens' democracy that the UNDP report describes, set against the backdrop of the concepts of human development developed by Amartya Sen's and Guillermo O'Donnell's theories on democracy, is an aspect of the democracy of institutions that I advocate as necessary and desirable for Latin America, in order to deepen representative democracy and its institutions.

One difference I would like to note between the report and my own views on the subject is that, in my judgment, what the authors of the UNDP report call "preconditions" (or prerequisites) for a well-functioning democracy in terms of its capacity to solve people's problems—principally in the economic and social spheres—should not be considered intrinsic elements of political or representative democracy or democracy of institutions. They are, instead, requirements that democracy must meet in terms of effectiveness or governance. As I argue below, I think these requirements or conditions for effectiveness relate more to the challenges of governance than to inherent attributes of democracy as a political regime. In fact, representative democracies that exist in the world coexist with different types of economic and social inequality, varying from place to place.

Finally, depicting representative democracy as democracy of institutions does not suggest a preference for one institution over another. Just as I reject claims of one-size-fits-all economic reforms, I also reject any such claims in the area of institutional reforms. In fact, a great institutional variety stands out in Latin America's recent history, where federal and unitary systems and proportional, majoritarian, and mixed electoral systems coexist, with different levels of institutionalization and fragmentation. Dani Rodrik (2007, 52) points out that at the institutional level in the economic sphere, the function is more important than the form. This translates to the formula, "one economics, many recipes," or the idea that "[institutional] function does not map uniquely into [institutional] form." The same can be said of political institutions, which can take many forms despite serving the same purpose or function.

Something similar occurs with the form of government and the apparent difficulty in reconciling presidential forms of government with multiparty systems (which has been sufficiently documented in the literature). One can find many examples of solutions to this in Latin America, including coalition presidentialism (see chapter 6). Instead of seeing Latin American presidentialism as a sort of anomaly, we should see it as a specific model situated in between U.S. presidentialism—a two-party system based on a very particular formula of checks and balances and a particular relationship between the executive and the legislature—and European parliamentarism, a form that is more in line with multiparty democracy. What is certain is that there are no ideal institutions. This extends to the question of the form of government (presidential or parliamentary) as well. There are a variety of institutions in Latin America, hidden among the menu of options aimed at ensuring adequate conditions of governance, that should lead us away from simplistic or dogmatic positions and towards a greater pragmatism. Rodrik (2008) argues that in the field of political reforms in developing countries, due to market or government failures in specific contexts that cannot be fixed in the short term, many times policymakers should opt for "second-best institutions" rather than "best-practice institutions." A variety of institutions exist in both developing and developed countries that serve particular objectives. In contrast to the "best practice" bias proposed by multilateral agencies such as the World Bank, the International Monetary Fund (IMF), and the World Trade Organization (WTO), reformers in the developing world operate in a "second-best environment." This suggests not that we should reject the search for best practices, but rather that we should recognize that reality is much more complex and diverse.

What matters beyond this or that particular institution is the combination of institutions or the type of institutional arrangements that allow us to advance towards the objective of governance, focusing on the reality of each country.


## DEMOCRATIC GOVERNANCE

Representative democracy, or democracy of institutions, is a necessary but not sufficient condition for democratic governance. Before moving on to a more detailed analysis, we should have an accurate idea of the concept of democratic governance. This term gains a certain complexity if we consider that "governance" refers to a democratic government's capacity to produce or ensure certain results in the economic and social spheres. Governance is linked more to policies than to politics, political processes, and political institutions. It refers to the question of delivery and performance, that is, the capacity of a democracy to ensure not only a certain legitimacy of political institutions but also certain results in the economic and social spheres from the standpoint of practical efficacy. Behind this conception lies a perception, as measured in diverse qualitative and quantitative studies of public opinion in Latin America, of the incapacity of political systems—and states—to adequately attend to the social demands of the populace. This brings with it the risk of a system-wide loss of legitimacy, eventually leading to ingovernability and the consequent search for alternatives to representative democracy and its institutions.

In the fields of political theory and comparative politics, various authors argue for the need to move beyond defining democracy as a political regime in order to include economic and social dimensions. For example, Przeworski points to the need to link the theme of "institutions" with certain economic and social "conditions" in the sense of substantive results—this is the old question, as he points out, of "social conditions of democracy" (1991, 26). Similarly, O'Donnell argues that a "democratic regime" is a "fundamental component" of democracy, but that it is "insufficient" for an adequate conceptualization of democracy (in O'Donnell, Vargas, and Iazetta 2004, 9). According to O'Donnell, political democracy (or polyarchy, or a democratic regime—they can be considered synonyms) is not sufficient for a complete understanding of democracy in terms of citizenship broadly defined, which includes the exercise of civil, political, and social rights. Scott Mainwaring and Timothy Scully offer a definition of democratic governance as the "capacity of democratic governments to implement policies that enhance citizen well-being and rights" (2008, 13). Thus, successful democratic governance comes from the government's capacity to maintain political practices of a reasonably high quality in terms of contributing to its country's economic progress and citizen security, while effectively facing major social problems like poverty, income distribution, and social services. It is therefore not only about democraticness, but also effectiveness—that is, not only the good health of democratic institutions, but also good state performance in the form of concrete results in the sphere of public policy. Finally, Payne, Zovatto, and Mateo Díaz (2007, 86) define "democratic governance" as "includ[ing] the capacity to adopt or implement decisions that adequately respond to a country's most pressing economic and social problems"—set against the background, they add, of Latin America's "political instability" and the "institutional weakness" from the 1950s to the 1980s.

Here I distinguish between the intrinsic qualities or attributes of democracy as a political regime and the economic and social conditions seen from the point of view of governance. In a broad sense, I understand democratic governance as a societal capacity to govern itself and, in a more narrow sense, the capacity of a political system and its institutions—and ultimately, the state—to peacefully and effectively absorb, channel, and process citizens' economic and social demands. It is particularly necessary to define governance conceptually in the case of Latin America, which currently faces a revolution of expectations within the framework of the political democratization, economic growth, and profound social changes that have occurred since the mid-1990s. This revolution of expectations implies greater impatience with or, put another way, a lower tolerance for the social inequalities that remain an element of continuity between the before and after of the most recent (and not-so-recent) processes of democratization.

As Latin America begins to further resemble middle-income countries through a process of integration into the world economy and profound changes in economic and social structures (see chapter 7), challenges to democratic governance impose certain requirements on democratic regimes that need to be fulfilled in order to consolidate political stability, economic progress, and social peace. The fact that various democracies with distinct levels of social and economic development exist in the world demonstrates that the requirements governance imposes on democratic regimes are not inherent to democratic regimes. This is generally true, especially in Latin America: "Latin America is the only zone that combines democratically elected regimes in all countries (except Cuba) with high poverty levels (40 percent) and the most unequal distribution in the world" (Zovatto 2007, 24).

## GRADUAL CHANGE AND LEGITIMATE HOPES

Democracy should not be understood only as a political regime (referring to the role of institutions), but also as a political process. The art of politics (Cardoso and Setti 2006) and that of governing consist of balancing democracy as a system of institutions and democracy as a political process. This brings us to the topic of democratic change and the rhythm, timing, depth, and methods of social change. Democracy does not exclude change—on the contrary, it makes change possible. Democracy does not ignore the conflict inherent in any given society—instead, democracy is, to a certain extent, the institutionalization of conflict. Inasmuch as institutions are autonomous, adaptable, complex, and coherent—according to Huntington's (1968) classical definition—they allow for the channeling of social demands and the peaceful and democratic resolution of conflicts. In order to avoid generalized conflict—that, depending on the conditions and circumstances, might devolve into a crisis, power vacuum, or, in the extreme, breakdown—institutions must work coherently, hand in hand (so to speak) with political and social processes. A representative democracy, or democracy of institutions, seeking adequate conditions of governance, must address the issue of the rhythm, speed, depth, or method of social change.

This is relevant to Latin America in light of our recent history. Political democracy extends throughout the region as never before. In the economic sphere, markets and growth play a fundamental role from a development perspective, while, in general and with different levels of advancement, economic and trade liberalization has moved forward in accordance with the requirements of globalization, from the perspective of a new insertion into the international arena. I am mindful, in this respect, of the conclusions of the final document of the Asia Pacific Economic Cooperation (APEC), which took place in Santiago, Chile, in December of 2004. The APEC document argues that economic and trade liberalization should be understood not as an end in itself but rather as a means to find "equitable and sustainable growth." Yet the persistence of poverty and inequality continues to be one of the most distinctive and characteristic realities in Latin America. The principal debates and differences in the region reside precisely here, particularly around the question of which development strategies and social policies are the most effective in dealing with poverty and inequality. The reconciliation of political democracy, economic growth, and social equity is the principal challenge that Latin American countries face.

The persistence of poverty and inequality becomes even more obvious and unacceptable as democracy and growth extend throughout the region. Democratization, urbanization, and globalization make exclusion more visible while also developing a greater consciousness of its economic and political costs. This gives the social issues a strategic importance in both the medium and long terms, which means that the continuity of public policies, beyond electoral cycles and short-term economics, becomes crucial to addressing those social issues.

The above implies a strategic choice for stability. The strategic meaning and continuity of social policies implies and demands a stable horizon in terms of both macropolitical (democracy) and macroeconomic (democracy without inflation) stability. Thus, just as the state has the obligation to guarantee certain public goods, such as security, it also has the obligation to ensure adequate macroeconomic stability, which has to be seen as a public good. Stability, in the positive sense, is a necessary but not sufficient condition for economic growth and the fight against poverty and inequality. With a history of political instability, as seen in the waves of democracy and authoritarianism experienced in the region, and economic instability (inflation, hyperinflation, chronic fiscal deficits, balance-of-payments crises, hefty external debt, among others), it is imperative on an ethical level to ensure political and economic stability in order to promote progress, welfare, and development in the region. Additionally, economic cycles of boom and bust and vulnerability to external financial shocks require a forward-looking view for the medium and long terms that establishes control over short term variables and electoral cycles. Fiscal responsibility, anticyclic economic policies, autonomous monetary authorities, the existence of market institutions—and of institutions that set clear, stable, and fair rules of the game, in general—and adequate economic regulations, accountability, and, above all, the construction of basic agreements are some of the challenges on the road to stability as democracies work to provide a certain level of predictability in citizens' daily lives.

Democracy is, in an important way, a race between hope and despair. It is therefore suspicious of immediate, short-term, overnight solutions (or the promise of solutions). The race requires an administration of the waiting periods that provide these intervals with the necessary legitimacy while moving towards the goal of ensuring adequate conditions of governance. Behind the (justified) dissatisfaction or malaise in Latin America lies the sum of injustice and impatience that, many times, translates into the search for a charismatic leader who provides citizens with a feeling of identity and belonging by promising the immediate satisfaction of social demands. What I propose instead is a way of governing that makes the wait credible (and legitimate), blocking the temptations of radical, revolutionary changes and easy populist promises while at the same time confronting their causes and removing their conditions.

This requires the process of institution building to go hand in hand with gradual change as a central aspect of what I call democracy of institutions. Such processes and institutions reflect the true nature of politics as the art of the possible in the Hirschmanian sense of possibilism. Hirschman (1973) points out the need to expand the limits of the possible within the logic of what it is possible to do and to gain. At the same time, he expresses his distrust in radical or revolutionary change, which he calls "voluntarism," and the role of the "pure economist" who ignores the political dimensions of things. As Hirschman points out, this argument should not be understood in a conservative sense, in defense of the status quo or of a certain social or political order. Democracy makes change possible, especially when it balances political institutions and processes of change. Possibilism justly attempts to go beyond the mere "probable," which is the realm of social science, in order to broaden the limits of the possible without bias or prejudice towards the depth of the changes. Instead, it ensures the sustainability of such changes. This is something like the "tunnel effect" that Hirschman describes, which gives legitimacy to the waiting; that is, to the extent that one is capable of seeing the light at the end of the tunnel and that other actors (vehicles) are moving in that direction, one will be in a better position to pay the costs of waiting in the short term. Certainly, following Hirschman's analysis of changing levels of tolerance in relation to income inequality, the previous metaphor presumes that one advances in the direction of the light at some point since, otherwise, when one is stuck or, even worse, moving backwards, things devolve into frustration and, in the extreme, rebellion against the status quo.

The region's development strategies and the necessary learning process associated with them have much to do with what Santiso (2006), following Hirschmanian logic, calls the "political economy of the possible." It is the opposite of both the "political economy of the impossible" that characterized Latin America in the age of utopias and global planning and the "political economy of impatience" that characterizes populist regimes. Ultimately, this concept of democracy is deeply suspicious of shortcuts, and if there is one thing we have learned from recent (and not-so-recent) Latin American history, it is that there are no shortcuts to development and democracy. Gradual reform is what makes social change possible, viable, sustainable, and legitimate in a democracy.

This has even more importance and significance in a region such as Latin America, which has turned away from—or so we want to believe—the paradigms and utopias that turned the region into a veritable social laboratory characterized by strong political polarization. The cost of these radical, revolutionary, or authoritarian experiments (and combinations of these) and the choice of a political economy of the impossible or of impatience generally ended with the people, especially the poorest and most vulnerable, paying the price. We are turning away from these paradigms and have moved (or should move) in the direction of a more pragmatic approach. Behind this issue lies the question of what type of equality we want: immediate results or effective opportunities. The waiting period is different for every case, as are levels of patience or impatience.

This points to the central question of what type of inequality democracy can tolerate. Efficient change is that in which some improve without others getting worse. The problem with neoliberalism—which often appears as neopopulism's counterpart (and sometimes a major antecedent)—is that there is no major support or worry for the "losers." Under democracy, especially in the age of globalization and because of the perceptions of uncertainty and insecurity associated with it, we must take charge of the losers and build social safety nets for those who live with uncertainty and insecurity. This is particularly necessary in times of crisis. Waiting is related to the capacity to hold on to certain shared convictions based on trust in institutions—rather than in personalist leaders—and in a financially stable system and efficient management of social programs. Thus, gradual or incremental change and the legitimacy of waiting become one of the principal challenges for Latin America today and in the future.

The argument I develop here should be understood as a critical reading of the determinist and reductionist theories that have permeated the social sciences since the 1950s, related to certain supposedly intrinsic requirements commonly associated with political, economic, and social processes and their structural determinants. Ultimately, I address an alternative focus that underscores the role of political actors, institutions, and policies. It is this triad that makes the difference between development and underdevelopment, between democracy and authoritarianism. Without ignoring the importance of underlying structural factors, we should recognize that there are alternatives and that Latin America is not doomed to authoritarianism and underdevelopment.

In his recent book, *The Spirit of Democracy*, Larry Diamond (2008b) studies the reversal of the third wave of democratization that began at the end of the 1990s, which some have referred to as the "democratic recession," and investigates hopes for and expectations of the future of democracy. He writes, "it is the policies and the collective will of the established democracies that could make the crucial difference" (13). I ask myself, along the same lines, what are institutions but the "collective will" of democratic regimes? Since the first chapter I have argued against determinism, maintaining that we are not doomed to any of the evils that Latin America has known throughout its history. While some of the structural arrangements that have existed in Latin America have evolved tensions between the double objectives of democracy and development—arrangements that include the international insertion that has characterized Latin America throughout its history, its political culture (cultural bedrock or ethos), the colonial legacy and the economic and social structures that we inherited from the Spanish and Portuguese, and the presidentialism that has characterized the region since independence, among others that I have described in this book—none have become insurmountable obstacles in terms of moving toward this double objective. These structural characteristics should not be taken in a deterministic, fixed manner or considered outside the context of historical processes, nor should we ignore the role of social and political actors, institutions, and public policies to the point where it seems as if the situation has no exit in terms of democracy and development, and political and economic stability.

This process, without doubt, is full of tensions and contradictions, set against the backdrop of poverty and inequality, corruption, and insecurity. In this context, there is no room for ingenuous posturing, for voluntarists or triumphalists, or for generalized and paralyzing pessimism. The challenge of strengthening markets, states, institutions, and civil society through efficient and innovative public policies directed at overcoming poverty and inequality and achieving transparency and the effective enforcement of the rule of law is at the center of the push to reconcile democracy and development. Neither the siren song of neopopulism nor the economic reductionism of neoliberalism have shown themselves to be capable of confronting the new challenges of economic growth and social equity under acceptable conditions of democratic governance. Beyond these two approaches, which tend to capture international attention, a new, more practical and less strident reality has emerged in Latin America that raises the possibility of coming closer (perhaps closer than ever before) to both democracy and development.

# WORKS CITED

Aguilar, José Antonio, and Rafael Rojas, eds. 2002. *El Republicanismo en Hispano-américa (Ensayos de historia intelectual y política)*. Mexico: CIDE-Fondo de Cultura Económica.

Bendix, Richard. 1977. *Max Weber: An Intellectual Portrait*. Berkeley: University of California Press.

Birdsall, Nancy, and Carol Graham, eds. 2000. *New Markets, New Opportunities? Economic and Social Mobility in a Changing World*. Washington, DC: Carnegie Endowment for International Peace/Brookings Institution Press.

Botana, Natalio. 2005. *El Orden Conservador: la política Argentina entre 1880 y 1916*. Buenos Aires: Debolsillo.

Brennan, Geoffrey, and Alan Hamlin. 1999. "On Political Representation." *British Journal of Political Science* 29(1):109–27.

Bulmer-Thomas, Victor. 2003. *The Economic History of Latin America since Independence*. New York: Cambridge University Press.

Burgos, Jorge, and Ignacio Walker. 2003. "Hacia el parlamentarismo." *En Foco* 4. Santiago, Chile: Expansiva.

Bushnell, David, and Neill Macaulay. 1988. *The Emergence of Latin America in the Nineteenth Century*. New York: Oxford University Press.

Cardoso, Eliana, and Alberto Fishlow. 1992. "Latin American Economic Development: 1950–1980." *Journal of Latin American Studies* 24: 197–218.

Cardoso, Fernando Henrique. 2008. "New Paths: Reflections about Some Challenges of Globalization." Unpublished manuscript based on conference held

April 3–5 at Watson Institute for International Studies, Brown University, Providence, RI.

Cardoso, Fernando Henrique, and Enzo Faletto. 1979. *Dependency and Development in Latin America*. Berkeley: University of California Press.

Cardoso, Fernando Henrique, and Alejandro Foxley, eds. 2009. *A medio camino: Nuevos desafíos de la dedesarrollo en América Latina*. Santiago, Chile: Uqbar Editores.

Cardoso, Fernando Henrique, and Ricardo Setti. 2006. *A arte da política: A historia que vivi*. Rio de Janeiro: Civilizacao Brasileira.

Cardoso, Fernando Henrique, and Brian Winter. 2006. *The Accidental President of Brazil: A Memoir*. New York: PublicAffairs.

Carothers, Thomas. 2002. "The End of the Transition Paradigm." *Journal of Democracy* 13(1): 5–21.

Castañeda, Jorge. 2006. "Latin America's Left Turn." *Foreign Affairs* 85(3): 28–43.

Cheibub, José Antonio. 2007. *Presidentialism, Parliamentarism, and Democracy*. New York: Cambridge University Press.

Chilcote, Ronald, and Joel Edelstein, eds. 1974. *Latin America: The Struggle with Dependency and Beyond*. New York: Schenkman Publishing Company, Inc.

Cohen, Youssef, and Franco Pavoncello. 1987. "Corporatism and Pluralism: A Critique of Schmitter's Typology." *British Journal of Political Science* 17(1): 117–22.

Collier, David, ed. 1979. *The New Authoritarianism in Latin America*. Princeton: Princeton University Press.

Collier, Ruth B., and David Collier. 2002. *Shaping the Political Arena: Critical Junctures, the Labor Movement, and Regime Dynamics in Latin America*. Notre Dame, IN: University of Notre Dame Press.

Correa, Enrique. 2007. "Gobernabilidad democrática en América Latina: Entre el entusiasmo por las posibilidades y el temor al desamparo." *Serie Estudios Socio-Económicos* 41. Santiago, Chile: CIEPLAN.

Cousiño, Carlos, and Eduardo Valenzuela. 1996. *Politización y monetarización en América Latina*. Cuadernos del Instituto de Sociología. Santiago, Chile: Pontifica Universidad Católica de Chile.

Dahl, Robert. 1971. *Polyarchy: Participation and Opposition*. New Haven, CT: Yale University Press.

Diamond, Larry. 1999. *Developing Democracy: Toward Consolidation*. Baltimore, MD: The Johns Hopkins University Press.

———. 2002. "Thinking about Hybrid Regimes." *Journal of Democracy* 13(2): 21–35.

———. 2008a. "The Democratic Rollback: The Resurgence of the Predatory State." *Foreign Affairs* 87(2): 36–48.

———. 2008b. *The Spirit of Democracy*. New York: Times Books.

Diamond, Larry, and Leonardo Morlino. 2005. *Assessing the Quality of Democracy*. Baltimore, MD: The Johns Hopkins University Press.

Diamond, Larry, and Marc Plattner. 2001. *The Global Divergence of Democracies*. Baltimore, MD: The Johns Hopkins University Press.

Domínguez, Jorge, and Michael Shifter. 2003. *Constructing Democratic Governance in Latin America*. Baltimore, MD: The Johns Hopkins University Press.

Dornbusch, Rudiger, and Sebastián Edwards. 1991. *The Macroeconomics of Populism in Latin America*. Chicago: University of Chicago Press.

Drake, Paul. 2009. *Between Tyranny and Anarchy: A History of Democracy in Latin America, 1800–2006*. Palo Alto, CA: Stanford University Press.

Edwards, Alberto. 1959. *La fronda aristocrática*. Santiago de Chile: Editorial del Pacífico.

Edwards, Sebastián. 1995. *Crisis and Reform in Latin America: From Despair to Hope*. New York: Oxford University Press.

———. 2007a. "Crises and Growth: A Latin American Perspective." *Journal of Iberian and Latin American Economic History* 25(2007): 19–51.

———. 2007b. "From the Alliance for Progress to the Washington Consensus." Unpublished manuscript.

Faletto, Enzo. 1985. "Sobre Populismo y Socialismo." *Opciones* 7 (September–December), 70.

Ffrench-Davis, Ricardo. 2005. *Reforming Latin America's Economies: After Market Fundamentalism.* New York: Palgrave Macmillan.

Ffrench-Davis, Ricardo, Oscar Muñoz, and Gabriel Palma. 1997. "Las economías Latinoamericanas, 1950–1990." In Leslie Bethell, ed. *Historia de América Latina* vol. 2. Barcelona: Crítica (Grijalbo Mondadori).

Flisfisch, Angel. 2008. "¿Hay alternativas a la democracia representativa? Democracia representativa, régimen e institucionalidad, la política y los políticos." Unpublished manuscript. Santiago, Chile: CIEPLAN.

Foxley, Alejandro, ed. 2009a. *Caminos al desarrollo: Lecciones de países afines exitosos*. 2 vols. Santiago, Chile: BID-Gobierno de Chile.

———. 2009b. "Middle Income Countries: New Problems, New Challenges." Unpublished manuscript.

Furtado, Celso. 1976. *Economic Development of Latin America: Historical Background and Contemporary Problems*. New York: Cambridge University Press.

Garretón, Manuel Antonio. 2003. *Incomplete Democracy: Political Democratization in Chile and Latin America*. Chapel Hill: University of North Carolina Press.

Gasparini, Leonardo, Matías Horenstein, Ezequiel Molina, and Sergio Olivieri. 2008. *Polarización económica, instituciones y conflicto: Dinámicas de la cohesión Latinoamericana*. Santiago, Chile: Uqbar Editores-Colección CIEPLAN.

Gerth, H. H, and C. Wright Mills. 1946. *From Max Weber: Essays in Society*. New York: Oxford University Press.

Graham, Carol, and S. Pettinato. 1999. "Assessing Hardship and Happiness: Trends in Mobility and Expectations in the New Market Economies." Working Paper no. 7. Washington, DC: Center on Social and Economic Dynamics.

Griffith, Ernest, John Plamenatz, and Roland Pennock. 1956. "Cultural Prerequisites to a Successfully Functioning Democracy: A Symposium." *American Political Science Review* 50(1): 101–37.

Haggard, Stephan, and Robert Kaufman. 1995. *The Political Economy of Democratic Transitions*. Princeton: Princeton University Press.

Hagopian, Frances, and Scott Mainwaring. 2005. *The Third Wave of Democratization in Latin America: Advances and Setbacks*. New York: Cambridge University Press.

Hall, Peter, and Rosemary Taylor. 1996. "Political Science and the Three New Institutionalisms." *Political Studies* 44, 936–57.

Halperin, Tulio. 1993. *The Contemporary History of Latin America*. Durham, NC: Duke University Press.

Hartlyn, Jonathan, and Arturo Valenzuela. 1994. "La democracia en América Latina desde 1930." In Leslie Bethell, ed. *Historia de América Latina*, vol. 2. Barcelona: Crítica (Grijalbo Mondadori).

Hirschman, Albert. 1963. *Journeys toward Progress: Studies Towards Economic Policy-Making in Latin America*. New York: Twentieth Century Fund.

———. 1968. "The Political Economy of Import-Substituting Industrialization in Latin America." *Quarterly Journal of Economics* 82(1): 1–32.

———. 1971. *A Bias for Hope: Essays on Development and Latin America*. New Haven, CT: Yale University Press.

———. 1973. *Desarrollo y América Latina: Obstinación por la Esperanza*. Mexico City: Fondo de Cultura Económica.

———. 1979. "Against Economic Determinants." In David Collier, ed. *The New Authoritarianism in Latin America*. Princeton: Princeton University Press.

Huntington, Samuel. 1968. *Political Order in Changing Societies*. New Haven, CT: Yale University Press.

————. 1991. *The Third Wave: Democratization in the Late Twentieth Century.* Norman: University of Oklahoma Press.

Inter-American Development Bank. 2005. *The Politics of Policies: Economic and Social Progress in Latin America.* New York: IADB.

————. 2007. *Outsiders? The Changing Patterns of Exclusion in Latin America and the Caribbean.* Washington, DC: IADB.

Kuczynski, Pedro Pablo, and John Williamson. 2003. *After the Washington Consensus: Restarting Growth and Reform in Latin America.* Washington, DC: Institute for International Economics.

Lanzaro, Jorge, ed. 2001. *Tipos de presidencialismo y coaliciones políticas en América Latina.* Buenos Aires: CLACSO.

Latinobarómetro. 2006 and 2008. www.latinobarometro.org.

Lemarchand, René, and Keith Legg. 1972. "Political Clientelism and Development." *Comparative Politics* 4(2): 149–78.

Levitsky, Steven, and María Victoria Murillo. 2005. *Argentine Democracy: The Politics of Institutional Weakness.* University Park: Pennsylvania State University Press.

Levitsky, Steven, and Lucan A. Way. 2002. "The Rise of Competitive Authoritarianism." *Journal of Democracy* 13(2): 51–65.

Lijphart, Arend. 1984. *Democracies: Patterns of Majoritarian and Consensus Government in Twenty-One Countries.* New Haven, CT: Yale University Press.

Linz, Juan, and Alfred Stepan. 1978. *The Breakdown of Democratic Regimes.* Baltimore, MD: The John Hopkins University Press.

————. 1996. *Problems of Democratic Transition and Consolidation.* Baltimore, MD: The Johns Hopkins University Press.

Linz, Juan, and Arturo Valenzuela, eds. 1994. *The Failure of Presidential Democracy.* Baltimore, MD: The Johns Hopkins University Press.

Lipset, Seymour Martin. 1959. "Some Social Requisites of Democracy: Economic Development and Political Legitimacy." *American Political Science Review* 53(1): 69–105.

————. 1960. *Political Man: The Social Bases of Politics.* New York: Doubleday and Co.

Love, Joseph. 1996. "Economic Ideas and Ideologies in Latin America since 1930." In Leslie Bethell, ed. *Ideas and Ideologies in Twentieth Century Latin America.* New York: Cambridge University Press.

Lowenthal, Abraham, ed. 1975. *The Peruvian Experiment: Continuity and Change under Military Rule.* Princeton: Princeton University Press.

Lustig, Nora. 2009. "Is Latin America Becoming More Inclusive?" Unpublished manuscript presented in Emerging Markets Forum, Bogotá, Colombia, 1–3 April.

Mainwaring, Scott, Ana María Bejarano, and Eduardo Pizarro Leongómez, eds. 2006. *The Crisis of Democratic Representation in the Andes*. Palo Alto, CA: Stanford University Press.

Mainwaring, Scott, Guillermo O'Donnell, and Samuel Valenzuela. 1992. *Democratic Consolidation: The New South American Democracies in Comparative Perspective*. Notre Dame, IN: University of Notre Dame Press.

Mainwaring, Scott, and Aníbal Pérez-Liñán. 2003. "Level of Development and Democracy." *Comparative Political Studies* 36(9): 1031–67.

Mainwaring, Scott, and Timothy Scully. 1995. *Building Democratic Institutions: Party Systems in Latin America*. Palo Alto, CA: Stanford University Press.

———. 2008. "Latin America: Eight Lessons for Governance." *Journal of Democracy* 19(3): 113–27.

———, eds. 2009. *Democratic Governance in Latin America*. Palo Alto, CA: Stanford University Press.

Mainwaring, Scott, and Matthew Shugart. 1997a. "Juan Linz, Presidentialism, and Democracy: A Critical Appraisal." *Comparative Politics* 29(4): 449–71.

———. 1997b. *Presidentialism and Democracy in Latin America*. New York: Cambridge University Press.

Meller, Patricio. 2000. *The Unidad Popular and the Pinochet Dictatorship: A Political Economy Analysis*. New York: Macmillan Press Ltd.

Méndez, Juan E., Guillermo O'Donnell, and Sergio Pinheiro. 1999. *(Un)Rule of Law and the Underprivileged in Latin America*. Notre Dame, IN: University of Notre Dame Press.

Ministerio de Asuntos Exteriores y de Cooperación. 2006. *Cooperación con países de renta media: Justificación y ambito de trabajo*. Madrid: ECI and ICEI.

Navia, Patricio. 2006. "La izquierda de Lagos vs. la izquierda de Chávez." *Foreign Affairs en Español* 6(2): 75–88.

Navia, Patricio, and Ignacio Walker. 2006. "Gobernabilidad democrática en América Latina: Instituciones y liderazgos." *Serie Estudios Socio-Económicos* 29. Santiago, Chile: CIEPLAN.

Nohlen, Dieter, and Mario Fernández, eds. 1998. *El presidencialismo renovado: Instituciones y cambio político en América Latina*. Caracas: Nueva Sociedad.

North, Douglas. 1990. *Institutions, Institutional Change and Economic Performance*. New York: Cambridge University Press.

Ocampo, José Antonio. 2007. "América Latina y la economía mundial en el siglo XX largo." Unpublished manuscript.

O'Donnell, Guillermo. 1979. *Modernization and Bureaucratic-Authoritarianism: Studies in South American Politics*. Berkeley: Institute of International Studies, University of California.

———. 1994. "Delegative Democracy." *Journal of Democracy* 5(1): 55–69.

———. 2001. "Reflections on Contemporary South America." *Journal of Latin American Studies* 33(3): 599–609.

O'Donnell, Guillermo, Philippe Schmitter, and Laurence Whitehead. 1986. *Transitions from Authoritarian Rule: Latin America*. Baltimore, MD: The Johns Hopkins University Press.

O'Donnell, Guillermo, Jorge Vargas, and Osvaldo Iazetta. 2004. *The Quality of Democracy: Theory and Applications*. Notre Dame, IN: University of Notre Dame Press.

Payne, Mark, Daniel Zovatto, and Mercedes Mateo Díaz, eds. 2007. *Democracies in Development: Politics and Reform in Latin America*. Cambridge, MA: Harvard University David Rockefeller Center/Inter-American Development Bank.

Pérez-Liñán, Aníbal. 2005. "Democratization and Constitutional Crises in Presidential Regimes: Toward Congressional Supremacy." *Comparative Political Studies* 38: 51–74.

———. 2007. *Presidential Impeachment and the New Political Instability in Latin America*. New York: Cambridge University Press.

Pierson, W. W., ed. 1950. "Pathology of Democracy in Latin America: A Symposium." *American Political Science Review* 44(1).

Posada-Corbó, Eduardo, ed. 1996. *Elections before Democracy: The History of Elections in Europe and Latin America*. London: Macmillan Press.

Przeworski, Adam. 1991. *Democracy and the Market: Political and Economic Reforms in Eastern Europe and Latin America*. New York: Cambridge University Press.

Reid, Michael. 2007. *Forgotten Continent: The Battle for Latin America's Soul*. New Haven, CT: Yale University Press.

Roberts, Kenneth. 1996. "Neoliberalism and the Transformation of Populism in Latin America: The Peruvian Case." *World Politics* 48(1): 82–116.

———. 2007. "Latin America's Populist Revival." *SAIS Review* 27(1): 3–15.

Rodrik, Dani. 2007. *One Economics, Many Recipes: Globalization, Institutions, and Economic Growth*. Princeton: Princeton University Press.

———. 2008. "Second-Best Institutions." Working Paper no. 14050 (June). Cambridge, MA: National Bureau of Economic Research.

Rojas Mix, Miguel. 1991. *Los cien nombres de América*. Buenos Aires: Editorial Lumen.

Rueschemeyer, Dietrich, Evelyne H. Stephens, and John D. Stephens. 1992. *Capitalist Development and Democracy*. Chicago: University of Chicago Press.

Santiso, Javier. 2006. *Latin America's Political Economy of the Possible: Beyond Good Revolutionaries and Free-Marketeers*. Cambridge, MA: The MIT Press.

Schedler, Andreas. 1998. "What is Democratic Consolidation?" *Journal of Democracy* 9(2): 91–107.

———. 2002. "The Menu of Manipulation." *Journal of Democracy* 13(2): 36–50.

Schumpeter, Joseph. 1942. *Capitalism, Socialism and Democracy*. New York: Harper and Brothers.

Sen, Amartya. 1999. "Democracy as a Universal Value." *Journal of Democracy* 10(3): 3–17.

Shugart, Matthew, and John Carey. 1992. *Presidents and Assemblies: Constitutional Design and Electoral Dynamics*. New York: Cambridge University Press.

Skidmore, Thomas, and Peter Smith. 2005. *Modern Latin America*. New York: Oxford University Press.

Smith, Peter. 2005. *Democracy in Latin America: Political Change in Comparative Perspective*. New York: Oxford University Press.

Sorj, Bernardo. 2007. *Latin America's Elusive Democracies*. E-book Series 2. Rio de Janeiro: The Edelstein Center for Social Research.

Sorj, Bernardo, and Eugenio Tironi. 2007. "Cohesión social en América Latina: Un marco de investigación." *Pensamiento Iberoamericano* 1(2): 109–10.

Stepan, Alfred. 1978. *The State and Society: Peru in Comparative Perspective*. Princeton: Princeton University Press.

Sunkel, Osvaldo. 1967. "Política nacional de desarrollo y dependencia externa." *Estudios Internacionales* 1(1): 43–75.

———. "The Precarious Sustainability of Democracy in Latin America." In B. Hettne, ed. *Studies in Development, Security and Culture* (vol. 1, *Sustainable Development in a Globalized World*). New York: Palgrave Macmillan.

Theobald, Robin. 1982. "Patrimonialism." *World Politics* 34(4): 548–59.

Thorp, Rosemary. 1998. *Progress, Poverty and Exclusion: An Economic History of Latin America in the 20th Century*. Baltimore, MD: The Johns Hopkins University Press.

Tironi, Eugenio, ed. 2008. *Redes, estado y mercados: Soportes de la cohesión social Latinoamericana*. Santiago de Chile: Uqbar Editores/Colección CIEPLAN.

United Nations Development Programme. 2004. *La democracia en América Latina: Hacia una democracia de ciudadanos y ciudadanas*. New York: UNDP.

Valdés, Juan Gabriel. 1995. *Pinochet's Economists: The Chicago School in Chile*. New York: Cambridge University Press

Valenzuela, Arturo. 2004. "Latin American Presidencies Interrupted." *Journal of Democracy* 14(4): 5–19.

Valenzuela, Eduardo, Simón Schwartzman, J. Samuel Valenzuela, Timothy R. Scully, Nicolás M. Somma, and Andrés Biehl. 2008. *Vínculos, creencias e ilusiones: La cohesión social de los Latinoamericanos.* Santiago, Chile: Uqbar Editores/Colección CIEPLAN.

Valenzuela, Samuel, and Eduardo Posada-Carbó. 2008. "Conference and Book Proposal: the Origins of Democracy in the Americas, 1770s–1880s." Conference at the Kellogg Institute for International Studies, University of Notre Dame, September.

Valenzuela, Samuel, and Arturo Valenzuela. 1978. "Modernization and Dependency: Alternative Perspectives in the Study of Latin American Development." *Comparative Politics* 10(4): 535–57.

Véliz, Claudio. 1980. *The Centralist Tradition of Latin America.* Princeton: Princeton University Press.

Waiss, Oscar. 1954. *Nacionalismo y socialismo en América Latina.* Buenos Aires: Ediciones Iguazú.

Walker, Ignacio. 1990. *Socialismo y democracia: Chile y Europa en perspectiva comparada.* Santiago, Chile: CIEPLAN-Hachette.

———. 2006. "Democracia en América Latina." *Foreign Affairs en Español* 6(2): 3–24.

———. 2008. "Democracy and Populism in Latin America." Working Paper no. 347 (April). Kellogg Institute for International Studies, University of Notre Dame. A version of this paper was published in 2008 as "The Three Lefts of Latin America." *Dissent* 55(4): 5–12.

———. 2009. "Por una democracia de instituciones para América Latina." *Estudios Públicos* 113: 267–93.

Weyland, Kurt. 2001. "Clarifying a Contested Concept: Populism in the Study of Latin American Politics." *Comparative Politics* 34(1): 1–22.

———. 2003. Neopopulism and Neoliberalism in Latin America: How Much Affinity? *Third World Quarterly* 24(6): 1095–1115.

Wiarda, Howard. 2001. *The Soul of Latin America: The Cultural and Political Tradition.* New Haven, CT: Yale University Press.

Wiarda, Howard, and Harvey Kline. 1979. *Latin American Politics and Development.* Boston: Houghton-Mifflin.

Wilde, Alexander. 1982. *Conversaciones de caballeros: El quiebre de la democracia en Colombia.* Bogata: Ediciones Tercer Mundo.

Williamson, John. 1990. *Latin American Adjustment: How Much Has Happened.* Washington, DC: Institute for International Economics.

————. 2004. "A Short History of the Washington Consensus." Paper presented at From the Washington Consensus towards a New Global Governance, Barcelona, September.

Wynia, Gary. 1984. *The Politics of Latin American Development*. New York: Cambridge University Press.

Zakaria, Fareed. 1997. "The Rise of Illiberal Democracy." *Foreign Affairs* 76(6): 22–43.

Zovatto, Daniel. 2007. "Balance electoral Latinoamericano." In C. Malamud et al, eds. *Anuario Iberoamericano*. Madrid: Agencia EFE and Real Instituto Elcano, Ediciones Pirámide.

# INDEX

249

Ignacio Walker

is a Chilean senior scholar of political science and
a practicing politician. He is currently serving as a senator
of the Republic of Chile and as president
of the Christian Democratic Party.